FOR the FIRST TIME EVER...

A FORMER TOP NEW AGE LEADER
TAKES YOU ON A DRAMATIC JOURNEY

INSIDE the NEW AGE
NIGHTMARE

Randall N. Baer

Huntington House, Inc.

Huntington House, Inc.
P.O. Box 53788, Lafayette, Louisiana 70505

Library of Congress Card Number 8-083851
ISBN Number 0-910311-58-7

Printed in the United States of America
Typesetting by Thoburn Press, Tyler, Texas

CONTENTS

Appendices

PROLOGUE

The New Age Movement was my life, my love for some 15 years. As an impressionable, rebellious teenager I became enamored with exotic Eastern mysticism, which eventually led to years of study to become a professional New Age teacher, holistic health practitioner, and activist.

But that was only the beginning. An uncanny sequence of dramatic events propelled a young, unknown man named Randall Baer into a meteoric rise to national, and even international, renown as an expert in "crystal power" and New Age philosophy. Before the age of 30, I had two acclaimed books published by a respected mainstream publisher, Harper & Row, a large teaching and research facility, and was able to write my own ticket on the national lecture circuit. I was riding high.

By becoming absolutely convinced that the New Age was the true path of enlightenment, love, and peace, I delved deeply into this movement and found myself on a fast-track to success, fame, and influence. But a horrifying encounter caused me to take a careful look at what I was doing.

There already has been a great deal written about this sorcery called the New Age. Most of it has been written by outsiders looking in. I want to tell you what it is like from the inside looking out — from the vantage point of one whose life was devoted to this movement.

What once was considered to be only a passing phenomenon by some observers is continuing to grow, gain influence, and capture the minds and allegiance of millions of young people and adults alike.

In the following pages, I want to help you separate fact from fiction, myth from meaning, and truth from a tempest in a teapot.

I want you to know exactly what the New Age Movement is about.

ONE

PORTRAIT OF
A SEDUCTION

Now I'd like to tell you exactly how a young man or young woman in high school, college, or post-college can become involved in the New Age Movement as they start to branch out into the world around them and explore new directions of adventure, self-development, and fulfillment. Perhaps in the reading of this story parents might be apprised of some of the strategies that the adversary uses through the glittery New Age temptations he dangles in front of young adults, and so be better forearmed to provide preventative and intervening counsel.

As well, I pray that more than a few young adults might read this story and realize the very real dangers that lay behind the oftentimes harmless-looking exteriors of so many New Age phenomena, so that they may never dabble or explore in these Satanic webs of ensnarement, and may always hold fast to the safety and victory of the Christian faith.

My own journey leading into the New Age and rising to heights of leadership is a classic portrait of spiritual seduction. Seeking after truth, I found only masterful counterfeits disguised as the truth. Yearning for inner fulfillment and peace, I found only glittering fragments and pieces that eventually would crumble to dust. So deep did the seduction lead that the bizarre became accepted as the norm, fantastical lies saturated my mind, and Satan's demons masqueraded as my guiding angels of light.

Most people involved in the New Age Movement today are so deceived by Satan's lies that they have absolutely no idea of the underlying sinister dangers. Personally, when I was a New Ager, such a

1

notion would have appeared to me as patently outrageous. I thank Jesus Christ that He delivered me from the New Age brainwashing that blinds a person to the horrors that lurk beneath the surface of the New Age.

After the Lord saved me from the counterfeits and lies that held me in glittery bondage, I saw the pattern of Satan's ever-so-cunning hand in pulling off an incredibly elaborate deception for 15 years of my life. In unraveling the thread of seduction woven into my life as a New Ager, I came to see Satan's wiles, strategies, and "tricks of the trade." I was aghast at his expert craftiness.

While this is so absolutely clear to me today in the Light of Jesus, as a New Ager who sincerely believed that he had found the truth, I was totally oblivious to the deception being perpetrated on me. When the eternal truth of the Lord seems to a New Ager to be utterly false, and the falseness of the New Age seems to be absolutely true, therein lies an intricate portrait of seduction. By sharing the portrait of how Satan seduced me, I sincerely hope that the tempting lies and clever shams of the New Age are laid bare and that it is shown clearly for the horrific abomination that it is.

AN ALL-AMERICAN UPBRINGING

Like many New Agers, I was brought up in a middle-to-upper middle-class home. Both parents were trained professionals — my father was a medical doctor and my mother a nurse. Family life was based on Christian morals, the Protestant work ethic, and an emphasis on education.

My father was a Navy doctor and, as a result, my roots were turned up every three to four years. This had advantages in exposing me to many types of people and situations. But I was a shy and introverted child who had difficulty adjusting to new schools, new sets of friends, and new neighborhoods.

Basically I was a good and obedient boy. Rarely did I venture into any serious transgressions, as my cautious nature prevented me from delving too far into "bad boy" territory. Cub Scout and Boy Scout involvements were a constant thread of experience. And, being an industrious and goal-oriented boy, I achieved much success in Scouting and top grades in school.

I was following a model all-American boyhood track.

In early teen years my inquisitive mind started to become interested in religion. I started to feel an emptiness inside and a hunger for truth. At home, we rarely discussed religious issues, mostly leaving such topics to be covered at Sunday school and church. However,

I never really felt any powerful experiences or encounters with Jesus, and my questions only multiplied as more and more doubts arose.

In pursuing a "God and Country" Scouting award, I became friends with a Navy chaplain, whom I felt could guide me toward truth. One day I approached my chaplain friend with great expectations of real dialogue and asked, "Can we talk about why some people are agnostics and atheists? I'd really like to know God, but I have so many doubts." His bewildered and somewhat irritated look instantly revealed to me that he was not receptive to my questions of doubt. "Perhaps some other time, but not now, Randall. You are too young," he replied.

My frustrations began to increase. I had to find "truth."

During the same time, I attended an adult Bible study and was the only teenager there. I was 14. One day I mustered up the courage and blurted out, "Why should I believe in God? Why should I read the Bible? Why should I attend church?"

The group sat in mute silence. I had asked forbidden questions and apparently no one there wanted to broach the subject because my questions were completely ignored.

Teenage Disillusionment and Exotic Explorations

Something snapped in me. I no longer wanted to attend what I perceived as sterile and lifeless church services and study groups. I suddenly knew that what I was searching for wasn't there. In the years ahead, I would hear many New Agers telling a similar story. I started going to various libraries searching for truth on my own. The realm of books, I felt, would open up the doors to new horizons.

The TV show "Kung Fu" caught my attention and, over a period of time, I became gripped by the allures of mysticism and exotic superhuman powers. Here were Eastern masters who had profound answers to the questions burning in my mind—"What is God?", "Who am I?", "Where do you find truth?" The hero image of Quai Chang Caine vividly demonstrated how to attain inner peace, oneness with the universe, and supernatural control over oneself and life's circumstances.

On regular trips to a bookstore in a neighborhood shopping mall, I found many books in the "Religion/Philosophy" and "Occult" sections on Eastern religious philosophy and "how to" books on Hatha *Yoga* and meditation. In the following weeks and months, I devoured the exotic "All is Oneness" philosophies, and taught myself how to perform yoga and meditation. This was the beginning of my New Age walk, and I had just turned 15.

I always had a close relationship with my mother and I could tell that she was alarmed. She gave me a serious warning to be very careful in my non-Christian pursuits. Though they voiced their serious concerns, neither of my parents forced me to stop my search. It was probably just a teenage "phase" that would be outgrown in time.

I kept up a good outward appearance. Only my closest circle of four high school buddies knew some of the details of my consuming search. At the time I was at the top 2 percent of my high school class, a member of National Honor Society, and enjoying successes in varsity tennis.

A Powerful Ally Helps Me Find the "Force"

During this time, I found another powerful ally on my truth-seeking path — marijuana — and it opened up a whole new world. Marijuana affects different people in different ways. For me, it would help "expand" my mind into many mystical types of "higher consciousness."[1]

One evening I felt that I had an encounter with what I thought was "God." While slowly inhaling the marijuana, all of a sudden the surrounding room disappeared. I found myself floating in the cosmos beyond all sense of time. The boundaries of my body and sense of identity miraculously expanded as I became the "light" and the "light" became me. Feeling like I was effortlessly soaring through infinity, I believed that I had met "god" and was one with the universe. This was what the Eastern religious philosophies were talking about — pure oneness and enlightenment.

How I dreaded it when the marijuana effects started to wear off, having to return to tiny planet Earth. In the days afterwards, my inner anguish and pain returned, but now I felt that I had found the true door to ultimate truth. I had hope.

My path branched out even more as my French teacher, whom I felt was "cool and progressive," formed a small group that met before school to study the works of Napoleon Hill, author of the best-selling books, *Think and Grow Rich* and *Grow Rich! With Peace of Mind*. Each of us set goals and learned the techniques for applying a "Positive Mental Attitude" to create whatever we desired in our lives. Little did I know then that Hill's philosophy was revealed by a "Council of 33 Masters" that spoke to him via mental telepathy to reveal the secrets of universal success.[2]

Back-to-Nature Through College

Upon graduation from high school I went to a highly respected liberal arts college near Minneapolis, Minnesota. During the first two years at this demanding academic college I chose classes that would help me understand mankind and his purpose for existence. Classes in anthropology, sociology, introductory religion, art, and biology further whetted my appetite to find the meaning of life. While studying other cultures from around the world, I became intrigued with primal cultures, American Indians, pantheistic religious views, and "getting back to nature."

My searching mind became engrossed in seeing "Nature" as the source of peace and truth. Somehow by mystically penetrating to the essence of Nature and becoming "one" with it, I felt that my questions and yearnings would be answered. It seemed to me that the Eastern mystics and primal cultures, like some of the more mystically oriented American Indian tribes, were the ones who had kept close to their roots in Nature.

I started to see Western culture as an artificial, "plastic" society that was divorced and separated from the rhythms of Nature, and was therefore increasingly sterile and lifeless.

The Transcendentalist teachings of Thoreau and Wordsworth became a major inspiration. Wordsworth wrote: "Come forth into the light of things, let Nature be your teacher." This became the driving theme of my search.

At the same time, I continued to smoke marijuana regularly, late at night after studies were finished. Still quite shy and insecure, I had a few friends, but none to whom I really revealed the depths of my inner search. The roof top of the dorm became a sort of late-night sanctuary. Smoking a joint, I would commonly have mystical and out-of-body experiences that would propel my awareness into "higher states of consciousness" where I would receive what I thought were profound cosmic insights that reinforced my developing New Age philosophy.

Little did I know that the seducers of Satan were laying out a red carpet of progressive ensnarement. As I took each step, a web of darkness was progressively being woven around me, weaving a spell of delusion and bondage.

Toward the end of my sophomore year, my intense yearning for a chance to "get back to nature" actually materialized. I had been applying Napoleon Hill's "Positive Mental Attitude" techniques fervently toward finding such an opportunity. This was a dream come true — an opportunity to be an assistant in a field biology project carried out in isolated national forest areas of northern Wisconsin. In this remote area, I was to assist a husband-and-wife team doing field studies of fishers, a type of animal in the weasel family.

Ah, now I could divorce myself from sterile, artificial Western culture and immerse myself in the eternal peace and supreme serenity of Nature.

During this time, after a half-day of checking traps and other duties, I was often free to read books on religion and explore marijuana-induced euphoria.

Yet a nagging problem kept re-surfacing day after day. I would mentally understand the mystical religious philosophy and even experience some of it on drugs, but waking up the next morning I would still have a strong sense of inner pain, estrangement, and anguish. I felt certain that I was on the right track to spiritual enlightenment and freedom from inner pain, but it seemed that I always ended up exactly where I started.

Perhaps I should have seen that what was artificial here was the direction my life was taking, but I didn't. In fact, every new drug experience and new philosophy book seemed to re-confirm that I was on the right track, and would find my answers if only I would persevere.

Because of the extreme isolation of the situation and my retreat into my own little mystical world, my work suffered and I experienced my first academic failure. This uncharacteristic failure should have been a red flag signalling that something was going wrong, but I ignored it and was determined to take a next major step—LSD and other hallucinogenic drugs.

Psychedelic Journeys to the Beyond

During the next year as a college junior, I had a chance to fulfill this desire. I moved into a college-sponsored "Asian studies special interest house," a collection of 16 people who had strong interests in Oriental culture and religions. Here I found a strong support group of people very similar to myself in many ways, all of whom were searching for truth and fulfillment by a wide variety of Eastern and psychedelic avenues. We even had a designated meditation room with a blue light to signify that everyone in the house should remain perfectly silent when someone was meditating. To others on campus, our group had a mystical mystique, which we enjoyed.

Most all of us were achievers from upper-middle-class backgrounds, and very inquisitive and explorative in these strange vistas of exotic spirituality.

Being cautious by nature, I spent lots of time in the library reading scholarly books on the effects of psychedelics, and how they helped sometimes in psychological healing (which I desperately wanted) and how they paralleled the mystical experiences of Eastern religions. I knew that this was the "big leagues."

The books and teachings of former Harvard professors Richard Alpert (later Ram Dass), Timothy Leary, Aldous Huxley, Dr. John Lilly, and others promoting variations on the psychedelic gospel of "turn on, tune in, and drop out" reverberated through my fascinated mind. I even was able to write a few papers on this research for a couple of religion classes I was taking. (I was by this time majoring in Religious Studies.) Talk about having your cake and eating it too.

Now I was ready to take the next step into the big league hallucinogens. From all that I had read, I couldn't wait.

A succession of experiences with LSD, mescaline, peyote buttons, psilocybin mushrooms, and hashish with others in my Asian studies house "blew my mind." Catapulted into extraordinary dimensions beyond my wildest dreams, I rapturously explored what I felt were the indescribable "heavens" of the supernatural realms. Incredible vistas of dazzling rainbow lights, beings of pure energy, and mind-expanding transformations unfolded with each new experience. I felt that the psychedelics afforded me access to the very essence of Nature and the cosmos. Here, I thought, I was privileged to know the innermost secrets of the universe known only to mystics, saints, and psychedelic voyagers.

Due to the overwhelming power of these drugs, it sometimes would take an entire day to "trip" and then another day to fully come down and reorient to the "3-D earth-plane," as well as to try to come to grips with these radically new experiences. When I would read some of the books in the college courses I was taking on Hinduism, Taoism, Buddhism, *Yoga*, and Western mystics, time after time my psychedelic experiences matched precisely with these traditions. Being a cautious sort, I had to consider the possibility that these "trips" were simply imaginary flights of fantasy or merely wild, cosmic, comic-book adventures concocted in my own mind. However, with the intellectual confirmation of Eastern scriptures and Western mystical writings, I felt that I was most certainly on the right track.

My experiences with the "mind-blowing" hallucinogens are really quite typical of a great majority of New Agers. The psychedelic doorway flashing the seductive neon sign—"Gateway to Nirvana: Instant Enlightenment"—has been (and continues to be) a major entry point into seeing reality the "New Age" way for millions of truth-seeking pilgrims. What I didn't realize then was that these drugs were blowing open "holes" in my mind that allowed demonic enchanters to further ensnare and brainwash my mind with glamorous psychedelic frauds.

Yet, at the same time, after coming down from psychedelic sessions I still felt fragmented inside. The inner anguish and hollowness were blotted out for a while but always returned after a time. I rationalized that I was a typical product of neurotic Western society. I figured that it would take me many years to work out of all the psychological knots and the sense of alienation that I inherited from a "plastic" and superficial Western culture.

But true enlightenment, according to Eastern religions, went far beyond just psychological balance and well-being. It is a much longer journey of spiritual realization built up over thousands and thousands of reincarnated lifetimes. With psychedelics, I thought that I had seen the mountaintop of spiritual enlightenment and communed with "god" there. Now I felt that the long task of hiking up the mountain was my lifelong direction and goal.

A few years later, though, I had an LSD experience that should have warned me of the deceptions that I had embraced. Shortly after gliding up a crescendo into the peak of the LSD "high," an overwhelmingly powerful demon-spirit took possession of me. I was no longer in control of myself and this demonic force took over the reins. While part of me watched helplessly, the demon-sorcerer cast a number of powerful spells and gave me visions of hideous darkness. After several hours of tremendous inner torture on this "bad trip," the demon "blew my circuits" and left me lying like a rag doll. I could not speak for two entire days, and the psychological damage took six months to heal.

In retrospect, I see that this gruesome experience should have been a sign to go no further on the New Age path. However, I made a decision that was only partly right—from that point forward, I vowed to myself never again to take any form of hallucinogenic drug, including marijuana. My goal now was to achieve personal healing and spiritual enlightenment by only "natural" methods. Thus, my New Age pilgrimage continued as I abandoned the psychedelic door while hundreds of other doors lay open for the experimenting.

BuÔÔhist ChANtiNG ChARMs

Within my college Asian studies house there were people experimenting in all kinds of spiritual paths. Being inquisitive, I tried several of them and had some interesting experiences.

A roommate and close friend really caught on fire with the practices of a Buddhist sect, named Nichiren Soshu Buddhism. He seemed really to grow past some personality flaws and sometimes even seemed to have a glow about him. I also was taking a religion course at the time called "Masters, *Gurus*, and New Religions." For a final paper and verbal report we were to investigate some type of unorthodox spiritual group. Figuring to kill two birds with one stone, I started to attend group meetings with my roommate every week in Minneapolis.

The group would all be on bended knees, chanting to a sacred scroll in front of the room. The chants were from an Eastern scripture called the "Lotus Sutra." There was a short, easy-to-learn chant which was the main focus of the religion.

I was instructed to chant this phrase for 30-60 minutes every day, and see if my life changed in any way. I did so and, to my great wonderment, I experienced a three-week time period of the most incredible luck and good fortune I can ever recall. It was absolutely uncanny. It was as though I had the "Midas touch" and everything I touched turned to gold. Money, amazing coincidences, and unworldly good fortune unfolded in my life like a royal red carpet. Here was power and tangible prosperity.

After a few weeks, though, the "Midas touch" that many other members of this sect also had experienced wore off. A couple of months later, having had my fill of this portion of the spiritual alternative menu, I completed a college paper on this organization, discontinued the practices, and whetted my appetite for more spiritual adventures.

Far-Out Mind Control

A little later, while on summer break between junior and senior college years, I saw a free introductory lecture on "Silva Mind Control" advertised in the local newspaper. I had been fascinatingly absorbing the writings of "Seth" at the time. Seth is a famous spirit channeled through the trance-medium Jane Roberts.[3] This spirit's writings intellectually outlined many of the psychedelic vistas that I previously had experienced, and showed how they relate to developing all sorts of higher psychic powers. This is exactly what Silva Mind Control promised to teach in a practical, step-by-step manner.

In a seminar taught over the span of two weekends, I learned an amazing array of mind power techniques for doing things like: acquiring inner spirit guides, intuitively diagnosing the health problems of any stranger, dream control, "mind-over-matter" techniques, psychic powers, using thought-power to control reality, trance-induction methods, and much more.

I tried some of these practices and they really seemed to work. Dreams could be controlled; psychic insights into people sometimes proved accurate; even clouds in the sky apparently could be influenced with mind-power. Again, like the Buddhist chanting, events in my life took a decidedly "golden" turn. I did not realize until many years later that Satan often gives apparently wonderful "gifts" when a person becomes involved with the New Age. With every gift received, the New Age practices seem to be validated as being true and positive. However, also, with each gift received, the New Age "hook" is set deeper and deeper inside the person.

So it was with me. While every indication told me that I was on the path of truth and fulfillment, an elaborate seduction really was beginning to overtake me.

One of the most intriguing practices taught by Silva Mind Control (today called the Silva Method) is the creation of an "inner retreat" or "inner sanctuary." After going through an extended step-by-step trance induction technique, we were told by the instructor to imagine ourselves to be in a house or dwelling of our own design. It could be anything we wanted, anywhere we wanted.

While many in the class imagined various types of idyllic wilderness retreats, I thought it would be interesting to visualize a high-tech lounge-and-laboratory on the ocean bottom, accessible via a luxury submarine. In my case, as the trance-induction technique deepened the trance, I would imagine myself in the submarine going deeper and deeper, deeper and deeper into the ocean depths. We were instructed to create an easy chair with every comfort feature we would imagine. On the right arm of the chair there was to be a control panel with switches that regulated various functions. In front of the chair we visualized a large screen, upon which to project various thoughts and desires that we wanted to create in our lives.

Extensive instructions guided us in creating every detail and exploring every aspect of our inner "home away from home." After many hours of repeatedly going through this process, the inner sanctuary actually started to take on a type of reality of its own.

The businessmen, housewives, professionals, policemen, and college students in the class started to have the distinct sensation of the "inner reality" taking on an eerily "real" status. We felt like astronauts of the "inner realms of higher consciousness." Any time we wanted to apply mind-power to create reality in the outer, physical world all we needed to do was to go to the inner sanctuary and vividly visualize our desire on the wraparound screen in front of the control panel chair.

This may seem fanciful, but 7-million people have taken this course, a goodly portion of them businessmen and professionals, and many have reported that they have remarkable results. In fact, there's a money back guarantee if a person is not able to exhibit certain intuitive powers by the end of the course.

Culminating this entire sequence, we were guided to go once again into our respective inner retreats and, after going through certain techniques, to invite or visualize one or more "inner counselors." These counselors could be in any shape or form, from the mundane to the bizarre, whatever we could think of; or in some cases, they simply materialized in front of one's awareness.

These "spirit guides" were said to have access to tremendous amounts of wisdom and knowledge which they would dispense to us upon request. They were to be regarded as friends and confidants who benevolently would guide us through life in a successful and prosperous way.

The instructor stated that he had a council of nine counselors; some of them being recognized celebrities like Einstein and Johnny Carson.

In my own experience, two guides suddenly materialized before my mind's eye. One was a tall, strong, wise-looking American Indian man and the other was a strikingly beautiful American Indian woman. After becoming used to the idea, the group was guided to acquaint themselves with their respective guides and to start asking questions. Most people in the group later shared that the inner counselors seemed to take on a vivid reality and that their dialogue seemed to have proven somewhat fruitful.

What I didn't realize at the time was that everything in Silva Mind Control was based on occult philosophy. The occult was simply repackaged in a de-religion-ised, Westernized format that would be acceptable and even appealing to middle-class America. The inner counselors are a type of biblically forbidden practice of "acquiring familiar spirits"; that is, inviting demons disguised as spirit-friends into one's life.

The Development of an All-American Yogi[4]

Shortly after beginning my senior year in college, I made a decision to take a year and a half leave-of-absence. While doing quite well academically, my usual enthusiasm for college studies was waning, as I was cutting corners and doing minimal work. At the same time, for all the advanced New Age classes I was attending and all the exalted spiritual experiences that were happening, inwardly, there was an alarming psychological deterioration taking place.

Greater degrees of inner alienation and anguish were building up to an intolerable degree. I always have been rather shy and quiet by nature, but now it became almost impossible to hold a conversation even with close friends. Something was fragmenting inside and I felt a desperate need for help.

During this time, I met a highly intelligent sophomore who was involved deeply in similar pursuits, and it was clear even to me that he had become quite psychologically unhinged. I went to a professor in the religion department who taught a lot of the Eastern religion courses I had taken. He had a mystique about him and was highly respected. He even had been college president for a time. Rumors

among some students and graffiti in the inter-dorm tunnels speculated that he was a *"bodhisattva"* (an enlightened one). Unfortunately, his schedule was swamped.

I decided to take time off from college to go to some yoga retreats
(also called *"ashrams"*). Here, I knew from extensive reading, were
places often removed from Western society out in the country where
I intensively could use advanced yoga practices to heal myself. In
effect, I regarded these *ashrams* as "spiritual hospitals."

After spending a couple of months painting houses to raise
money (my parents would fund a college education but not this kind
of thing), I drove from Texas to California. My eventual destination
was a well-known and respected Yoga center, under the leadership of
a famous *Swami*.

First, though, the *Swami* was holding a weekend seminar on
"Superconscious Living" in San Francisco, which I wanted to attend.
This was my first real exposure to the Yoga subculture. Meditation
beads, astrological arm bangles, people in white or orange outfits,
sitars, pictures of Yoga masters, and people in pretzel poses during
breaks filled my mind with excitement at delving into new and exotic
lands and peoples.

In the midst of the weekend, I happened to be browsing through
the Yoga paraphernalia on sale, and came upon a completely compelling drawing of a Yoga master named Babaji. I had read of this
mysterious high master in the classic book, *Autobiography of a
Yogi*, by the well-known Eastern guru, Paramahansa Yogananda.
Babaji is said to have resided in the remotest regions of the Himalayas
for over 2,000 continuous years, in a 20-year-old body. A force
about the picture drew my attention magnetically.

Mesmerized by the power and the strange feeling of familiarity
that seemed to emanate from it, I immediately bought a copy and
started to meditate on it at various times during the weekend. I felt
that I was receiving a spiritual "call" from this "high Yoga master" to
be his disciple. Even though my rational mind wanted to be cautious
and reserved about this, the impact of what I was feeling in deep inner
levels gave me a certainty that this was what I had been yearning for.

At the very end of the weekend seminar, the *Swami* stood at the
exit while every one of the 300 attendees lined up to receive a "divine
glance" from him. As I drew nearer, I noticed that the people receiving the divine glance became limp and relaxed all of a sudden, and
then a couple of moments later went away with a wide smile on their
faces. When I stood face-to-face with the *Swami*, his eyes were completely absorbing. It was as if I was suspended in time, totally embraced by serene eyes that connected to a universal power beyond
time and space. Then, in a flash, I was back within myself and need-

ing to focus on moving my physical body away from the line. I found that I, too, had a wide, relaxed smile and felt warm and blissful inside. This, for me, was the final confirmation that I had found what I was looking for and that at the Yoga retreat I would find more answers and be healed of my psychological afflictions.

Little did I know then that I had fallen for one of Satan's oldest tricks—the use of guru-figures as demonic puppets through which to transmit blissful forces that seduce even as they veil the consuming face of darkness behind it all. I had walked right into a web of darkness that appeared as a luminous rainbow of divine promise.

With excited anticipation, I drove for an hour and a half northeast of San Francisco to the rural area where the Yoga community sits on several hundred acres in the rolling foothills of the Sierra Nevada Mountains. There I saw many large domed buildings, tepees scattered all about, and scores of busy people attending to their tasks. I was there on a work/study program. Half the day I was to be an apprentice in the village's organic gardens. During the other times I would attend classes in their Yoga Teachers' Training Program, do extensive meditation and Hatha Yoga, and have fellowship with all the yogis around.

The people there were clean, friendly, and helpful. They had their own version of the Ten Commandments—"*Yamas* and *Niyamas*" (the five do's and the five don'ts). Drugs, alcohol, extramarital sex, etc., were expressly forbidden. Days were very structured and disciplined, from 5 A.M. to 10 P.M. A Yoga church service was held for the whole community of 200-300 on Sundays. Everyone was vegetarian, with some being fruitarian (fruits only), and some aspired to breatharianism (no food, air only). (Though I heard much talk about breatharianism in many circles of the New Age, I never did find anyone who actually could pull it off.)

The rigor and discipline of the daily routine helped my own personal healing and stabilizing process to some degree, though not as much as I had wanted. The Yoga system prides itself on being a "science of higher consciousness"—the idea that by applying certain cause and effect Yoga practices through thousands of lifetimes a person eventually would create his own wholeness and ultimate salvation. In such a system, I realized that it might be a long, long time before I attained inner healing and everlasting peace. It wasn't very good news.

Pocono Bound

After four months my money ran out and so I went back home to Texas. After a few months of housepainting, I was keen to move on to my next spiritual adventure. The heading was eastward this time.

Destination: another well-known Yoga community situated in the Pocono Mountains of Pennsylvania.

A huge former monastery in rural backcountry, this serene setting was overseen by the guru of the entire national organization. This *Swami* had achieved a certain amount of renown in some scientific circles when he proved, at the highly respected Menninger Foundation, that he has certain mind-over-matter abilities. I quickly found a mystique, involving thousands of alleged miracles and mystical marvels, permeating the community. All bowed to their glorious and adored guru, who acted as a god-on-Earth, benevolently bestowing wisdom, gifts, miracles, and salvation to all his supplicants.

Again, as at the previous Yoga community, the lifestyle was regimented, orderly, clean, and in accordance with the five do's and five don'ts. Though I now look back on these people as being deluded by a messianic pretender, their dedication, organization, sincerity, and kindness made for a pleasant stay.

The better part of every day was a routine of early morning group meditation and devotions, followed by breakfast and morning studies. Afterwards, there were a couple hours work, lunch, and then afternoon studies and group meditations. Evenings sometimes had planned activities and classes. Otherwise we were on our own and had fellowship or retired to our individual rooms for study and more meditation.

Emphasis in this community was on "detached self-observation" — a kind of self-induced psychological splitting of the inner self into a totally detached observer and the rest of the self who thought, felt, and acted. To the detached observer part of oneself, it doesn't matter what the "lower self" is doing or experiencing — the observer remains totally non-involved and unconcerned.

The observer simply watches and goes "Hmm, that's interesting" to everything, no matter if the person is experiencing a third-degree burn or smelling a flower. This kind of psychological split makes for a rather emotionless, joyless placidity. It's somewhat like having a community of people aspiring to be like "Star Trek's" Mr. Spock.

I also experienced a Yoga initiation by one of the sub-gurus of the community. As a visitor I did not merit initiation from the *Swami* himself. The sub-guru was in a stage of deep meditation when I entered the room, seemingly oblivious to my presence. After a time, he called me over to sit beside him in an eerily deep voice. He positioned himself so that his mouth was several inches away from my right ear. Then he enunciated a *mantra*[5] directly into my ear several times. There was a peculiar penetrating quality to the sounds. It was as though they were being seeded deep within my being.

He had me vocalize the sounds myself, and informed me that this was my personal *mantra* that linked me to the ancient lineage of this community's gurus. Strangely enough, I felt almost lighter-than-air walking out of the room, and experienced a continuous, extremely pleasant, blissed-out state of mind for two whole days.

Again, a demonic link was seeded within me, sugar-coated with short-term bliss and peace. My seduction was growing deeper and more complex with each new spiritual adventure. While my scrapbook was filling up, I was sinking into Satan's gilded mire.

One Last Skirmish in College

Having quenched my appetite for Yoga *ashrams* for a while, I decided to go back to college and finish up my final two trimesters. The domain of college academia seemed now to be an alien environment, somehow irrelevant to real life and quite "ivory towerish." Still, the general pursuit of knowledge and the academic study of various religions was an enjoyable interlude.

In a final senior thesis paper, reviewed by all Religion department professors, I challenged what I perceived as antiquated, out-of-touch Western religious orthodoxy and presented an eclectic alternative of psychedelically expanded Eastern mysticism and American Indian shamanism. It was ill-received (though passing), but I fully expected this. My voice of defiance in the face of what I then perceived as entrenched orthodox authority was the beginning of my future New Age activism.

I walked away from college with a B.A. in Religious Studies in one hand and Yoga meditation beads in the other. In retrospect, I can't know if it would have made a difference but I wish one of my professors (most of whom were Christians) had taken off their objective, academic hats and sat me down and given me the simple witness of the faith in Christ that even a child can understand. In all the complexities of religious intellectualism, I totally had missed the ultimate truth.

Exploring Career Options in the New Age

My dedication to becoming professionally involved in some aspect of the New Age Movement was by now firmly established. Inwardly, I still felt incomplete and in need of much healing. Combining both deep personal need and career direction, I decided to pursue the profession of holistic medicine. Also called holistic health, this is a major branch of the New Age, one that is extremely widespread and well-developed throughout America and the rest of the world.

Looking through ads in New Age periodicals, over a hundred choices of schools and learning centers in the holistic healing arts

were available. I felt that by learning how to heal myself with holistic
health practices, I then could apply that knowledge to helping others
heal themselves in the future.

While in the midst of sorting out choices, I received a letter from
the director of the Yoga Teachers' Training Program that I had attended in California. He said that he had received my image in
meditation after asking his guru for guidance in picking a program
assistant. Perceiving this to be a "sign from above" and feeling
privileged to be asked to such a position, I agreed. Within the
month, I was on the road again to California.

This assistant teaching position proved valuable as a beginning
New Age leadership experience.

In unraveling the thread of Satan's seduction in my life, I see how
he provided certain "signs" that I would respond to in pointing me
further down the road of well-intentioned delusion. Most every New
Ager can recount a long series of uncanny "coincidences" occurring
in their lives, leading them further and further along the New Age
path. What I see today is that the adversary plots to lead people more
and more deeply into the New Age by providing "signs" and "coincidences," like laying a trail of cheese in front of lab mice running
a maze.

After finishing the three-month program assistant stint, I saw a
vision in meditation pointing me to a holistic health retreat I had
been reading about. Situated on Orcas Island off the coast of Washington, this remote and storybook-beautiful island was home to a
small settlement of New Agers who offered various kinds of retreats
and classes.

I chose a seven-week program designed to give a person the "full
treatment." On a diet heavy on sprouts, wheatgrass juice and morning "liver cleansers" containing liberal amounts of garlic, one's
gastro-intestinal condition certainly did get the "full treatment."
Soon I was introduced to a wide assortment of techniques designed
to "break you down and then build you back up."

One practice was to get up in the morning and quickly drink an
entire gallon of heavily salted water. Why? So you immediately could
regurgitate it all back out. This "atomic cleansing" technique was for
clearing stomach mucus out of the body. If you can imagine a bath-
room full of people doing this at the same time, it's certainly a fine
way to start the morning. Even then, as a New Ager, this was a bit
too much for me.

During the first afternoon's class, our group of 16 paired off and
the instructor led us through a bodywork technique supposed to
"realign our body's energy field." At the end of the technique each
person giving the treatment was provided with a tissue, and we were

then instructed to put pressure at the very tip of the tailbone of our partner. This was not sexual in nature, but it was one heck of a way to get to know someone the first day.

Then there were the "jackhammer" bodywork sessions (my term for them). Some schools of New Age bodywork[6] feel that psychological traumas also are lodged in the deep muscle tissues. Therefore, to release these traumas and restore body harmony, it becomes necessary for the practitioner to grind fists, fingers, elbows, and knees deeply into virtually every major muscle group in the body of the hapless recipient.

This is *severely* excruciating, to say the least. The howls, shrieks, and murderous screams that would fill the air in the community eventually became "normal," though during the first few weeks the place sounded at times like a torture chamber.

Then it was MY TURN. Sometimes a couple of assistants were required to hold me down while the practitioner tried to make my calf muscles "one with the table" via extreme elbow pressure. This is a series of treatments profoundly etched in my memory.

There were other less-severe practices, but these were the most memorable. Everyone in the group followed the entire regimen. Looking back, so much of this appears completely ludicrous. At the time though, everything was presented professionally, with lots of rationale behind it, and it seemed to make sense. When doubts arose in my mind, I thought: "Since you've already paid your $1,700, you might as well give it a shot."

Several small groups of 15-20 individuals were involved in different classes at any given time at this center, and it is noteworthy to point out that many of the participants were successful professionals in a wide variety of fields, New Age and otherwise.

I later discovered that the members of this community were all disciples of yet another Indian guru, supposed to be "God" in the flesh. While they did not advertise it, this was their spiritual link-up with Satan's forces. Yet again, the guru-connection had played a guiding role in my pilgrimage into seduction.

A Survival School Vision Quest

My next venture (after a time of recuperation from all the "healing" I had experienced) veered off onto a different tangent. I have had the innermost feeling since an early age that the times in which we live today are the end times. While I had a different perspective on the end times as a New Ager than I do today as a Christian, at the time I read many prophecies foretelling severe disasters and worldwide tumult in the relatively near future. I thought it imperative to

learn how to survive under adverse circumstances and to live off of
nature. I also was looking for an ultimate test of my personal mettle
plus a chance to undergo what American Indians call a "vision quest."
A survival school, based in Provo, Utah, provided a perfect opportunity to satisfy this piece of my pilgrimage puzzle.

Being as enamored with American Indian religions as I was then,
I felt that my spiritual journey would not be complete without my
own version of their vision quest.

This quest is a "rite of passage" from boyhood to manhood, in
which the young Indian boy is left alone in a sacred place to fast, do
rituals, pray for a "vision" of his life-purpose, and to acquire spiritual powers. In many ways it is a kind of initiation into the supernatural realms. This is a fairly popular practice in the New Age, and
I felt that I would find some answers to my burning desire for finding
inner peace and my life's greater purpose.

I quickly found that this outdoor survival school was indeed a
kind of "ultimate challenge" that would test my personal mettle to
the very limit. The first three days of the program were called *Impact*,
and this phase certainly did make an intense impact on the 50 participants. Getting out of the bus in the remotest badlands of southern
Utah, for these first few days we were allowed to have only the
clothes on our back, a knife, a fork, a cup, a plastic trash bag, and a
sweater. This was to be a real initiation into a real survival situation,
as we had no food, no canteens, no tents.

Strenuous forced hiking for 12-14 hours per day through some of
the worst badlands I have ever seen and up and down mountains
quickly took its toll on some of the less fit of the group. Dehydra-
tion, vomiting, exhaustion, and severe blisters, among other side
effects, afflicted some, but we still had to move on. There was no
food to be gathered from the badlands, and water was extremely
scarce. At times we would have to brush away the layers of scum
covering a small pocket of water in the sandstone. Most of us were so
desperately parched that we drank such water thankfully.

On the last day of the three-day Impact phase, a 28-day program,
we hiked well into the night and still had a long way to go to reach our
destination. There was a stream at our destination, so we had a lot of
motivation to get there. Having had no food and little water for three
days under such extreme conditions, most all of us were walking wrecks.

I still was using this situation as a vision quest, and had been
meditating whenever possible and calling out to the spirits of the
Indians for a vision. Then, something very unusual happened. Instead
of feeling severely exhausted and beleaguered like the others, I became filled with a power that completely erased all fatigue and made
my steps easy and light.

Started marking this page

When we reached the destination around 2 A.M., half the group was near a state of total collapse. Numerous people were vomiting, one was having real medical problems, and most simply drank some water and dropped asleep where they knelt. Still feeling this extraordinary energy surge, I helped some of those in need for a time. After everyone had gone to sleep, I was so energized that sleep was impossible, so I sat down in the Yoga *lotus* position to ride the energy out in a state of meditation. After a couple of minutes, I felt like the "lid" of my mind was opened and my awareness soared into the starry heights.

This was a mystical experience of "cosmic consciousness" like none I'd ever had before. I saw in my expanded mind's eye a hawk-spirit, that seemed to span the entire galaxy, come to alight over me. For what felt like hours I heard hawk cries that seemed to reverberate through every atom of my expanded consciousness. I had received my vision, and was ecstatic.

Waking up in the morning after two hours' sleep, I felt normal again, and extremely fatigued, like the others. The energy surge had come and gone.

At the time, I felt that "God" had answered my spiritual cry, and that this experience confirmed that my life was going in the right direction. I felt that truth had been revealed to me in a very special way, and that I was one major step closer to personal healing and spiritual enlightenment.

In unraveling the story behind my seduction, though, I see now that by calling out to the spirits of American Indian pantheism and following the pattern of the vision quest ritual, I again had unknowingly opened myself to the wiles of Satan. I had asked for a "vision" and "powers" and got both. By crossing into the Biblically forbidden territory of occult practices (Deuteronomy 18:10-12), I had ventured onto Satan's turf.

The enemy and his demonic legions masquerade many times as angels of light and servants of righteousness (2 Cor. 11:13-15). This was a constant thread through all my New Age experiences, happening time and time again. What I was absolutely convinced was truth was actually an extended series of masterful counterfeits. The powerful experiences and elegant philosophies in the New Age can be so utterly convincing to even the most well-intentioned persons. This is what is so sad about so many people involved in the New Age.

In this experience, I had gone through yet another mystical doorway into further reaches of Satan's New Age landscapes. I also acquired a "familiar spirit"—a demon masquerading as the spirit-hawk with which I felt such a close affinity. In a way similar to the American Indians, I had acquired a "power animal," my "spirit helper."

This demon parasite attached itself to me in the masquerading appearance of a spirit-hawk. By now, with all the yoga initiations, guru-connections, "inner counselors," and a "power animal," I was enmeshed firmly in Satan's web of luminous darkness.

Within the next week I re-injured a problem knee, had a terrible case of intestinal problems (from the raunchy water), and had to hitchhike back to Provo, Utah. In all fairness, the participants in this program were given fair warning about the severe conditions and steep challenge of the program. Survival we wanted, and survival we got.

A year later, still very concerned about obtaining further survival skills for the cataclysmic times I felt to be ahead for the world, I attended a two-week Security and Survival Training seminar. In it I learned about martial arts, military-style strategies for scouting, evasion, and defense, nuclear fall-out measures, living off the land, water purification, and a host of other bottom-line techniques for survival through world-shaking times. While many of my New Age friends thought that they could meditate and fast through such a crisis period, I figured to cover all possible angles, from the spiritual to the bottom-line practical.

Becoming a Holistic Health Professional

Now I was ready seriously to pursue vocational training in holistic health. This was an area in which I further could pursue my New Age beliefs. It promised to teach me further how to heal myself, and also lead to a professional career. I found a holistic health learning center with a two-year program leading to an N.D. (naturopathic doctor) degree. The program was set up to have several in-residence learning sessions at the school each year. For the rest of the time we were given substantial assignments to do on our own.

In keeping with its "natural" approach to health care, the school was located in the beautiful backwoods of northern Minnesota, with the classroom overlooking a lake where we would sometimes see bald eagles and golden eagles hover overhead and dive for fish. It was all quite idyllic.

The school was run in a very professional manner, with a serious and disciplined approach. A significant portion of my fellow students were nurses and former nurses who were disillusioned with orthodox medicine. All of us were aiming toward a fairly well-paying job in the fast-expanding holistic health field. This was and is one of the strongest and most well-developed branches of the New Age Movement, and the job opportunities were plentiful.

This program had a very different focus than the sometimes loony approach I encountered at the health retreat a while back (those won-

derful "jackhammer" bodywork sessions and other such practices).
There were several world-renowned figures who would fly in to instruct on occasion, and several M.D.s were on the faculty. Holistic
health is basically an attempt to use natural substances (such as
herbs, juices, etc.) and natural treatment methods to heal the whole
person—body, emotions, mind, and spirit. This movement is radically
opposed to much of what orthodox medicine has to offer.

Over the two years I completed a course of study that included
such subjects as: Trauma-free exercise; Iridology; Fasting; European
Weight Reduction Programs; Diet and Nutrition; Stress Management;
Body-Mind Integration Techniques; Swedish Massage; Postural
Integration Bodywork; Trigger Point Therapy; European Health
Rejuvenation Techniques; Martial Arts; Spiritual Awareness Enhance-
ment; and Herbology.

Holistic medicine is one of the trickiest areas to sort out the New
Age from the non-New Age. This is to say, a holistic professional
might recommend that a person do aerobic exercise and take a multi-
vitamin, but doing the exercise and taking the vitamin is not necessarily New Age. This important issue of discerning and separating
what is and is not New Age in the field of holistic health is often a
complex and subtle one requiring extensive examination.[7]

The primary point here is to note that the large majority of people involved in the program, including the head instructor, had an
underlying New Age philosophy. Yet never in all the school's literature and clinical hand-outs was the term New Age used. There was a
conscious and careful attempt to package and market holistic health
in a more scientific and mainstream-acceptable way so as to appeal to
the broadest possible number of people. This was done with good intent, as it was believed that holistic health is totally beneficial to all
people. But the essential problem is that New Age philosophy lies at
the core of much of the holistic health field.

My educational experiences there led to an even more subtle
seduction. By seeing how the New Age could apply to so many different aspects of life—exercise, nutrition, body therapies, emotional
health, stress management, etc. with sometimes remarkable effectiveness—I saw that the New Age had a host of practical, down-to-
Earth, positive effects (though, there are many dangers implicit in
some holistic health practices). In fact, I experienced significant psychological healing and enhanced physical health by applying some of
the techniques over several years.

I also saw that a few aspects of holistic health—particularly some
of the exercise and nutritional information—have a scientifically
verified basis. The M.D. instructors at the school (a couple of whom

occupied highly respected positions in the medical community) lent a greater air of authority and mainstream respectability.

The area of holistic health is one of the most subtle and sophisticated areas of the murky merging of the esoteric and the mundane, the metaphysical with the mainstream, the pseudo-scientific with the scientific, the non-New Age with the New Age.

I was fascinated with my studies and felt that I really had found my life's calling. On a professional level I couldn't even remotely think of anything else that I would want to do with my life.

Comfortable and secure in this knowledge, I could not yet even *IMAGINE* the astounding turn my life shortly would take.

Notes

1. In New Age terms, "higher consciousness" basically means a supernaturally expanded frame of mind that supposedly embraces a grander understanding of universal truth that transcends rational thought.
2. See *Grow Rich! with Peace of Mind*, by Napoleon Hill (New York, NY: 1967). pp. 158-159.
3. Trance channeling is a phenomenon in which the medium allows a spirit to take over the mind and body. During the channeling session, the spirit's personality (usually very different from that of the medium) is evidenced by their words, body movements, style of speech, etc. The medium is usually totally unconscious of whatever happens during the session. Afterwards, the medium will then "return."
4. A "yogi" is a person who is dedicated to the discipline of Yoga.
5. A *mantra* is a word or short phrase that is repetitiously sounded in meditation. Many *mantras* are names of various Hindu deities.
6. "Bodywork" is a general term referring to a wide variety of massage and massage-like holistic health treatments.
7. For an in-depth analysis on this subject, see *New Age Medicine: A Christian Perspective on Holistic Health*, by Paul Reisser, M.D., Teri Reisser, & John Weldon.

THE RISE TO NEW AGE LEADERSHIP

Somehow, the startling sequence of events that was to overtake me shortly seemed as if destiny already had charted out this bizarre but astonishing rise to New Age fame. Miraculous "coincidences" kept opening up doors for a totally unknown young man—me—virtually to be catapulted into a meteoric New Age career.

In the midst of all the uncanny, overwhelming, bizarre, and wacky happenings detailed in this chapter, powerful forces were at work to raise me up to a position of leadership. In deep delusion at the time, I thought that the "Force" was simply very strong with me, and that the cosmic gods were paving the way for me to do important work in bringing about a revolutionary New Age "One World Order."

It never, ever occurred to me that Satan could be in back of all of this. Such a thought would have seemed absolutely outlandish at the time. The New Age, I thought, was the veritable stepping stone into the kingdom of heaven. It is hailed as the final solution to all the world's woes, and the bearer of a planetary super-Renaissance of human consciousness, government, and science. To suggest otherwise, I thought, was pure ignorance, and to suggest that the plans and forces of the Antichrist lurked beneath this "super-Renaissance" was absolute folly.

The deluded of the New Age are not aware of their delusion. This is what is so pitiful—and so potentially dangerous.

So much of the New Age felt so good, so true, so awe-inspiring. Oh, the cleverness and finesse of the adversary, who devises schemes within schemes and wraps them within other entrancing schemes.

To follow this tale of deception, brainwashing, and bondage is to see the enemy at work, as an angel of light, beautiful on the outside but rotten at the core. May the reader be alerted to Satan's strategies, and so be better buttressed against them. Forewarned is forearmed.

In the unfolding "inside story" of a former New Age leader, a panorama of alien, farfetched, and even shocking New Age landscapes are exposed. By coming to perceive this weird, brainwashed New Age mentality, the reader is better forewarned of the motives and goals of New Agers, as well as some of the deceiving strategies of the Antichrist forces.

Meeting a New Age "Soul-Mate"

Freshly graduated from holistic health school, holding high hopes and enthusiastic visions of a successful career, I had no idea of the even more radical twist my life was about to take.

For a while events unfolded as I had foreseen. I went about opening up a "Natural Health Center" in a medium-sized city in East Texas. In a small, business-zoned house, I offered personalized health care programs, bodywork treatments, weekly "Awakening Your Potential" classes, iridology analysis, meditation and Hatha *Yoga* classes, health care products, and a host of other products and services. I even had a carefully planned "deep relaxation environment" in one room where a special arrangement of colors, plants, aromas, art, subliminal tapes, and New Age music was created to induce "therapeutic deep relaxation." Business was slow, but I knew it would take time to build up a practice.

In a local bookstore, I came across a flyer advertising the New Age Awareness Center. It looked like something right up my alley. It would be nice to find some metaphysically like-minded people to New Age around with.

I called the number and talked for a while with a sweet-sounding lady who was the director. She informed me that this Center was composed of a loosely affiliated group of people who would attend free-of-charge lectures and programs on various New Age topics. There was no membership, no fees, and no commitment necessary. During the conversation, I offered to give a free evening lecture on holistic health sometime. She agreed and we set a date.

Later, after the presentation, Vicki, the director, and I chatted for a while after every one else had gone. She told me in a light but honest way that she virtually detested health foods and all that holistic health craze. She much preferred a diet heavy on Twinkies, Ho-Ho's and Ding-Dongs. I tried to take all this in stride, but a *real* New Ager to my mind was a fastidious vegetarian who never would stoop to eating such outright "garbage." I thought she was a pleasant person, but definitely not my type.

In regularly attending the New Age Awareness Center meetings, I got to know "Miss Twinkie," as I secretly referred to her in my mind. Little did I know that she saw me as "Mr. Natural Self-Righteous." There was definitely some static behind our friendly demeanor toward one another, but strangely enough there was a growing spiritual attraction. Somehow, we would find ourselves talking late into the night after a meeting was over, even as we carefully positioned ourselves at very opposite ends of a long couch.

Time after time this would happen. There was no romance involved in this at all—the "chemistry" was just not there. But there was a mutual spiritual attraction that was growing so strong that it started to frighten us.

Over several weeks we searched in our meditations for direction regarding this alarming situation. We came to have a powerful feeling that we were being spiritually "called" to join together and do New Age "light-work" together. We felt that a "mission" had been divinely bestowed on us. Because of this, we became a spiritual soulmate "couple."

The Crystal Connection

Vicki had received a small but perfect quartz crystal from an American Indian medicine man—one of his "power objects."[1]

One day when doing New Age meditation, she was instructed by her "spirit guides" to give me the crystal and to ask me to meditate with it. This was bizarre. The idea of meditating with a hunk of rock sounded patently ridiculous.

After laughing about the idea for a couple of days, I decided to give it a shot. It couldn't hurt, could it?

Only minutes after focusing on the crystal in a state of trance-like meditation, my consciousness was catapulted into electrifying domains of extra-natural light the likes of which I had never before perceived. The upper part of my head felt like it wasn't there, like it had become invisible, as my awareness raced upwards at the speed of light. From a high distance, I could see in my mind's eye that my body was trembling and shaking as the power of the experience rattled through it.

This was my "crystal initiation" into an entirely different supernatural realm. Wow! Was this "crystal power" or what?[2]

For the rest of the week my crystal-aided meditations brought vivid visions of strange high-tech machines and contraptions all using crystals in different ways. It was like stepping into a science fiction novel about technologies on an alien planet. I also saw visions of a high-crystal-tech holistic health clinic with lasers, holography, color beams, glowing liquids, and more in this mind-boggling sci-fi film.

Several close friends remarked on a distinct change in my demeanor. Somehow, they said, I was more charged and outgoing. I felt blissful, as if I had found an entirely new part of myself. Sadly, though, in reality I blindly had entered an entirely different realm of Satan's high-tech, dazzling deceptions. Sure, all this was a blast and I was riding a high like I had never known, but later there would be a very dear price to pay for all this occult adventurism. A dear price indeed.

With seemingly providential timing, a man called the New Age Awareness Center to see if the center would sponsor his 1-day crystal workshop. Vicki and I marveled at this uncanny coincidence.

I couldn't wait to see what mysteries would be unveiled.

For the most part, the workshop consisted of guided meditations somewhat like those in Silva Mind Control (remember the inner sanctuary), except this time we were to project our minds *into* the crystal held in front of the forehead (where the occult "third eye"[3] is located). I thought that this was a crazy idea, but went ahead and tried it anyway. In the first guided meditation I wasn't really getting the hang of it, but starting with the second one I felt that my mind somehow was focused inside the crystal. We were guided to explore various sensory perceptions of the crystal structure—are there any sounds, how does it feel, what do you see, etc. Almost everyone in the workshop experienced some perceptions, though they were all different from each other.

In a later guided meditation, I saw a vision of a large library composed solely of different sizes and shapes of crystals, each containing volumes of stored information, like a sci-fi, futuristic concept. I also saw elaborate crystal computers glowing and scintillating with multicolored electric charges. Alien beings of short stature and enlarged heads attended to a large complex of high-tech crystal instruments and machines that did ultra-advanced things I couldn't comprehend. Funny thing about the alien technicians, they worked together wordlessly like a bunch of bees in a coordinated group synchrony. This was getting a little crazy.

After the workshop, my mind was reeling with the new ideas, trying to comprehend this new world that was opening up inside of me. I really was getting hooked on crystals.

Shortly thereafter I went to a psychic fair in Dallas. Amid all the usual psychic readers I came upon a man calling himself "Saint" who wore a tag identifying himself as a "gemologist." He was not giving psychic readings about people, but rather about crystals. He said that he could tell you the history of the crystal, what kind of information it contained, and what its best uses were.

Here was my next step along the "crystal connection" seduction that started to take the place of the "guru connection" that Satan had used to lead me onwards in previous years.

"Saint" and I felt an immediate affinity—as though we were long-lost brothers. He had been involved in crystals for a number of years already, and knew much more than I did. At the time—the very early 80s—crystal power was still very much a lesser-known, unpopular topic. For hours after the psychic fair ended, he regaled me with tales of UFOs with which he was in constant communication, inside knowledge on how the UFOs were preparing to make themselves known to the world, and even a time when he was beamed aboard a spaceship to receive an Emerald Ray initiation and a crystal implant in his body (shades of Whitley Streiber's best-selling book *Communion*).

I really had never thought much about UFOs before, but the stories were utterly fascinating. Little did I know then how large a role the UFO-connection would play in my own life and in the 1980s New Age as a whole.

"Saint" loaned me his "master stone" to help me "activate my consciousness onto a higher Light-frequency." It was a strange-looking, blackish, ovoid-shaped stone with thousands of tiny spines sticking out all around it. Years later I found out that this was a rock called tektite, the unusual characteristics of which still cause debate among scientists as to whether it is a type of meteor. I carried this stone "power object" throughout the next few dramatic months.

Aligning into New Directions

The 1982 Grand Alignment was fast approaching. A precursor of the infamous 1987 Harmonic Convergence, this major New Age event, was based on a highly unusual astrological alignment of planets that was supposed to usher in a new level of "cosmic light" to the Earth. Such times always seem to bring out the most dramatic experiences in New Agers.

We were no different. As the moment of Grand Alignment came to pass, Vicki and I both independently came to a decision to move from East Texas. We did what many New Agers would do—we got out a map of the USA and used a pendulum to divine our next destination.

The pendulum indicated one of the hottest New Age hot spots of the early 1980s—the Santa Fe, New Mexico area.

We also decided that because of the deep bond we shared in doing our New Age light-work that we should be married. That there was no romance between us was secondary—we just felt that we should be together. It was an unusual strain of New Age thinking, to be sure.

We planned a "spiritual marriage ceremony." And, typical of New Agers, we wanted to do it in a mystical location. Having recently heard of the "Marfa lights" near the tiny town of Marfa, West Texas, we planned to do the private ceremony on the trip to New Mexico. The Marfa lights are sightings of strange luminous appearances that seem to center around Marfa, dating back to American Indian times. Many myths and legends surround this unexplained phenomenon. (New Agers love this kind of thing.)

Over the next couple of months we planned our move to the promising metaphysical horizons of Santa Fe. Though we had little money, no jobs waiting, and little idea of what we actually were going to do there, we simply trusted in our inner guidance and the tail of the pendulum.

We did the spiritual marriage ritual in this utterly desolate location. However, we didn't see the Marfa lights.

We felt like intrepid metaphysical voyagers seeking out new vistas, charting new lands. Little did we know that our years in northern New Mexico would exceed our wildest dreams—and we could dream pretty wildly.

The Spirit World Reveals Its Plans for Me

In the early 80s Santa Fe was regarded by many New Agers as a particularly hot "vortex area." A vortex is supposed to be a special area where the power and magnitude of mystical energies is unusually high; a place in some ways "closer" to the heavens than the other locations of "lower vibrations." Wherever a vortex is, you can be sure that New Agers will be flocking there in droves to absorb and bask in the "rarefied vibrations." Mt. Shasta, California, Maui, Hawaii, and Sedona, Arizona are other prime examples of such metaphysical magnets.

Santa Fe in those days—the late 70s to early 80s—was really like an isolated microcosm of the New Age Movement. In some ways it was like a miniature Southwest version of the leading-edge San Francisco-based New Age subculture. If something New Age really was happening it would be happening in Santa Fe. The metaphysical menu was always extensive and dynamically changing. For the exploring New Ager, this was a paradise.

We lucked into an unusual opportunity to live in a low-rent/great-view house. The unique Southwestern combination of high desert, mesas, and mountains, as well as the smell of pinyon in the air, can be breathtaking at times.

The first thing we did was to take two weeks off for a type of "spiritual honeymoon" — lots of the spiritual, but no passion (by mutual choice).

Exploring the mystical landscapes of the Southwest was our quest. There was much to explore and many surprises.

The spiritual honeymoon was a head-turning one, though a most New Age one. While the daytime visits to marvelous tourist locations and vortex spots were fun, it was the nighttimes that "blew my mind."

The spirit world began to speak to us explicitly and directly. All of a sudden Vicki would go into a trance. Then a spirit would come into her body and animatedly speak. I couldn't believe what was happening.

These electrically compelling spirits would come in and identify themselves, and then proceed to convey some august universal message of great import. I found that I even could converse with these "high and wise" spirit-entities. They would answer my questions with what sounded like great wisdom and supernatural prescience. The variety of spirits coming and going was astounding — I talked with spirits identifying themselves as "Moses," "Mozart," "White Eagle," "White Cloud," "Serapis Bey," "Ascended Master Kuthumi," "Mary," "Golden-Helmeted Ones," "Green Ray Master," and a host of others. The power emanating from these spirits was overwhelming and entrancingly intoxicating.

For hours at a time, spirit after spirit would come into Vicki's body and speak through her. She was totally oblivious to what was being said and done. It was like she was tucked away somewhere while the spirits temporarily would "use her vehicle," as they said, to speak to me.

I was flabbergasted by what they told me. Distilling the volumes of information, essentially this array of exalted "Universal Masters" and "Servants of the Light" told me this: that Vicki and I, and a few select others like us around the world, were receiving a "grand dispensation" to be the vanguard "Bearers of New Age Light" to lead the world into the fast-approaching "Golden Age of Oneness."

They told us to start to call out in our meditations to the "Space Brothers," who allegedly were highly advanced extraterrestrial intelligences stationed in our solar system. These "Space Brothers" had come from a variety of galaxies, and were part of a collective "Intergalactic Space Federation" working together to assist planets like Earth to go through a "purification process" preceding a quantum leap into a new evolutionary stage of human development — a New Age of "Heaven-on-earth."

The Space Brothers were said to work in conjunction with the "Great White Brotherhood" (also known as the "Spiritual Hierarchy of Light"), a universal hierarchy of Ascended Masters, archangels,

angels, and other types of spirit-beings who administrate and control all aspects of creation.

I was told that our task was to help bring the advanced teachings of the Great White Brotherhood to those people who would be receptive to New Age consciousness and also to share techniques (many of them using crystals) so that these people could be "activated into a higher consciousness of Light." I was informed that my path already had been charted out and decreed into action by the "Higher Councils of Universal Masters," and that I should therefore expect many dramatic doors to open in the coming years.

Unbelievable! The cosmic "gods" were speaking directly to me, saying that Vicki and I were "chosen ones" specially hand-picked to lead the world into the New One-World Era.

I was stunned for days by these overpowering experiences and revelations. I thought that I was pretty far out before all of this. But as the weeks and months unfolded, several of these spirits' pronouncements actually materialized in uncanny ways, plus in Vicki's and my meditations we started to receive startlingly clear transmissions from spirit-sources identifying themselves as Space Brothers.

This was getting to be like an episode from the "Twilight Zone." But the power of these experiences felt good, our lives were fun and exciting, and the words of "peace, light, and brotherhood" seemed totally enlightened and benignly love-filled.

The higher plateaus of my seduction and bondage were set into motion here with full force. I had been enticed with visions of high cosmic drama and promises of world-shaking spiritual work to be done, while the powerful charms of luminous demons masquerading as angels of light conspired to mesmerize and brainwash me to deeper levels of bondage.

Channeling of this kind is really quite common in many New Age circles. Many who are true-believers maintain successful professional careers even as they fully indulge in the New Age. What to some would appear verging on the insane (or inane), appears to these true-believers as high truth beyond the reckoning of the less evolved.

In retrospect, I see that the sometimes overwhelming power accompanying these experiences that I thought then was heavenly love and light was actually an entrancing force put forth by demonic deceivers so that a type of open-eyed, light-to-deep hypnotic trance occurs in the recipients. Being much more vulnerable and suggestible in this state, even as the person feels wonderful and "light-filled," brainwashing influences can then be subliminally seeded.

Recall how easy it is for professional hypnotists to hypnotise a group of people all at once. Once in this trance state, the people can be implanted with all kinds of normal-to-bizarre hypnotic suggestions that they will perform at the command of the hypnotist.

With regard to New Age channeling, a parallel dynamic takes place, though the mode of hypnotising and the suggestions implanted are of a very different variety. The fact that channeling is one of the hottest phenomena in the New Age today is no happenstance — it is an integral part of the enemy's power-play to induce larger magnitudes of delusion in the millions of people composing this fast-growing movement.

"Cutting My Teeth" on the New Age

Up to this point, I was a student, basking in the comfort of the pursuit of knowledge while not yet being tied to the full gamut of adult responsibilities. Now I had to go out and make an actual living in the real world of bills to pay and duties to fulfill. More than anything else, the next years were a transition into married manhood. It was indeed a learning experience.

With a fair amount of perseverance, fortitude, and resourcefulness a New Ager with some type of professional New Age training can eke out a passable living. Over the next two years I was involved in a fairly wide spectrum of activities, including the following. This list is a partial study of New Age inroads into some branches of mainstream society:

- Teaching hatha *yoga* classes at the local YMCA.
- Teaching "Dynamic Relaxation" classes through the Continuing Education branch of the state university.
- Giving lectures at the public library on "Quartz Crystals and Self-Transformation."
- Giving "crystal healing sessions" at a popular local metaphysical bookstore.
- Teaching aerobic classes at the YMCA.
- Being a staff member of a local holistic health school.
- Giving "natural health care" lectures to the general public.
- Offering "Maximizing Wellness" personalized holistic health consultations.
- Coordinating a city-wide "New Age Networking Guide to Santa Fe."
- Organizing a New Age "Festival of Light."
- Participating in various New Age conferences and expos in Santa Fe.
- Selling crystals at flea markets.

- Selling crystals at psychic fairs.
- And having a few garage sales to make ends meet.

On the side, we organized a New Mexico version of Vicki's Texas-based New Age Awareness Center. The flyer presented it as a "service-based, non-path-oriented forum for all spiritual expressions." Various metaphysical and holistic health speakers would give free evening presentations. The smorgasbord of New Age topics would include such things as:

- Peruvian whistling vessels (occult whistles for inducing trance-states).
- Group channeling sessions.
- Bach Flower Remedies (the "vibrational essences" of flowers for healing purposes).
- New Age art.
- Acupuncture.
- "Meeting Your Soul-mate."
- A "Come As You Were" party (costumes of past life incarnations).
- Past Life Regressions.
- UFO contact sessions.
- Guided Imagery for Success and Prosperity.
- Stress Management.
- And many more creatively varied topics.

We were quite the New Age activists, dedicatedly propagating the wonderful news of the New Age to as many as would listen. On several occasions we even participated in world-peace demonstrations in the imposing city of Los Alamos—what we called a "bastion of mad scientists' technological horrors"—where a world-class scientific community has been established since the birth of the Manhattan Project which developed the atomic bomb.

While all this was happening, powerful forces were continuing to guide and groom me for future works of much greater magnitude. These first few years in the Santa Fe scene were as a local apprenticeship leading up to national-level New Age seership.

A Warning Not Well-Taken

Before detailing these formative forces and events, it is interesting to note a certain visitor who appeared one night at our doorstep unannounced. A clean-cut young man, about 18 or so, asked if he might come in. Hesitatingly, I allowed him in and offered him a seat.

He came right to the point: "God told me to come here and tell you that you're masquerading as the light. Your master is darkness."

Rather taken aback by such an unexpected comment, I asked him to repeat this—maybe I had not heard him correctly. He did so, and I heard it the same as before.

Trying to be reasonable, I asked him if he would care to elaborate on this statement—could he prove this in any way?

He simply repeated his statement: "God told me to come here and tell you that you're masquerading as the light. Your master is darkness."

Understanding this was all he was going to say, I politely thanked him for relaying the message, and assured him I would ponder it. After he left, I simply dismissed the event as being from a crank. After all, I only recently had been having personal conversations with the higher ranks of cosmic "gods," and if I was masquerading as the light, they certainly hadn't brought it up.

Now, in retrospect, I wonder if Jesus Christ sent me a messenger that night to gently but firmly deliver His truth and a way out of my glittery bondage before I became even more deeply imbedded in it.

Hooked on "New Age Science"

Within the first month of arriving in Santa Fe, some acquaintances told us of someone we *had* to meet. Going by the very New Age handle of "Marco Atlantis," this magnetic personality was on the same "wavelength" as the one called "Saint" that I had met a while back.

A swirl of dramas surrounded this man: calling down UFOs to land; plans for building "healing temples"; blueprints for super-scientific breakthroughs; revelations about government conspiracies and UFO cover-ups; and dates for divine intervention and world deliverance. The man was like a human vortex of cosmic happenings.

He used a lot of advanced-sounding scientific terms mixed up with an unusual metaphysical jargon. When asked about the source of this, he brought out his "bible," a 600-page volume called *Keys of Enoch*. When I started leafing through its pages, a surge of energy gripped me. There was a vague but profound feeling of *déjà vu*, a feeling that this book was very familiar to me, and that it held the keys to unlocking incredible cosmic doors. I was so enthralled that I cut the meeting short and made a bee-line for the closest metaphysical bookstore. If I would have had to drive 500 miles that day to get this book, I would have done so. Fortunately a copy was available at a metaphysical bookstore 15 minutes away.

Over the next two months I was obsessed thoroughly with the *Keys*. The author is a man with many highly respected scholarly and scientific credentials (including more than one Ph.D. degree) who claims to have been translated bodily into the highest heavens and given a scripture for the New Age. In this "bible" I found an unparalleled level of sophistication and way of viewing the "big picture" of the cosmos, the magnitude of which I never had perceived before.

I had read thousands of religion and metaphysical books, but this one was in a class by itself. The author claims that it is written in a *coded* language that helps to "unlock the mind-gates" to the "Great White Brotherhood" (also called the "Spiritual Hierarchy of Light"). Time after time, upon reading certain passages I would have visions come before my mind's eye or spontaneously would go into a state of trance-meditation filled with racing thoughts and higher inspirations. My mind-gates were indeed being unlocked, and I was being re-circuited into a whole new dimension of New Age higher consciousness.

The *Keys of Enoch* claims to be a complete cosmic synthesis of the spiritual and scientific realms. With a peculiar blend of scientific concepts and esoteric principles, this book proposes to have the 64 keys to the "Higher Science" (or "Sacred Science") of totally reconstituting the Earth and its peoples into a New Age.

Interestingly, as I became more and more re-circuited, I came to be fascinated with scientific principles and many areas of leading-edge high technology. This was new to me, for I never really had cared for the dry world of science. In *Keys of Enoch* I read that startling advances in such diverse scientific fields as genetic engineering, telecommunications, supercomputers, nuclear fusion technology, artificial intelligence, solid state physics, quantum physics, advanced holography, laser optics, astrophysics, and others were to be combined with New Age spiritual philosophy in creating a utopian New World Order.

This "Sacred Science" claims to be a revolutionary super-science capable of linking with the infinite powers of the universe, all applied to completely re-create the planet into a paradise and its populace into gods. Thus, a grand "Second Genesis" would generate a super-Renaissance global utopia. At least, this is what *Keys of Enoch* and much of New Age philosophy proposes.

In reality, under the guise of light, peace, and love, the New Age seeks to re-make the world into a utopian society that is actually set up by the false Messiah—the Antichrist—leading to attempted world domination.

This New Age spiritual-scientific worldview became the guiding force behind all my future work. For some uncanny reason, I had a special affinity with all this that seemed to just blossom forth from within. It was like I had a special talent that, heretofore, was totally untapped. My own self-perception at the time was that I simply was tapping into the New Age higher consciousness and my own innate "god-powers." In reality, I was undergoing a profound level of brain-washing into some of Satan's more sophisticated-looking delusion-ary traps.

If you think that any person like this is so "cracked" that his life would be a wreck and an obvious candidate for a straitjacket, you would be only partially right. Outwardly, my life was very demand-ing but the challenges of being a New Age activist and a career man were being met quite well. I was basically a happy and fulfilled per-son, though a significant feeling of inner emptiness persisted.

In the New Age circles all around the country it is not unusual at all to find *many* people moving through all kinds of such radical higher consciousness transformations. Most of them continue to deal with life's challenges adequately, some better and some worse.

Shirley MacLaine and John Denver, the two most well-known New Agers, are prime cases in point. They both have made public some of their life-changing higher consciousness transformations, and both still enjoy prolific and highly successful careers. In my own case, within three years of moving to New Mexico, I would come to write two popular New Age books that were published by Harper and Row, a major mainstream publishing house. One can be enmeshed deeply in New Age lies, and at the same time still lead an apparently sane and productive life. This is part of what makes the New Age movement so dangerous.

A Crystal Power Book Materializes from "Heavenly Places"

Approximately three months after moving to the northern New Mexico area, my "spirit guides" gave me instructions to write a book on the subject of crystals. It was only a year or so since my very first crystal experiences, and I had no idea how I could accomplish such a task. This was back in 1982-1983 when there were only a few meager and obscure crystal books on the market. It was just a year or two before the massive crystal craze would start to sweep the New Age like a raging wildfire.

The spirit guides told me to take 12 quartz crystals and lay them out in a circle, to tape another one to the occult "third eye" and to suspend a large pyramid overhead. I was to sit in the very center of the crystals with my head underneath the pyramid. This was sup-posed to create a "crystal energy field" having amplified "higher vibrations" for receiving channeled thoughts from the spirit guides.

To my amazement, as I would enter a kind of semi-conscious trance, discernible thoughts, inspirations, and pictures would appear in my mind. All this was not my own doing—the spirit guides were transmitting their thoughts and influences to me. My job, effectively, was to take notes and then shape up the material into book form.

Over a period of three months I would take my position in the crystal circle for 10-12 hours per day and receive and transcribe this information. With some library research on the history of occult crystal use plus orthodox science's uses of man-made crystals in various technologies (like computers and lasers), the manuscript was complete.

Uncannily, a major publishing house was actively searching for "crystal power" manuscripts at the time. Out of hundreds of publishers, I chose 15 of them to send manuscripts. Thirteen were returned with a flat rejection notice. One small company was somewhat interested. And, after nine months of deliberation, the major publisher chose my manuscript. I couldn't believe my good fortune, but what the spirit guides had promised actually had come to pass against incredible odds.

Honestly, at times before this happened, especially when things got a little rough, I was inclined to doubt the revelations and prophetic projections of the spirit guides. In some ways I am a practical person and, if a philosophy is true, it should also work in the "real world" of mainstream society. But signing a contract with a publisher of blue-chip stature and eventually seeing the book in bookstores all around the country was pretty solid confirmation to me.

I was unaware, though, that the power of Satan can work quite effectively in bottom-line reality, too. It was not yet clear to me then that if something "works" that doesn't necessarily mean it is ultimately true. The enemy can perform "counterfeit miracles, signs, and wonders" (2 Thess. 2:9) that "work" but are not truth in the least.

The book, entitled *Windows of Light: Quartz Crystals and Self-Transformation*, launched me onto the national New Age scene. Released in 1984, the subject of crystals really was beginning to catch fire. Mine was one of the very first modern-day books on this topic to be released. It sold very well, and generally was considered to be the best book in the field for a number of years. As more and more crystal books cascaded forth in the coming years, my book was considered by most to be consistently among the top three books in the field.

At this time, I started to give weekend seminars in numerous major cities across America. The stage was set for the rise to national leadership.

Even as this book first was reaching bookstores and my national New Age career germinated, voluminous notes were being compiled for a second book. With each passing month, the information was becoming more advanced and elaborate. It was as if I was advancing through different grade levels in a cosmic schoolhouse.

For instance the crystal power ritual techniques were becoming much more complicated. Many of them involved attempts to stimulate and activate what the New Age calls the various psychic power centers located in the brain so as to awaken super-human higher mind-power abilities.

I also started to receive visions of hundreds of different crystal-based inventions. These inventions were not confined just to crystals; they also included pyramids, magnets, sonics, New Age music, color, lasers, electronic devices, computers, high-tech trance-induction machines, and others. Many were quite intricate; some even involved elaborate room-size set-ups involving hundreds of crystals and pyramids, among all the other elements. I was tapping into what seemed to be a mother lode of New Age sacred science.

Though the subject of sacred science is a most complex one, basically this aspect of the New Age is an attempt at a type of modern-day, high-tech sorcery and white magic.[4] This aspect of the New Age Movement was one of the "hottest" fields arising in the late 1970s and 1980s. Thousands of Ph.D.s from diverse scientific fields plus myriad independent thinkers and inventors have made this field a major up-and-coming force having a powerful influence in the New Age Movement today. With a unique blend of a) high-tech devices (like lasers, computers, etc.), b) modernized New Age sorcery, and c) futuristic scientific vision, New Age "sacred science" claims to be the way for man to technologically control the powers of the universe. By "awakening your own spiritual god-powers," sacred science claims that the entire universe can be manipulated by a human-based "Master Science" of extraordinary sophistication, a super-scientific revolution to manifest fully when the New Age dawns.

The fatal flaw (among other defects) of sacred science is that it is a human-devised technological pretender to the throne of Jesus Christ and His way, His truth, and His life.

In a similar way that the Antichrist will set himself up as a god proclaiming that he has all corresponding sovereign powers to rule the universe, sacred science is New Age man's attempts to have god-like technological control over himself, his destiny, and the entire cosmos. "Push-button miracles" become a tool of New Age man's higher consciousness in order to extend his rulership from Earth to the heavens. It is nothing less than an attempt at a modern-day Tower of Babel.

Essentially, New Age science is the attempt to manipulate reality in increasingly more powerful ways via an occult-based sorcery of sorts. To the orthodox scientist sacred science is a fringe-element pseudo-science. To those in the New Age, though, this topic is subject to much speculation and theorizing. Some of these inventions and techniques are experienced subjectively as being effective, some-times extremely so, in pursuing New Age goals.

Is New Age science just another *Alice in Wonderland* fantasy? Does it involve the placebo effect? Is it a mad scientist's dream? Why are Satan's demons leading more and more New Agers along these lines? Does it have any connection to the UFO issue? These and many other tantalizing questions arise about this strange "Twilight Zone" area of the New Age.

No matter whether sacred science works to some degree or not, I can testify today that it is based on occult principles and practices that are all forbidden, either explicitly or implicitly, in the Holy Bible (Deut. 18:9-12).

This is the ultimate flaw of New Age sacred science. It proved later to be one of my most difficult lessons of all to learn.

Project Beam-Down

To go back a little in the storyline, while going through the lengthy process of waiting for the publisher's acceptance of the first book (nine months) and the pre-release publication process (six months), there was a dynamic series of events and experiences con-tinuing to forge my New Age involvements.

At an upscale, nationally known resort outside of Santa Fe, I met the third in the series of high-energy macro-cosmic figures.

First, there was "Saint," then "Marco Atlantis," and now "John."

I had heard of him through the Santa Fe grapevine and it sounded as though he was on a "heavy cosmic trip."

Arranging a meeting at the resort where he resided, I was swept quickly up in the high excitement of John's dramatic plans.

He claimed that the resort area was the site of the region's most active vortex—a veritable bridge spanning the gap between the heav-ens and Earth. John said he had been "divinely guided" to move to the resort and commanded to coordinate the planet's first direct link-up with the Great White Brotherhood and the Intergalactic Federa-tion (UFOs).

He had an impressive array of highly elaborate, sophisticated-looking sacred science devices involving pyramids, crystals, lasers, electronic apparatuses, computers, psychedelic-type New Age music, subliminal cassette tapes, and exotic trance-inducing aromas. These devices were set up in a large symmetrical grid arrangement in a very spacious conference hall.

The idea, according to John, was to use sacred science to create a type of "space-time warp" (kind of like going to warp-drive in Star Trek) so that spirit-beings and extraterrestrials could materialize and interact directly with the people who were within the conference hall. In addition, John said that all this was leading up to further stages of extraterrestrial beings "beaming down" to Earth as well as "beam-ups" of the New Age elect to spaceships waiting above. The elect were to undergo cosmic initiations and "Light-body activations,"[5] so as to receive various advanced psychic powers, universal knowledge, and revolutionary high-tech tools. They then were to beam back down to Earth and help lead the world through a transition period into the One World Golden Era—the New Age.

Had I come to the right place? What Saint, Marco Atlantis, my spirit guides, *Keys of Enoch*, and many channeled New Age books were all talking about, seemed to be happening before my very eyes. In fact, when the word got out, people came flocking to the resort to "tune into" the celestial happenings. Marco Atlantis, who had been living in Albuquerque, even moved onto the resort lands. This was "hot" property indeed.

What added to the excitement was that people started to report "angels" materializing and increased UFO sightings around the northern New Mexico region. Was it hysteria? Fantasizing? Lying?

Many felt a profound subjective experience of "consciousness warping" in the sacred science set-up (like one's mind going to warp speed). Was it wishful thinking? The placebo effect? Or demon-controlled delusion and brainwashing?

John relayed his ethereal experience of receiving the "Divine Plan"[6] for all this. He claimed that he physically was beamed up to a command spaceship and was greeted by the fleet commander, a space-woman named Semjaza, originating from the Pleiades star system. Semjaza put him through a series of high-tech "chambers" to "activate his Light-body." She then appointed him to coordinate the Plan on the earthly end of things.

Electric anticipation filled the air for several months. Project Beam-Down (also called "Project Second Genesis") finally was about to happen after many millennia of waiting through lifetime after re-incarnated lifetime. We felt that we were on the threshold of the climax of the ages.

As so often happens, personality friction started to build up. Especially when it came to the issue of who was in command—John or Marco Atlantis. A rift of tension eventually tore the situation apart, even as the appointed date of the Beam-down came and went.

Though somewhat disappointed, I went away from this involvement feeling much more knowledgeable about sacred science and the UFO-connection. As I cut off all ties with John and Marco Atlantis, I felt that their egos had botched the situation and that John had been accurate about some topics but was in error with the setting of dates for the Beam-down.

Looking at this scenario today, I see that my early guru-connection by now had been replaced by a 1-2-3 punch of the UFO-connection, the crystal-connection, and the *Keys of Enoch* connection. All three New Age connections now had become my most powerful links of delusion. By now I was in deep trouble but was absolutely unaware of it. At this point:

- The lies of demons masquerading as "Ascended Masters" and "extraterrestrials" had cast a brainwashing spell.
- Occult-based New Age practices revolving around crystal idols mesmerized the mind.
- The allures of the modernized sorcery of sacred science worked its delusionary demon-conspired magic.

You might think that surely all this totally bizarre New Age UFO drama is probably just an isolated incident. But, in fact, it's not really that uncommon a New Age scenario at all. Would you believe that more than 75 percent of New Agers hold a completely unshakable belief in the reality of UFOs? Actually, 75 percent is probably an understatement. It's most likely around 85-95 percent. Even further, a solid percentage of New Agers—I'd estimate 50 percent or more—truly believe that they *are* alien or angelic beings that have reincarnated today into human form.

For instance, John Denver has made public the belief that he originated from a place near the Lyra nebula. In Shirley MacLaine's bestselling book and TV miniseries, *Out on a Limb*, the UFO-connection plays a major role in her cosmic vision quest. MacLaine's mentor, David, claims to have had a romantic and spiritual involvement with an alien woman named Mayan.

In general, believing that you're from the Orion, Sirius, or Pleaides star systems, among others, are very popular New Age self-concepts. Personally, I was convinced completely that my celestial home was Orion.

In fact, the question of whether UFOs are real is rarely contested or questioned. This belief is part and parcel of much, though not all, of the New Age mentality. UFOs are involved quite heavily in their concepts of the world's deliverance from a time of suffering and tribulation into an enlightened "One World United Government" (that is, the New Age).

Most New Agers hold firmly to the view that hundreds, if not thousands, of UFOs already are deeply involved in rendering aid to planet Earth in subtle but highly significant ways. But, because of a kind of "prime non-interference directive" (like on Star Trek), the extraterrestrials cannot intervene directly or render explicit assistance until humanity is *ready* for their help. These extraterrestrials are believed to have a highly evolved spiritual philosophy (akin to New Age philosophy) and extremely advanced technologies, both of which form the foundation for the New Age One World Order.

As wacky as all this sounds, there are many millions of New Agers who absolutely are convinced of this view. In fact, in most New Age circles, a person is considered a bit weird or "out of it" if he *doesn't* believe in all this.

What one might call a "UFO virus" has infected a huge sector of the New Age subculture. From past personal experience, I can say that the influences felt while I was in the grips of this "virus" were utterly compelling and convincing. Whether UFOs are "real" has not been determined scientifically as yet; whatever is happening here, there is a demonic power in back of the entire phenomenon.

In commenting on this topic in his book, *Angels: God's Secret Agents*, Billy Graham states: "Some reputable scientists deny and others assert that UFOs do appear to people from time to time. Some scientists have reached the place where they think they can prove that these are possibly visitors from outer space. ... many people are now seeking some type of supernatural explanation for these phenomena. Nothing can hide the fact, however, that these unexplained events are occurring with greater frequency around the entire world and in unexpected places."[7]

Also, in *Confronting the New Age*, Douglas Groothuis reports: "Those supposedly contacted by the UFOs often display traits common in other kinds of occult phenomena such as a trance state, automatic writing, peering into crystals, the poltergeist effect, levitation, psychic control, psychic healing and out-of-body experiences."[8]

Whatever is going on when people receive "telepathic communications" and "channeled information" from "higher entities" claiming to be extraterrestrials, it is powerfully demonic in nature. What I see clearly today in light of the Holy Bible is that the UFO virus is yet another aspect of the end times "powerful delusion" spoken of in 2 Thess. 2:9-12:

"The coming of the lawless one will be in accordance with the work of Satan displayed in all kinds of counterfeit miracles, signs and wonders, and in every sort of evil that deceives those who are perishing. They perish because they refused to love the truth and so be saved. For this reason God sends them a powerful delusion so that they will believe the lie and so that all will be condemned who have not believed the truth but have delighted in wickedness."

It's so easy to be deceived by all kinds of counterfeit miracles, signs and wonders, as I was. So deeply so that I was totally blinded to the Resurrection and the Life of Christ Jesus.

The ultimate paradox for New Agers is that they believe the lie that they're heading for the New Age kingdom of heaven-on-earth. All the while, they're really following a Satan-conspired path to destruction.

Looking back on when I used to believe in the New Age lie, it is nothing less than utterly terrifying. The demonic power behind the seduction is dazzling to the point of blindness.

Had Jesus not delivered me from the powerful delusion of the New Age, I certainly would have been shocked to the core at the time of judgement. For without salvation through Jesus, I surely would have been cast into the lake of fire, and experienced the "weeping and gnashing of teeth" (Matt. 13:42). Not a very pleasant fate, to be sure.

Meeting the "Lord Maitreya"

Word got around Santa Fe New Age circles that a man claiming to be the "World Teacher" recently had located himself and his operation in Albuquerque. Marco Atlantis was, for a short time, living at his small headquarters in the suburban sections of this arid New Mexico city. He put in a word about Vicki and me, and we were granted a personal audience.

Buzzing with excitement about being in the presence of a Universal Master, we entered a nondescript, medium-sized suburban adobe house. Finding two blissfully smiling young women waiting to usher us to the "Great One," we first were led into a meditation room filled with pictures of "Maitreya" and other Eastern religious symbology, and instructed to "prepare our minds to receive the Maitreya in our consciousness."

Hosted into the room, the "Lord Maitreya" sat in cross-legged position on top of a double-mattress arrangement with dirty, wrinkled sheets. We were to sit on pillows on the floor, directly in front of him. He was a smallish man, Middle-Eastern-looking, and rather nondescript in appearance. Here he was, an enlightened Master. What divine dewdrops would he bless us with?

After about 30 minutes, both Vicki and I had clued in to the fact that this guy perhaps was well-intentioned but seriously deluded about himself and his supposedly supreme universal stature. This "Lord Maitreya" person had some degree of polish to his New Age rap, but we felt that he definitely was not a world-messiah. We started to ask him a few trick questions, and he seemed oblivious to the fact that he was providing answers about concrete facts of our personal life that were totally incorrect.

There was definitely, though, a buzz in the atmosphere of the place. For some, he might serve as an attractive guru-figure, but to increasingly seasoned New Age observers, he just didn't measure up.

Such a totally enlightened "World Teacher" would have read these thoughts in our minds, but we were polite and he actually thought we had bought into his exalted status. His followers repeatedly called us afterwards, trying to firm up what they thought to be our converted discipleship. They kept asking us for favors and money, which we politely fended off.

Over the next year, we received a couple of mail-outs containing the World Teacher's proclamations and directives for all of his followers. Later, we heard no more from him, nor do we know what became of his female entourage.

I don't know if the Lord Maitreya who I met is the same mysterious Lord Maitreya of international intrigue who ran full-page ads in newspapers around the world proclaiming, "In answer to our call for help, as World Teacher for all humanity, the Christ is now here." This highly touted 1982 occurrence claimed that this "Christ" would be heard telepathically by all peoples in their own language.

Apparently the world was not ready to receive his royal New Ageness, and he did not appear as promised.

Benjamin Creme of the Tara Center, the Maitreya's leading spokesperson, claimed that the World Teacher was working *in cognito* in London. In the years since, no one, not even anyone in the New Age Movement, has confirmed any of this, and it remains a mystery.

On January 12, 1987, a full-page ad in *USA Today* added another installment of this drama, proclaiming: "The Christ is in the world. A great World Teacher for people of every religion and no religion."

Did I meet the real Lord Maitreya or merely a pale imitation? To this day, I do not know. Maybe so, maybe not. There are thousands of false prophets and false christs rampant in the New Age landscape. If I did in fact meet the one being trumpeted so grandly, I can see why he would not come out of the closet. The sham would be all too obvious. He would fare no better than one of his early predecessors—a man by the name of J. Krishnamurti.

In the mid-1920s this young wunderkind dazzled audiences in India with reported coronets of brilliant blue appearing over his head as he spoke of himself in the first person as a god. As he attempted to extend his reign, he arrived to thunderous cheers in Europe. But as he sailed to America his charisma and occult powers mysteriously left him, and a writer for the *New York Times* reported that Krishnamurti was virtually incoherent during an interview, and characterized him as "a shy, badly frightened, nice-looking young Hindu." Krishnamurti's messianic claims quickly fizzled.

There are thousands and thousands of false prophets and false christs springing up in the New Age Movement today. In fact, the New Age serves as a prime breeding ground of sorts for Satan to groom and raise up a wide variety of these agents of deception, from the more obvious ones to the more subtle, slick, and sophisticated.

I see clearly now that the more obviously false prophets and christs like Krishnamurti, "Saint," "Marco Atlantis," Ramtha, Maitreya, Lazaris (the most influential spirit being channeled today), and a host of others are in some ways a diversionary tactic of Satan's. In his schemes within schemes wrapped within other schemes, the enemy lays out a full array of false prophets and false christs, the more obvious ones relatively clearly and easily are identified as such.

The potential problem here, though, is relaxing one's guard by stereotyping the characteristics of Satan's obvious forerunners as applying to all the rest of them. The more obvious ones are actually set-ups so that as many people as possible will think that's what *all* false prophets and false christs are like. Then it becomes all the easier for slick, urbane, sophisticated wolves-in-sheep's-clothing—the Antichrist and his immediate forerunners—to fool great numbers of the world population.

Meeting a False Christ of National Renown

About six months later there was a buzz around town—one of the hottest channels in the country was bringing her program to New Mexico. For considered reasons, let's dub the woman channel "Ms. S" (short for Ms. Seductress) and the spirit being channeled "Master D" (short for master of deception). Little did I know when I paid my $125 for the 3-hour program that I was about to get an education of quite a different sort than anticipated.

With the session starting 45 minutes late, the crowd of 175 or so had an edge of high anticipation and irritated edginess. The grand entrance of Ms. S, already in trance and in character as Master D, was suitably regal. After all, here was a spirit claiming to be a "god," one who had attained full cosmic enlightenment, and who could boast of tens of thousands of avid (or is it rabid) followers.

Suitably enthroned on a kingly looking chair up on a high platform, Master D surveyed the entire room silently for 5-8 minutes, ostensibly to see all and know all about everyone in the room. First-timers like myself were seated in the front rows, and possibly we were to be granted the opportunity to ask Master D any question we wanted. Here was my big chance, if he (she?) would only call on me.

To my great surprise, Master D turned straightaway to me.

As I opened my mouth to ask the first question, I felt a force envelop me, putting me somewhat off-guard and a little fuzzy-headed.

Recovering my balance a bit, the thought quickly passed my mind that this must be the power of this spirit's love embracing me. Though I was to find out later that Master D customarily spends only 3-4 minutes with each person, he dialogued with me for a good 20-25 minutes.

Actually, it was more a monologue. I had asked a couple of questions about my New Age spiritual work and its future directions. What I received was an extended discourse on the misdirectedness and futility of my current projects and goals. I was stunned both rationally and by a force that made me quite passive and virtually unable to challenge what was being said. I watched myself turn into a yes-man, just nodding my head in a kind of open-eyed trance while the entire group watched.

After Master D finally turned elsewhere, I felt like I was run over by a cosmic locomotive. My mind still was extremely passive and unable to form focused thoughts, and my body was numb and somewhat limp. The trance-inducing abilities of many demon-spirits are quite potent indeed.

What was going on here? Master D had negated everything that the other Universal Masters had been relaying to me for two years. I thought, "Didn't these Masters confer with each other up there in the heavens so that the right hand knew what the left hand was doing? This doesn't make sense at all. There has to be something else going on here."

After the program ended, while walking toward the exit one of Ms. S's assistants ran up to me. He informed me that Ms. S was quite impressed with me, and thought I had a lot of potential for doing New Age light-work. And, if I were interested in pursuing a position in the organization, to contact him. Well, I thought, this is quite a turnabout.

Driving back home, it finally struck me. I really had not given much notice to the four program assistants who regulated logistics around the front platform. Now I remembered—they were each blond-haired, blue-eyed males, all in their mid 20s to early 30s. Well, I fit that description also. After being discredited in front of my peer group, a miraculous job opportunity knocked at my door. A year later, I confirmed my suspicions while talking with a former aide— Ms. S has quite a fondness for young men of a certain type. Here was another type of seduction indeed.

What had happened is a perfect example of the dynamics of the relationship between a trance channel and the spirit(s) that use the trance channel's body to work their deeds of deception. In essence, the trance channel "sells their soul" in return for lots of attractive benefits—money, power, fame, and even satisfaction of other desires. In return for providing these things, the spirit gets to take over the reins of the trance channel's soul. The channel must dance for his new master upon command like a puppet on a string, and for the rest of the time the channel gets to enjoy all the fringe benefits.

My Cosmic Vision Quest: "Healing Temple One"

It is not at all uncommon for a New Ager to receive a "grand cosmic vision." Inevitably, these visions are quite glorious, exalted, and seemingly world-shaking in importance. Believed to be "divine revelations" received directly from the heavens, they can take many and sundry forms:

For some, it's a pursuit of high mystical adventure of self-discovery and/or cosmically important planetary healing via New Age rituals done at "vortex areas."

For others, it's a self-image of cosmic power, mystery, and glory.

For some, it's an evangelic job with the "Spiritual Hierarchy of Light"—as agents, messengers, teachers, or contactees of this Universal Council.

For others, as it was for me, it's the manifesting of a New Age retreat or some other type of New Age center of activities and services.

I'd like to insert an observation at this point concerning the material in the rest of this chapter: Almost all of this material will seem so bizarre as to be outlandish, insane, unbelievable, or a combination of all three (in case the material up to this point hasn't seemed so). The important point to keep in mind is that the following material is *quite typical* of the inside story of heavily involved New Agers. If you happened to see or hear about Shirley MacLaine's TV mini-series, "Out On a Limb," you will notice a few parallels between her "cosmic vision quest" and my own, though there are certainly many differences as well.

Though the exact content of many New Agers' beliefs along these lines varies, the depth of the powerful delusion is so profound as to be virtually unimaginable to a non-New Ager. In understanding some of the dangers of this movement, it can be most helpful to see certain insights into the weird New Age mentality from which their convictions and actions arise.

My own cosmic vision quest was certainly grandiose. Though I laugh at this grand vision today, it appeared very real to me at the time, and I pursued it with vigor and enthusiasm.

My vision's name was "Healing Temple One." This was the guiding force and direction of my life's work as a New Ager at this time. The Ascended Masters and Commanders of the Intergalactic Space Federation, in overseeing my efforts, kept feeding me detailed ideas and blueprints on a clear and regular basis during my trance-meditations and out-of-body experiences.

Essentially, the vision was that of a veritable spaceship-come down to earth. Not any old 30-foot diameter spaceship, but one to be hundreds of yards in diameter — a macro-ship, or what New Agers would call a "mothership." The New Age concept of a mothership likens it to the hub of a wheel that a host of smaller spaceships rely upon for directives and other supportive assistance.

Healing Temple One (get ready for this) actually was supposed to come down from the intergalactic heavens — a super-spaceship landing on Earth. Also called a "temple-ship" in New Age terms, the Divine Plan was that Healing Temple One would come down to earth accompanied by a substantial host of other space vehicles and motherships all around the world. This act of divine intervention was to bring salvation from a time of acute world turmoil, followed by the establishment of "planetary healing" and a New One-World Order, all to occur sometime before the year 2000.

It is important to note here that not all New Agers would agree fully with the type of scenario illustrated by Healing Temple One. There are many other prophetic variations on the millennial New Age theme. The scenario represented by Healing Temple One does, though, represent a large percentage of those who believe in the existence of UFOs. A solid 70 percent plus of the New Age subculture believe that spaceships will descend en masse from the skies at some point in the relatively near future.

The depth of the New Age brainwashing that this Healing Temple One scenario reflects demonstrates the power of Satan's demons in back of this branch of New Age thinking. You would be surprised at the *millions* of New Agers in all walks of life who believe the Healing Temple One scenario or some variation thereof.

Let me quote from select parts of the 8-page prospectus for Healing Temple One that I wrote:

"The time has now arrived to establish temples and academies of the sacred sciences. ...

"On many levels, mankind is approaching a gateway of transformation leading to a New One-World Order, an era of quantum advancements both in man's own consciousness and in high technology that are breathtaking to consider. ...

"Both the Spiritual Hierarchy of Light and the Intergalactic Federation are to use Healing Temple One as a primary operational base through which to do the high-level Light-work that is needed at this crucial time in Earth's history. ...

"Healing Temple One forms a gateway between the heavens and the Earth, thereby catalyzing the revelation of scientific knowledge and technologies that will revolutionize the entire world."

This is representative of a fairly standard variety of New Age thinking occurring with many believers in UFOs.

A futuristic view of New Age science was an integral part of this Healing Temple One vision. In the "Golden Aquarian Age" technological wonders and miracles brought to Earth by Healing Temple One were supposed literally to remake the world—a grand Second Genesis. The prospectus claimed: "The revolutionary technologies to be used and further developed in this project lay the foundation and form a gateway through which the heavens and the Earth are united in one vision, one reality, one divine manifestation."

Let me draw a couple of examples of the futuristic technologies from the Healing Temple One prospectus:

"'Light-body activation therapy' involves a sequence of treatments through a series of high-tech activation chambers. ... Envision, for example, an activation chamber humming with harmonically elevating sounds, bathing the spirit, mind, and body with tranquility. As the sounds gradually increase in intensity, a stream of multi-colored light-beams are projected into each *chakra*-center[9] in rapid pulses of computer-orchestrated colors. After this is completed, the body is gradually freed from gravity through the action of gyroscopic crystal and anti-gravity devices until it is floating inches off the therapy table. Computer-generated holographic energy-fields are projected via laser-beams into each *chakra*, transforming them into crystalline spheres of Light."

Another super-high-tech healing chamber was designed as a New Age "Fountain of Youth":

"A Pyramidal Cellular Harmonizing Chamber. ... This long-sought 'Fountain of Youth' is based upon the integrated use of the sacred sciences of pyramidology, crystallography, anti-gravity technologies, radionics, sonics, laser science, intelligent supercomputers, and electro-medicine."

High cosmic-tech comes to Earth—the primary theme of New Age science. A New Age brings a New Science.

In back of all these enticements lay the lies and delusionary powers of demons—seducing the mind into an ultra-futuristic "golden calf" idolatry.

The Ascension Chamber

Over thousands of hours of research and development, I even built my own one-room prototype of a part of Healing Temple One called the "Ascension Chamber." It was certainly a very scaled-down version of the billion-dollar visions of Healing Temple One. No supercomputers, no electro-medicine, no anti-gravity technology. Though primitive compared to grand future-science prophecies, the Ascension Chamber was still fairly elaborate. Its stated intent was to "use sacred science to activate New Age higher consciousness." In essence, it claimed to: "Use New Age science to accelerate spiritual growth so that in a matter of hours, many lifetimes of evolvement can occur, like a time-lapse photography sequence. You no longer need to trudge slowly along your spiritual path like an ox-cart along a dirt road. This was for the old age—this is the New Age. Why not take the high-tech spiritual fast-track to instant enlightenment?"

The Ascension Chamber room was filled with hundreds of crystals in geometric configurations, and close to a hundred pyramids hanging from the ceiling and walls. The purpose for this supposedly was to "create a concentrated energy field of ultra-high vibrations." Lasers, magnets, specialized electronic devices, computers, and aromatic agents were added in specific ways to help "amplify, enhance, and control the energy field." Further, an orchestrated multi-media presentation of rotating multi-colored designs, films of occult symbols, mystical New Age music, and swirling colors that filled the entire room (somewhat similar to a laser show) all were combined to induce a trance-state in the recipient. This type of trance-induction or hypnosis deeply affected many of the recipients. Many occult-based New Age practices also were applied to induce mystical and out-of-body experiences, as well as channeling experiences.

There were also some sophisticated "brain-drive" machines. Such high-tech devices all are the rage in the New Age today. Having names such as MC^2, David I, Alpha-Stim, Neuro-Pep, Bio-Pacer, Isis, Somatron, and Graham Potentializer, they are readily available, ranging in price from $300 to $6,000.

Advertisements for these various mind-power machines are one of the hottest items in national New Age magazines, especially since late 1987/early 1988. Most of these devices use goggles (for flashing light input) and headphones (for sound input), and have control consoles that coordinate the light and sound in order to induce controlled trance-states and psychedelic-like experiences. They are very popular due to their deeply relaxing effects in addition to the dazzling psychedelic experiences. Here we have high technology's latest contribution to the New Age Movement—machines that control and pleasurize the mind with power, precision, and efficiency. It's similar to Aldous Huxley's *Brave New World*.

Also used in the Ascension Chamber were subliminal cassette tapes and videos. In short, subliminal technology inserts messages into the mind of the individual without the person being aware of the mind-programming process. This highly developed modern technology has been around for many years. In the process, it also has become quite sophisticated, so much so that it has blossomed into a real high-tech hazard. What I see today that I did not understand then is that even though the stated purposes of most all subliminal cassette tapes are apparently positive and benign (e.g., losing weight, gaining self-confidence, overcoming fears and phobias, etc.), the *method of "unzipping" the mind* without the person being aware of the process as well as the many potential misuses of such a technology (on individual and mass scales) hold many serious dangers best avoided.

In short, the Ascension Chamber was a modernized form of white magic and sorcery applied toward a trance-inducing, hypnotizing procedure for inducing mystical experiences, out-of-body experiences, and "reprogramming the mind with positive and evolutionarily advanced thoughts." While today I do not know if all the crystals and pyramids really made a difference, the trance-inducing methods (New Age music, subliminals, brain-drive machines, films of occult symbols, and swirling light-shows) did indeed produce powerful experiences and effects in a large percentage of the treatment recipients.

Over the years, my intense interest in this field of New Age sacred science led me to set up a large teaching and research complex containing five different types of Ascension Chambers, each separate chamber having an elaborate design for performing different functions for "activating the Light-body" or "communicating with the Great White Brotherhood."

With deep regret, I must report that over a thousand sessions were given over a period of three years. In fact, the Ascension Chamber and its four other variations proved exceptionally popular among certain New Age circles of Santa Fe, and it was actually one of my "claims to fame" on the national scene.

What I realize today that totally was veiled to me while enmeshed in webs of delusion is that such chambers (this one, and others similar to it that are available in the New Age today) can be DEMON'S DENS of temptation, ensnarement, delusion-weaving, and brainwashing.

While in a trance-state, a person is highly vulnerable to demonic intrusions that perpetrate their dark web-weaving. Behind the modernized New Age gloss, Biblically forbidden occult-based principles and practices are at the foundation of New Age phenomenon like Healing Temple One and the Ascension Chamber.

I testify in humility and repentance today. They are harmful. They are an abomination. They are a fast-rising New Age phenomenon to be avoided like the plague in the years ahead.

A Meteoric New Age Career Rise

While in the midst of pursuing my Healing Temple One vision and doing Ascension Chamber sessions, an entirely new level of national exposure was opening up. National seminar tours that followed on the heels of my first book, *Windows of Light*, met with good response, but now I was on Satan's fast-track for promotion into the big time during this next sequence.

In late 1985, my second book — *The Crystal Connection: A Guidebook for Personal and Planetary Ascension* — was published and released by the same mainstream publisher, Harper and Row. About 400 pages in length, it set the standard in the thriving field of crystals. By this time crystals were "hot," were "buzzing." One of the top three national New Age magazines, *East-West Journal*, reviewed the book and pronounced it "light-years beyond the rest."

The book was marketed as: "An essential reference, *The Crystal Connection* is a landmark achievement in the field of crystal-based sacred science."

With a follow-up national seminar tour, speaking to enthusiastic audiences of many hundreds in each city, I rode the crest of a wave of crystal popularity. Though there were over a thousand crystal teachers by now in cities large and small, I was widely held to be one of the top three international authorities in the field. One of the others (who is still active in the field) is named Marcel Vogel, Ph.D., who is a retired senior research scientist at IBM, claiming over 60 patents in his distinguished career. At a later date, I was on the television program, "20/20" in a segment on the "crystal craze."

By now I also was offering a variety of week-long advanced study programs at my New Mexico headquarters. The primary course offered was called the "Advanced Crystal Energetics Training Program" — a course for advanced studies in crystal power and sacred science.

You might be surprised at some of the attendees — an astrophysicist, a noted solar scientist, scientists in several other disciplines, many chiropractors, dentists, some Fortune 500 businessmen, some M.D.s, many holistic health practitioners, numerous nurses, and quite a few highly successful professionals of other varieties, including a couple of media celebrities.

Other week-long courses offered included: "The Sacred Science Program," "Advanced Sacred Science Intensive," "Vortex Visitations," and "The Keys of Enoch Seminar." In effect, my teaching and research center became a type of college of sorts, training people to begin or further develop professional careers in the New Age.

Invitations to national-level New Age expos and retreats were coming in.

I had a third book — 500 pages in length — in the offing.

At this point so many opportunities were opening up that I could write my own success ticket. I had hit the big time, and the horizons of my career looked spectacular.

Yes, I was riding high, but there would be a price to pay for all this later — a painful price indeed. I was a rising New Age star. But the meteoric rise eventually would come to a burning halt. Satan always exacts his pound of flesh, sooner or later. This I learned well in the later stages of my season of New Age success.

A Picture of a Modern-Day New Ager

As explained earlier, not all New Agers can be easily picked out of a crowd. Some you can tell a mile away by the crystal pendants, rainbow clothes, and "Visualize World Peace" bumper stickers on their VW busses. But just as many others appear as normal as any other mainstream American.

I'd like to provide a quick thumbnail sketch of myself during my New Age years as I outwardly appeared then. The main point is that there were few obvious external indicators that I was involved in the movement. You can't necessarily tell that a person is a New Ager by his outer wrapping.

Home was classically middle-American — clean, tidy, regular-looking furniture, etc. There were no metaphysical pictures on the walls, no bevy of crystals everywhere you looked, no strange incense smell in the air, no New Age paraphernalia lying about. Walking into the home, a person would have few external indications of my New Age involvements.

I gave seminars dressed in high-quality suits and ties, and gave my week-long advanced classes in professional apparel.

I had medium-length hair and no external indications of New Age-iness (though I wore a crystal pendant inside the shirt and carried other crystals in a pocket).

To every outward indication, I was a successful professional in some field (what a lot of neighbors thought). All this was not done as a conscious deception at all. Rather, it was the result of a lifestyle inherited from childhood plus a strong commitment to bringing a highly professional approach to my career and to reach as broad an audience as possible.

Many people would be surprised at the number of closet New Agers there are throughout every level of American society, from the business office to the hospitals to the laboratories. By all external indicators, an observer would find it very difficult to discern that such a person is a New Ager. The point here being: New Agers who blend into the mainstream cultural landscape are everywhere in our society.

I also would like to point out here, in a parenthetical statement, that not all New Age activities are cults. Some certainly are, but a solid percentage of New Age organizations, seminars, etc. are definitely not cults. Most of these operate along the lines of regular businesses in terms of how they offer their products and services.

My own business was a case in point. I am an exceptionally private person, and greatly love solitude. The more well-known I became, the more people would want to attach themselves to me and my work in one way or another. Vicki and I wanted no part of starry-eyed hangers-on or advantage-seeking opportunists. Over the years of being involved in the Santa Fe and national New Age scenes, we developed an ingrained skepticism and somewhat jaded view of the veritable circus of New Age people and their trips.

Living remotely outside of Santa Fe, we created a rather well-developed system for keeping an arm's length distance even from people we liked. I met many leaders, teachers, and businesspeople who had a similar approach as myself. I mention all this to emphasize the fact that in discerning whether something is New Age, it is helpful to keep in mind that not all New Age phenomena are cults.

Tripping the "Light" Fantastic

In the midst of my New Age career rise, while so much outwardly was demanding my attention, my inner journey took on new magnitudes of intensity. With each passing month, I found myself going into states of extended solitude whenever time allowed.

If I had an evening off, for example, it would be spent alone, having trance-meditation and out-of-body experiences[10] and receiving knowledge from my spirit guides in the Ascension Chamber well into the late evening and early morning. The mind-blowing cosmic power, the glittering good feelings, and the amazing revelations experienced during these times completely captivated me. While holding down the responsibilities of my New Age career, this overriding desire to travel deeply within the heavenly spirit-world became a virtual obsession.

Two events resulted from this. One is detailed in the next chapter section, and the other is that Vicki and I decided to divorce. While ours was an unusual passionless marriage, at least I was *around* as a best friend and companion as well as co-worker. Now, I was becoming more and more absorbed into the spirit-world, leaving Vicki with little-to-no companionship or emotional support. So, an amicable divorce was effected so that she was free to pursue her interests and I

was free to pursue what I perceived as an "inner voyage to the ultimate supernatural realms of Infinite Intelligence."

In New Age morality, there are no prohibitions against divorce.
Whether a married couple stays together is based mainly upon "soul
growth compatibility." That is, if after a time two souls who are married start to grow in different directions, then it is appropriate, if
desired, to dissolve the marriage and find other more spiritually compatible soul-mates.

Though our friendship was a bit strained for a couple months
over this, Vicki and I remained the best of friends and continued in
our dedication to do light-work together. Feeling the divorce was our
own private business and being reluctant to severely disappoint our
parents, we kept it to ourselves until Vicki met her new husband two
years later.

Out-of-Body Leads to Almost Out-of-Mind

In my New Age days, I was quite adept at inducing and expanding the limits of mystical and out-of-body experiences—this was one
of the big reasons for much of my success. I would mount myself up
with all kinds of New Age inventions and crystals, and then thrust
myself into trance-induced higher states of consciousness. It would
feel like I was being transported by winged angels and loving forces
to an incredible variety of dazzling extra-natural domains. The sensation of my spirit being released from Earthbound, bodily restric-
tions and freed to roam the unlimited expanses of the cosmos was
breathtaking. Here it was, the freedom, the light, and the truth that I
had been searching for all my life. I had found the keys that opened
the heavens before my very eyes.

But the ultimate seduction had overtaken me: What I thought
was "up" was actually "down." What I thought was "heaven" was actually "hell" wrapped in Satan's finest counterfeit garments. What I
thought were Ascended Masters, extraterrestrials, and angels were
actually demons in cunning, glowing disguises.

The Bible states: "Put on the full armor of God, that you may be
able to stand firm against the schemes of the devil. For our struggle is
not against flesh and blood, but against the rulers, against the powers,
against the world forces of this darkness, against the spiritual forces
of wickedness in the heavenly places" (Eph. 6:11, 12). And: "Satan
disguises himself as an angel of light. Therefore it is not surprising if
his servants also disguise themselves as servants of righteousness;
whose end shall be according to their deeds" (2 Cor. 11:14, 15).

Yes, I actually was getting a guided tour of some of the "spiritual
forces of evil in the heavenly realms" by demons masquerading as

"servants of righteousness." Though some of my experiences may have been just imaginary fantasy, I am fully convinced that most of them were ventures into some of Satan's most beautifully deceiving spirit-domains of glittery bondage masquerading as our Heavenly Father's kingdom of heaven.

The popular Christian book, *The Beautiful Side of Evil*, by Johanna Michaelsen, is very aptly named. Darkness can have an outer covering, so to speak, of luminosity that can appear to be inexpressibly beautiful. The power of darkness can feel wonderfully beauteous, too. Satan and his demonic legions are masterful counterfeiters who can make darkness appear to be light, untruth appear to be truth and hate appear to be love. The luminosity of darkness can be so bright that it bedazzles to the point of blindness and mesmerizes to the point of brainwashing. This is exactly what happened to me, and what is happening today to all those involved in the New Age Movement.

One night, while in the Ascension Chamber, my spirit was roaming some of the farthest reaches of "heavenly light" that I had ever perceived. That night I had an experience that would change my life forever.

During this experience I was surrounded by a virtually overwhelming luminosity—it was as if I was looking straight into the sun. Waves of bliss radiated through my spirit. I was totally captivated by the power.

Suddenly, another force stepped in. It took me by complete surprise. In the twinkling of an eye, it was like a supernatural hand had taken me behind the scenes of the experience that I was having. I was taken behind the outer covering of the dazzling luminosity and there saw something that left me literally shaking for a full week.

What I saw was the face of devouring darkness! Behind the glittering outer facade of beauty lay a massively powerful, wildly churning face of absolute hatred and unspeakable abominations—the face of demons filled with the power of Satan.

For a moment that seemed like an eternity, I realized that I was in major league trouble, for this devouring force was now closing in on me.

In absolute, stark terror I felt powerless to stop what appeared to be inevitable doom. Horror filled me like a consuming flame.

Then, miraculously, the same supernatural hand as before delivered me from the jaws of this consuming darkness, and hours later, I found myself waking up the next morning in the Ascension Chamber. It felt like I had a peaceful nights sleep but, upon waking, the horror of the past night's experience had left me terribly shaken. My mind was racing uncontrollably in all directions at what felt like the speed of light. My body was shaking involuntarily, sometimes rather violently. This nightmare continued without respite for a full week. I thought that I was going stark raving mad. In a month's time, though, my grave situation gradually settled down to some semblance of sanity and normalcy.

What I didn't know at the time was that it was JESUS who had intervened by His greater grace into my life. At this point, though, I only knew that some force greater than that of the devouring darkness had done two things: 1) it had shown me the real face of the New Age "heavens" and "angels" that I was so deeply involved with, and 2) it had delivered me from certain doom.

What I knew at this time was that I had made some serious errors in my New Age involvements. I also knew that if those errors weren't corrected that I might face the same horrific experience again. And quite possibly the next time I wouldn't get away.

An openness to reconsider my New Age involvements arose in me out of desperate need. This openness would help me, over the following months, to find a Way, a Truth, and a Life that I had never known before—Jesus Christ.

But this journey was not to be an easy one. For Satan does not relinquish those he has in bondage without a struggle, as I was about to find out.

Notes

1. "Power objects" have a long history of occult uses. Ranging from talismans and crystals to eagle feathers and "magic wands," all types of witches, wizards, alchemists, medicine men, shamans, and other occult figures have used "power objects." These objects, when ritually consecrated, are supposed to contain or attract different types of occult power that can be applied in occult pursuits.
2. The concept of "crystal power" is discussed in more detail in chapter 7. Essentially, though, on the one hand there is no conclusive scientific evidence to confirm this strange notion. On the other hand, the use of crystals as "power objects" has a long history, and millions of New Agers have had the subjective experience of some type of occult energy amplification and focusing when involving crystals in New Age practices. Wishful thinking? Wild fantasies? The placebo effect? Whatever is going on, the point here is simply to note that New Agers do believe in "crystal power" (however unsubstantiated).
3. The "third eye" is an occult belief that a center of psychic powers is located at the forehead between the two (physical) eyes.
4. "White magic" is a branch of witchcraft that claims to be based on peaceful, positive occult principles; but which is strictly forbidden in the Bible (Deut. 18:9-12).

5. The New Age commonly refers to the "Light-body." This term also is used when referring to the "Higher Self." Both these phrases basically mean "New Age higher consciousness," supposedly a more "enlightened" state of being.

6. Often, New Agers refer to the "Divine Plan," or simply as the "Plan" in referring to the sequence of events overseen by the "Great White Brotherhood" leading into the New Age.

7. Billy Graham, *Angels: God's Secret Agents* (Waco, TX: Word Books, 1986), p. 20.

8. For more discussion on the topic of UFOs, plus quotes from other Christian authorities, see chapter 5, "New Age Sorceries and Idolatries."

9. "*Chakras*" are an occult concept asserting that there are seven major "energy centers" in the etheric human anatomy along the spine that control all aspects of human functioning.

10. See chapter 5, for an explanation of "out-of-body experiences."

THREE

THE BONDAGE
BROKEN

The testimony I offer in this chap-
ter of my life bears yet another lost soul's great rejoicing in receiving
the Good News. Yet upon conversion, my story did not become an
immediate "and he lived happily ever after ..." Would that it were so
easy, some type of classic storybook ending. To jump the gun a bit,
yes, I received Jesus as my Lord and personal Savior. And as all
reborn Christians know, this is a glorious new beginning that words
can only begin to describe. I had been freed from Satan's bondage.

But as I was to find out shortly in my walk with Jesus, struggles,
persecution, and mistakes were still to come.

Billy Graham's observation really rang true in my own experience:
"In our attempts to share the faith we have given the impression that,
once you have accepted Christ as Savior and Lord, your problems
are over. That is not true. Becoming 'new' in Christ is a wonderful
beginning, but it isn't the end of pain or problems in our lives. It is
the beginning of our facing up to them. Being a Christian involves a
lifetime of hard work, dedicated study, and difficult decisions."[1]

What I found as a struggling Christian was that the Good Shepherd takes care of His sheep, even through the "valley of the shadow
of death," even if they stray for a time, and even as they err and re-
pent. My path as a newborn Christian was a most humbling and
stumbling one—a very far cry from the glory days of New Age leadership. Time after time, the Holy Spirit would convict my heart and
show me my errors, and I would come to the Lord on bended knee,
asking His forgiveness. Sometimes, I honestly feared that He would
not forgive me, sinner that I am, but each time coming before Him in

repentance, I found a loving Shepherd and my best Friend. He would rebuke and then raise me up in His arms, salve the wounds, give comfort and guidance, provide restoration, and send me on my way like a loving parent. I had never had such a personal relationship before. No matter what hardships and struggles I went through then (and now), this unbreakable, eternal relationship is the source of my strength, hope, and life everlasting. This is my testimony.

Through all the events that were about to transpire, these words of the apostle Paul came to have great personal meaning: "neither death, nor life, nor angels, nor principalities, nor things present, nor things to come, nor powers, nor height, nor depth, nor any other created thing, shall be able to separate us from the love of God, which is in Christ Jesus our Lord" (Rom. 8:38, 39).

A Lost Soul Goes Searching: The Journey Continues

Badly shaken by my brush with "spiritual wickedness in heavenly places"[2], I set about a sweeping re-evaluation of my New Age philosophy and activities. There were obviously some major flaws here.

The first thing I did was to declare a personal moratorium on all mystical excursions into the spirit realms. I was not going to jeopardize myself like that again.

I also had to sort out the shocking realization that the light that appeared so heavenly was really a counterfeit front for a devouring darkness. How could this be? Could all my cherished spirit guides' guidance, all the wonderful mystical experiences, all the sophisticated books that I had read, all the enlightened ones of Eastern mysticism, and all my respected New Age friends' experiences be based on a grand delusion?

Was it just me? Was it the entire New Age movement? Or was it just select parts of the movement? This was all so mind-boggling.

Everything that I was as a New Ager: everything that I knew I had found, I had accomplished, was now totally up in the air. All things New Age were subject to intense scrutiny in an entirely different way than I had ever scrutinized them before.

In retrospect, I see that this was the key to opening up a new possibility of accepting Jesus Christ into my life—the willingness to question the fundamental assumptions of the New Age, and to be willing to really see untruth if it were there to be found.

Most all New Agers are *really* not willing to admit the possibility of falseness in their fundamental beliefs. That was certainly true of me. But because of my harrowing experience, and what I learned from it, I was ready to admit the possibility of deception.

The demands of a busy New Age career continued to occupy a large portion of my daily life. There were commitments to be met, responsibilities to fulfill, and bills to be paid. Still feeling rather weak and shaken after being bedridden for a week, I managed to gather enough strength to get on with the work at hand, even as all my questions and doubts echoed within. Feeling like the walking wounded, I made it through the next weeks while recovering strength and basic stability.

After regaining strength, I continued giving lectures, seminars, and programs, but began to have a different perception of the material and the people. While speaking, part of me would be questioning everything coming out of my mouth. Some areas started to ring hollow, though it was just a vague feeling at the time.

As for the people, their rampant flakiness and self-centeredness that I had already noticed for years started to become more and more irritating. With each passing week, a sense slowly grew that things in the New Age and myself were definitely not right.

During this time, at home a quirky change was coming over Vicki. (Though divorced by now, for financial and family reasons we lived under the same roof—an acceptable arrangement by New Age standards.) On Sunday mornings, I would be making brunch for myself, and there she would be watching Christian televangelists for an hour or so. The funny thing was that it seemed like she was listening to them seriously.

You must understand, a *real* New Ager wouldn't be caught dead watching televangelists, much less taking them seriously. To the New Age, Christians generally are regarded as "old age," people who have yet to awaken to the "higher realities of New Age consciousness."[3] In fact, I must confess that I teased her to no end when she would repeat this scene week after week. All she would say was, "Why don't you just listen to them for a while with an open mind? They're making some sense to me." I scoffed at her and thought she was being quite weird.

About four or five weeks into this scenario, the thought came to me: "If you're really open-minded, as you claim to be, then you should at least give this a fair chance—it couldn't hurt."

So one Sunday I sat down with Vicki and watched two Christian televangelists for an hour, switching the TV channels back and forth. I noticed myself becoming somewhat interested and my appetite was whetted for more.

With each passing week, I became a little less resistant and a little more interested. Scanning through the available channels, I found a defininte preference for some religious programs over others.

At the same time, I started to study the Bible with fresh eyes. In New Age philosophy, the Holy Bible is accepted, but only conditionally, it being taken only as one scripture among many others. Also, I began to see that New Age philosophy picks and chooses what it likes and doesn't like from the pages of the Bible. It also re-interprets these select passages with a metaphysical New Age slant. Now I tried to put as many of my preconceptions as possible aside, and started to study the Holy Bible to see what it revealed on its own terms.

The more of the Bible I read, especially the Gospels, the more I saw that the teachings of Jesus plainly were at variance with New Age philosophy on many key points. A few of these issues included:

- The sinful nature of man (the New Age says that man is inherently perfect and a "god").
- Man's need for redemption through Jesus Christ (the New Age says that there is no need for redemption).
- The final judgment (the New Age holds that each person is ultimately his own judge, and that the "lake of fire" is a myth).
- The personal and visible Second Coming of Jesus Christ (the New Age maintains that another "Christ" [not Jesus Christ] and/or "Christ consciousness" will lead the world into the New Age).

The more I read the Bible and recalled some of my Christian theology classes from college, the more I saw that the philosophies of Christianity and the New Age had gaping, irreconcilable differences between them. New Age thought claims to embrace the essential truths of all religions and all scriptures into a greater whole.

What I saw now was that the Bible was most definitely not compatible with this "greater whole," and that New Age philosophy has to do a lot of very selective hand-picking of pieces and snippets of the Bible in order to assimilate Biblical Christianity under the New Age umbrella.

The New Age claimed to embrace the Bible, but I saw that the Bible just doesn't fit into the New Age. Logically, both sides could not be right. One side was right, and the other side was wrong.

Now I had to decide *which* side was right.

On a strictly intellectual level, this is an incredibly difficult question to answer. Without an assumed absolute standard of values, philosophical argumentation is relativistic and equivocal. In fact, the more I thought about all the issues involved, the more confused I became. I didn't know how this was going to come to a conclusion.

As several months of watching selected Christian televangelists passed, an increasingly alarming situation arose. By this time I had regained my strength, but for no apparent reason, I felt a growing deterioration within myself. Psychologically, there was an erosion of positive emotions, self-confidence, self-image, and other vital areas.

Spiritually, I sensed an inner hollowness growing to unprecedented degrees. Overall, it felt like life was being drained out of me, and that I had no control over the forces in motion. In some ways it was like a spiritual "cancer" progressively filling my being and causing deep corrosion from the inside out.

Frantically I tried to apply any and every "advanced" New Age technique to try to stem the tide of these forces. Try as I might to use crystal power, healing through visualization and affirmation techniques, "create your own reality" methods, *chakra*-system balancing, polarity therapy, and a host of other techniques, nothing was working to stem the wave of inner deterioration. Things were getting very scary. To not be in control of the situation, and to have exhausted almost every possibility I knew of, was becoming acutely alarming.

In fear, I had turned to that in which I felt most knowledgeable and secure — New Age practices.

One day Vicki, who was very concerned about my situation, suggested that I pray as the Christians do. Well, this was a possibility that had not yet crossed my mind. So, with a sincerity born of deep need, I prayed as best I knew how. These SOS prayers were along the lines of "If you're there, Jesus, I *really* need your help." I felt no discernible response, but continued these prayers several times a day for a couple of weeks.

Much to my dismay, the condition only worsened. It now became quite clear that some type of negative spirit-force was in back of all this, and that it definitely had the upper hand. I only could watch helplessly as it felt like this spirit-force was taking more and more control of me, draining my energy as I became entrapped in its tightening tentacles.

Had my spirit guides and the Ascended Masters and the Space Brothers abandoned me? Or, a virtually unthinkable thought, were all these apparently loving, enlightened spirit-beings actually counterfeit fronts for the consuming darkness that I saw before?

Over the next week gruesome thoughts and visions started to infiltrate my mind and dreams. Resistance to the pressures exerted by this spirit-force was waning. Even my vision and other sense perceptions were being distorted. I had heard of demonic possession, and even had seen a few cases, but had never considered the possibility that it might happen to me. At this point, I knew that this was exactly what was occurring.

My SOS prayers took on an increasingly acute urgency. I was fighting a losing battle, and knew it. It was only a matter of time before all will-power and strength was drained. For days I was in an unspeakable living nightmare. Vicki prayed, too, but nothing seemed to come of it.

All through these desperate times I continued to watch a few select Sunday televangelists, and found more and more of their essential Gospel message to hit home in my heart. Toward the end of this period I had to spend increasing amounts of time in bed, just trying to fend off the waves of darkness invading my being. Often passing the hours by watching TV to take my mind off the anguish, I also came upon a couple of weekday Christian tele-ministries.

Up until this point when the Christians would ask the viewers to pray with them, I felt self-conscious and somewhat silly, and would focus my attention elsewhere until they were through.

One day, while watching the *700 Club*, I was in awful shape. Pat Robertson called on unsaved viewers who were in need of deliverance from bondage to pray a prayer with him. I was in such a state now that I was way past feeling self-conscious or silly.

There was something about the way Robertson was speaking and looking into the camera that felt like he was talking directly to me. Such a sensation never had happened before, and there was a clarity and conviction that came upon me as I got up from the bed and knelt on the floor with my hands on top of the TV. Somehow I knew with absolute certainty that this was very real, and it was my chance to get out of this maddening bondage.

I don't remember the exact words repeated along with Robertson, but I do have a vivid recollection of what transpired.

As the prayer progressed I felt the hand of Jesus reach deep into my innermost being with an almighty power that was both piercing to the core yet completely gentle at the same time. By the end of the prayer I was so filled to overflowing with the power of His presence that a powerful but gentle quaking in the Spirit happened in every fiber of my being. Weeping uncontrollably, I gently dropped to the floor. As this happened I felt the conviction of the Holy Spirit pierce my heart and wept in acute repentance as the quaking in the Spirit continued for almost an hour. Continuously, prayer poured forth from my lips in repentance and in praise of His majesty and saving grace. I had never prayed like this before—it was like an effortless stream of sweet water pouring through me in rejoicing and honoring Christ Jesus as my Lord and personal Savior.

The Lord had cut through my horrific Satanic bondage and set me free as He received me into His Body as He washed my scarlet sins as white as snow. I was captive, but now I was free.

With an absolute certainty, I knew that this was what I had been looking for all my life and never had found till now. This made even the most powerful mystical New Age experience completely pale in comparison of our Heavenly Father's infinitely greater power and glory. Satan's glowing counterfeit fineries are as cheap, filthy rags compared to the Truth.

A Time of Restoration and Great Rejoicing

For the next week or so I cancelled all work and enjoyed a "honeymoon" with Jesus. Words beg description of the inexpressible joys, loving restoration, and sweet communion of this time.

Much happened during this week of rejoicing. A prodigal son had returned home, destitute and unworthy, but was met with loving arms and a wonderful feast. It was hard to fathom the greater love of Jesus that can forgive so much sin.

Continually, this Bible passage kept coming to mind, reminding me: "I am the way, and the truth, and the life; no one comes to the Father, but through Me" (John 14:6).

One morning I opened the Bible and prayed to be led to an appropriate passage. Turning to Revelation 22:12-15, I read:

"Behold, I am coming quickly, and My reward is with Me, to render to every man according to what he has done. I am the Alpha and the Omega, the first and the last, the beginning and the end. Blessed are those who wash their robes, that they may have the right to the tree of life, and may enter by the gates into the city. Outside are the dogs and the sorcerers and the immoral persons and the murderers and the idolaters, and everyone who loves and practices lying."

Impressed in my heart, I knew that had I remained in the New Age I would have been one of those condemned to be outside the gates along with all manner of other sinners, to be cast into the "lake of fire" and experience the "weeping and gnashing of teeth."[4] This passage also moved me with tremendous compassion for those still in the New Age who are bound by chains they are completely unaware of. So many of these people were my friends, my own brethren.

I also felt profoundly, as so many other Christians have, that today's times are the end times, and that the personal and visible return of Jesus is near, though we know not the day or hour.

I could not bear the thought of the multitudes of well-intentioned New Age people who I knew were walking a path leading to destruction—they were as blissfully deluded as I had been before my conversion to the Christian faith.

Who would warn them? In 15 years as a New Ager I had come across only one person witnessing to me of Jesus Christ. Having been in most major cities giving lectures and having kept my finger on the pulse of the national-level New Age Movement for the previous five years, I was not aware of a single Christian outreach program formulated to take the Christian witness directly into the New Age subculture. To make matters worse, a New Ager converting to the Christian faith is an extreme rarity—I never personally had met one in 15 years. Satan's deluding power in the movement is powerful indeed. The more I thought about this, the more the feeling arose that I could not turn my back on people involved. My heart became heavily burdened with the task of doing the best I knew how to bring the Good News to the New Age.

While getting a handle on all that had happened and fervently studying the Bible, another wonderful event happened. Vicki also came to accept Jesus into her life. Perhaps this was catching. Praise the Lord!

A Foretaste of New Age Reactions to Come

In sharing what had happened in our lives with friends in the Santa Fe area, I was to get a foretaste of things to come. The Good News goes strongly "against the grain," especially in those who have been involved heavily in the New Age for some time. Reactions of annoyance, irritation, agitation, anger, frustration, and even revulsion kept cropping up. We kept our testimony simple and did not try to impose it on anyone, but this would be a recurrent pattern of my witnessing experience throughout the New Age subculture in the year ahead. Though I was never known as a particularly magnetic person, my mild manner and gentle politeness generally was liked. This had not changed. The only factor that had changed was that I was a new man-in-Christ bearing His testimony.

What I was to find out over the next year is that, in Satan's New Age delusion, the first thing he targets is a person's openness to the only Truth—Jesus Christ—that can set the person free from the enemy's clutches. Time and time again I would find that the simplest testimony that I would offer would meet with an inordinately negative response, sometimes from very kind, gentle, and peaceful individuals.

Many New Agers pride themselves on being tolerant of all spiritual differences—they say, "All spiritual paths lead to the same place." Such is not the case when it comes to Biblical Christianity, "the faith which was once for all delivered to the saints."[5] There is an inherent adversarial relationship between the two. When this comes to light, it sometimes takes New Agers by surprise because they are often not even aware of the anti-Christian sentiment that Satan has planted within them. It would make sense that the only power that can destroy the adversary—Jesus Christ—would be targeted the most heavily.[6]

After meeting with such a strong negative response, and also starting to become aware that demons were attacking with increasing force, we decided to move from the northern New Mexico area and regroup.

Taking the Christian Witness to the New Age

Moving to Hot Springs, Arkansas, Vicki and I moved into separate residences, but continued to work together. We always had worked well together, and found a new dimension of friendship-in-Christ that would provide much-needed mutual support in the trying times that lay just ahead. About a year later, Vicki would marry Thomas, a former New Ager converted to the Christian faith.

Though we continued to lead separate lives, we maintained a friendly working relationship, dedicated to spreading the testimony of Jesus to the New Age subculture.

After settling into new circumstances in Hot Springs, with much deliberation I decided to use an already-planned national seminar tour as a platform for proclaiming the Christian witness. My popularity was still riding the crest of the international crystal craze and the release of my second book, *The Crystal Connection*. It looked to me like a prime opportunity to bring to the New Age Movement what it so desperately needed. I didn't foresee, though, the severe tribulations looming on the horizon.

While studying the Bible and a few select televangelist ministries, I tried to discern the basic principles of sharing the Good News. Among others, one principle stood out clearly. Jesus Christ told his disciples: "freely you received, freely give" (Matt. 10:8).

I remembered from childhood church-going and also saw on the tele-ministries that this directive from the Lord was indeed a foundational principle of Christianity. But what is commonplace and expected in Christendom is a totally radical concept to the New Age. As elaborated in chapter 6, "Behind the 'Rainbow-colored Glasses,'" the practice of free-giving service is rare-to-non-existent in the New Age subculture. Everything has a price tag — everything.

Notwithstanding this entrenched price-tag mentality, I decided that it was imperative to follow Christ's directive on this important matter, no matter what the consequences. So, all flyers and advertising for the national seminar tour carried the message: "Free Admittance" At the bottom of the flyers, it stated: "Donations are accepted and appreciated, but definitely not required."

This approach, in and of itself, caused quite a stir. It was virtually unheard of for any New Age leader to offer anything free-of-charge.

In fact, the novelty of all this stimulated many people to come to the seminars just to see what in the world was going on.

Audiences up to 500 at a time attended these weekend seminars in many major U.S. cities. What they didn't realize until very shortly into the program was that there was something else unique and unheard-of going on—the witness of Jesus Christ. Though I did so imperfectly, my own personal testimony was given, along with the key concepts of repentance, man's sinful nature, the judgment, the uniqueness of Jesus Christ as Lord and personal Savior, the need for man to be redeemed through the blood of His sacrifice, the need for baptism, and other fundamental Christian principles. All this was the very first order of the day.

I was not prepared for the response. Somewhere inside of me, I had nurtured the idea that some significant percentage of New Agers rejoicingly would receive the Lord into their lives. I knew from the previous witnessing experiences in New Mexico that the going would be tough. But with the miraculous things that had happened in my life, and with the full realization that "He is the only Door" (John 10:9), into the true kingdom of heaven, I hoped that there would be numerous New Agers who would embrace the Good News as whole-heartedly as I. It broke my heart to find that this was not to be.

The exact response I received in New Mexico was the same in every single city. Except now it was on a much larger scale. I kept noticing that, within 10-15 minutes at least half the audience would be noticeably edgy and irritated—some so much that they would rudely stalk out of the room. Others had glazed-over looks in their eyes. This response was a first for me. Sure, I had given a few boring lectures in my time, but people only would yawn or nod off. They didn't become agitated and rude.

During breaks I would overhear biting comments. Some would come up to me and start shouting and making a scene. Friends and long-time supporters were stunned and confused. By the end of the seminar, an audience of hundreds usually had dwindled down to less than 50. Of those who remained, most did so out of friendship, loyalty, or curiosity.

Gone were the glory days of cheering crowds, giving autographs, and fending off eager supporters. I felt alone, isolated, and shunned. But Jesus made His presence powerfully felt, and I knew that I was not really alone. If I had to give up everything that I had worked for in my life for the Christian cause, I would do so with rejoicing and without reservation.

Absolutely nothing else mattered but giving my testimony to New Agers. I knew that the Lord would give me all the strength and support that I needed, no matter what else happened.

The relatively few people who did accept Jesus into their lives, though, were a marvel to behold. Satan's chains broken, seeing with new eyes, singing praises to Jesus, being cleansed of past sins, these people spoke or wrote to me and told of the miracles that He had wrought in their lives. Seeing this sparked tremendous inspiration in me to carry on with renewed energy.

On another level, things were heating up. Exactly corresponding to the time of this seminar tour, demonic attacks started to mount with increasing severity. I was venturing into the adversary's New Age turf and causing some waves. Multitudes of demons made sure to get Satan's point across to me by all manner of oppression, harassment, and mean tricks.

I know that some people don't believe that demons are real, but they certainly are. They are powerful and have a wide variety of cunning tricks they use in their perverse trade. Among many other things, I was involved in several freak incidents where I came within a split second of severe injury or death.

Later, Vicki had a different set of similar weird, quirky incidents. She also came close to dying three times from what doctors said were run-of-the-mill, non-life-threatening health problems. The doctors never did understand her illnesses.

For more than a year we persevered through hardships too numerous to detail. At times we identified fully with the feeling expressed in 2 Corinthians 4:8-10:

"We are afflicted in every way, but not crushed; perplexed, but not despairing; persecuted, but not forsaken; struck down, but not destroyed; always carrying about in the body the dying of Jesus, that the life of Jesus also may be manifested in our body."

Amidst the adversity came many blessings. Being so heavily afflicted, I knew that it would be *only* by the power of Jesus that protection, strength, and peace would come to pass. With constant fervent prayer born out of severe need, plus totally giving all situations over to His control, my personal relationship with the Lord grew immensely. I came to feel His presence every day as a constant Teacher and Friend. To me, this was a blessing far surpassing anything else that was happening at the time. Still being a newborn Christian, I also felt His hand of rebuke, correction, and forgiveness in leading me toward becoming a better disciple.

My Three Big Mistakes As a Newborn Christian

In order for this testimony to be complete, I also must reveal my errors, my sins. In so doing I hope that my Christian brethren will come to better understand the plight and the unique problems that face former New Agers who are newly converted to the Christian faith.

Hindsight is so often 20/20. Mistakes of the past seem so clearly error-filled when viewing them from the present, but at the time you were doing the best you could. I am not offering excuses for past mistakes—they were wrong, plain and simple. But the wonderful news to me, looking back on all this, is that Jesus did not abandon me. His all-embracing love unswervingly stood by me through thick and thin, and He patiently used His shepherd's crook to rebuke, correct, and guide me along the way.

Now I see clearly that the first mistake after conversion was in not seeking out a Christian church, with pastoral guidance and fellowship. It is, of course, critically important for any newborn Christian to have appropriate support and guidance in this new walk.

While this is obvious now, it did not even occur to me for over a year. Analyzing the situation today, I see that while I had accepted the Christian faith, there were still many New Age stereotypical views of the Christian community that were retained. Unless a person actually has been deeply involved in the New Age, it is extremely difficult to comprehend how astoundingly alien a world it can be.

After conversion my first thoughts were of bringing the Christian witness to New Age friends and supporters. The Christian community already was well apprised of my marvelous discovery. However, the New Age subculture had been my home for 15 years—I literally grew up in it, and all my friends and the ties of a lifetime were there. Also, I knew of no Christian outreach programs into the New Age subculture. My thoughts, therefore, were to try to help change the New Age from the inside out.

It is also important to point out that New Agers have certain stereotypical views of Christians, just as Christians have their views of New Agers. In chapter 9, "How do New Agers View Christians?: A Study of Stereotypes, Arrogance, and Potential Dangers," this subject is developed more completely. In short, New Agers generally view Christians as judgmental, unforgiving, and rigidly dogmatic. While I see that this is a very unfair stereotype, it is the perception of most New Agers. Therefore, these people often will go out of their way to avoid unnecessary contact with Christians. Even as a converted Christian, I still had this type of habitual avoidance pattern. I knew that my Heavenly Father loved me, but I honestly didn't know if Christians would—especially being a former New Age leader. In fact, I had a strong fear and defensiveness about the Christian community.

Thus, my first major mistake was made—not finding appropriate Christian leadership and fellowship.

The second mistake revolves around the use of crystals and sacred science.

There are a number of explicitly forbidden occult practices delineated in the Bible, the most comprehensive list of which is located in Deuteronomy 18:9-12. Here it prohibits such practices as: "passing through the fire," divination, observation of times (i.e., astrology), being an enchanter (sorcery), witchcraft, necromancy, being a charmer, consulting familiar spirits, and wizardry. I started to speak out against them quite strongly in my seminars, including taking a highly unpopular stance against one of the strongest trends in the New Age—trance channeling and the acquiring of familiar spirits (that is, having spirit guides).

Here's where my error started: I viewed my approach to crystals and sacred science as a scientific one, and I saw no inherent contradiction in applying these disciplines while being a Christian as long as they were not used in conjunction with Biblically forbidden practices. This is untrue, but it took me a while to understand it.

Here's the line of reasoning I used: It is a fact that modern technology employs crystals (most of them man-made) in a huge variety of common technological devices, from computers to lasers to watches to satellite communications. The field of orthodox crystallography (crystal science) is a major scientific discipline in which thousands of orthodox scientists around the world are involved.

To apply a specific example to the issue at hand: The tiny silicon chips used in computers are a type of crystal which is the essential building block of most computer technology. Without using the silicon crystal and its technological variations, the better part of our civilization would come to a grinding halt.

Basically, I saw that computers are a neutral tool—they are not inherently Christian, nor are they inherently non-Christian. Christians use computers all the time, so do non-Christians. Therefore, the use of silicon crystals in computers is not an inherently religious issue. It is not the computers or silicon crystals that are good or evil in and of themselves; rather, whether computers are put to good or evil purposes depends on the *human* factor.[7]

I applied the same type of reasoning to the sacred scientific use of crystals. I figured that crystals are a neutral tool and, like computer silicon crystals, they could be put to good or evil purposes depending on the human factor.

On the one hand, if a crystal is being used, for example, in fortune-telling or "tuning in to spirit guides in trance-meditation" or divination, obviously they are being applied in conjunction with Biblically forbidden practices. Using crystals in such ways would, then, be most inappropriate.

On the other hand, in some *apparently* non-occult-based applications, some alleged effects of crystals include: helping to concentrate the mind, to release stress, to alleviate headaches, to build up vitality in the body, and others. Here, I figured, with these types of apparently non-occult-related purposes, it was possible to be a Christian and still use crystals. After all, I thought, I could use a computer and still be a Christian, as long as the computer was utilized within Christian ethical guidelines. Same with crystals, right? Wrong.

It took a good while, but eventually the Holy Spirit convicted my heart and showed me the error of my thinking.

First, all claims about allegedly non-occult-based uses of natural crystals for releasing stress, alleviating headaches, etc. have no orthodox scientific proof, and therefore are to be considered mere speculation until proven otherwise. If there really is something to the notion of crystal power, then it is potentially dangerous to apply it without scientific testing, verification, and development.

Second, and most important, sacred science (and its use of crystals) is fundamentally different in nature from orthodox science. Though in some ways this becomes a very complex issue, the crux of the matter is that all aspects of sacred science involve obvious-to-subtle Scripturally forbidden principles and practices. My final conclusion was that sacred science (and all that it encompasses) is an attempt at modern-day sorcery, white magic, and wizardry, which the Bible states is all an abomination in the sight of the Lord.

Once the Holy Spirit helped me see this, I renounced all involvements with the field of sacred science and its applications of crystals. I testify that this entire field of knowledge should be categorized as New Age.

My third (and I hope last) major mistake was the outcome of intense persecution, feelings of isolation, and misjudgment.

I was involved in giving highly controversial national seminars, as mentioned earlier, to New Agers and it was a period of extreme hardship and persecution.

The sometimes gale-force demonic attacks, severe erosion of supporters, and fall-out from disenchanted friends began to take their toll. For over a year the persecution and hardships were constant and were increasing. My co-workers—the married couple, Thomas and Vicki—and I felt like the walking wounded. Being strong people, resolutely committed to our Christian faith, the erosion of supporters, loss of so many friends and near financial ruin was taken in stride. But we really were taking a bad beating from the demonic attacks.

Earlier, I related the incidence of a series of quirky close brushes with extreme danger. Also, consistent bad fortune at every turn and daily feelings of strong, unearthly oppression also weighed down heavily on us. It was only through the strength and comfort that the Lord provided that allowed us to bear this burden.

Also, at this point Thomas was ministering to Vicki virtually 24 hours a day as she suffered terribly for over three months from some unknown illness. As I mentioned before, she came close to death several times as doctors were mystified at what appeared to be a simple, non-life-threatening health problem. They could not discern the underlying cause—not surprisingly, since it was the enemy's evildoing behind all of it. Praying in tears over these months, sometimes for many hours a day, on her behalf—my friend and sister-in-Christ—I came to receive strong and repeated impressions in my heart that it was imperative to totally exit from the New Age subculture, and that we had to cut every single tie with it.

This was to be one of the biggest lessons I learned from the entire experience. I had tried to be a Christian and yet still live and work within the home that the New Age subculture had been to me for so long. Yes, I was an unwelcome rebel within this subculture, opposing it as I tried my best to share the Christian testimony. But, even as uncomfortable as it was becoming, this was still home.

On the other hand, I perceived the Christian community as a strange and alien land. It was safe to watch the few select Christian tele-ministries that ministered to me because they could be kept at arm's length. At this time, I still had some stereotyped views of the Christian community as being judgmental and unforgiving.

Honestly, I was *afraid* of being stigmatized and harshly treated because of my past sins as a New Age leader. I feared too, for the welfare of Thomas and Vicki, who were struggling so desperately and who could not bear the increased weight of any more potential hardships.

However, in prayer I kept being impressed with an unmistakable conviction that total, absolute separation from anything and everything having to do with the New Age subculture was an answer to my months of prayer. While studying the Bible, I came across a passage that confirmed further the necessity of taking this course of action. Second Corinthians 6:14, 15 states:

"Do not be bound together with unbelievers; for what partnership have righteousness and lawlessness, or what fellowship has light with darkness? Or what harmony has Christ with Belial, or what has a believer in common with an unbeliever?"

I began to see clearly that to try to live in the midst of the New Age subculture while being a Christian was quite inappropriate as well as being very damaging in many subtle, yet profound, ways. I came to know with penetrating clarity that the New Age subculture is Satan's turf—a demonic den of iniquity under the enemy's control—

and that to involve oneself within it (to be yoked together with unbelievers) is tantamount to spiritual suicide.

It was time to leave home. My former New Age home was (and is) an infested viper's den to be exited with all due haste and avoided at all cost.

In leaving, I decided to share one last message of testimony with as many New Agers as possible. Therefore, a farewell message was formulated and sent out to every person on our extensive mailing list.

In this farewell message, two basic statements were made — one accurate, and the other containing an error.

To encapsulate the *first statement*: I shared the conclusion that I had reached — that there are sophisticated powers of darkness behind every aspect of the New Age Movement, deceiving people with false philosophies of love, light, and peace. That the only way to salvation is through the Way, the Truth, and the Life of Jesus, and that it is absolutely imperative to remove oneself immediately from all New Age philosophies, practices, and ties.

Most of my New Age supporters thought by now that I really had flipped out. Mainly because, in the New Age context, converts to Christianity are rare; and former leaders converting to the Christian faith were unheard-of. To totally cut all ties with the subculture seemed a radically backward spiritual move to make.

The *second statement* (containing a grievous mistake) was that a church-based support-group was being organized for former New Agers who had converted to the Lord and desired assistance and support in fully extricating themselves from all aspects of these involvements. As the one to whom these few former New Agers looked for the leadership role, I was to be the leader of this group (the mistake). What became of this short-lived church-group was a learning experience for all, particularly for me.

Out of the many thousands to whom the farewell message was sent, about 100 requested more information. A short booklet was sent to these 100 that detailed some basic Christian principles and a strong anti-New Age stance. Over this group's short life of about four months, less than 15 sent in applications for membership.

Most members were at-a-distance, scattered all around the country — a few diehard converts, who felt as isolated as I did, and as in need of support.

About two months after the church-group was formed, the Holy Spirit strongly convicted my heart. It became clear that it was most inappropriate for me to be in a leadership role. I had been a leader in the New Age Movement, but it was a grievous error to take a leadership role as a Christian. Immediately thereafter, the members were informed that I would no longer be the leader, and that the format would be more along the lines of a simple support group with everyone sharing responsibilities as desired.

Each person in the group felt the same kind of deep apprehension and fear of reaching out to the Christian community. Memories of national church scandals and feuds only reinforced our misgivings. So, because of this superficially stereotyped view of Christians, we felt caught betwixt and between two worlds. On the one hand, it was imperative to remove ourselves totally from the New Age. On the other hand, the Christian community seemed alien and foreboding. Most everyone in the group had been experiencing various sorts of traumas, upheavals, and persecution due to their conversion to Christianity, and many simply desired some support with their difficulties and their transition out of the New Age subculture. The support group offered a helping hand.

Mainly through membership newsletters and tape-recorded discussions, primary efforts were directed toward the difficulties and subtleties of fully extricating oneself from all New Age connections and associations. Christian books and booklets critiquing the New Age by Dave Hunt, Joseph Carr, Texe Marrs, Douglas Groothuis, the Spiritual Counterfeits Project, T. A. McMahon, Karen Hoyt, John Ankerberg, John Weldon and others proved immensely helpful.[8]

Also, many aspects of lifestyle and daily living were re-examined fully—things like re-evaluating friendships with those still in the New Age, getting rid of all New Age-related clothes, music, aromas, jewelry, mementos, paraphernalia, and stopping the use of buzz words (such as high vibrations, higher consciousness, and the like). These and other topics were applied as a type of self-evaluation and de-programming procedure. It is a real job ridding oneself of a lifetime of New Ageiness.[9]

This group continued for another couple of months before disbanding. During this time, a number of people started to sense that we should begin exploring the Christian community in our respective cities. Many of the group members had stabilized their lives, having experienced a lessening of persecution as well as much-needed healing and restoration. If we were to be met with rejection or harshness, then at least we had regained our strength to face it.

A few preliminary excursions to Christian meetings and church services brought in positive reports of friendly, concerned, loving receptions. More excursions met with the same kind of response. There was a bit of what sociologists call culture shock—that is, a type of uncertainty experienced in a very new environment. But, no one seemed to hold our New Age pasts against us, or reject us as outcasts.

It appeared that our perceptions of the Christian community were to be one of the last remnants of views that needed re-evaluation.

Gladly! What a relief to see that we were not as alone and isolated as we thought.

As this process unfolded it gradually became apparent that our support group had served a purpose of being a sort of half-way house for a beleaguered bunch of former New Agers adjusting into a new world of Christianity. But now the time had come to disband and to seek out Christian leadership and fellowship in our respective communities around the country. Though an emotionally difficult decision — we all had fought through an intense spiritual battle together — it was time to move on and find our places in the Body of Christ. So we did.

Praise the Lord for all His love, forgiveness, and guidance in delivering this small, struggling group of people from the clutches of Satan's New Age Movement. Surely, it was only through His saving grace and greater mercy that we were able to be reborn into everlasting life.

Retrospective

Looking back on my 15 long, intensive years in the New Age, it is clear how Satan tempted a naive, searching teenager, seduced a well-meaning, but blinded truth-seeker, and bound a man in chains with each step of a meteoric New Age career. The tragic poignancy of this entire scenario is that I truly believed through all this that the New Age did indeed hold ultimate truth and spiritual supremacy.

Not until I had a dramatic encounter with the devouring face of darkness behind all of the beautiful counterfeits did I *begin* to suspect that Satan is the author of the New Age. The saddest part of all is that millions and millions of New Agers today haven't a clue to the fact that they are caught up in a masterful, powerful delusion[10] that leads only to the lake of fire.[11] Today, my heart still breaks when I think of all the people, young and old, who are flocking toward the false light of the New Age like moths to a flame.

I marvel today at the amazing grace that saved a sinner such as me. Certainly I did not merit salvation in the least. But the Lord gave His victory to me anyway through His greater grace. People still involved in the New Age desperately need to hear the Christian witness. Souls hang in the balance. There is a huge New Age "wilderness area" within our own society with people in grave trouble who are not even aware of it. I invite Christians who feel the Lord's call to evangelize the New Age subculture to please read chapter 11, "A Call for More Christian Outreach Programs to the New Age" (and Appendix B).

I also would like to express deep gratitude to the *televangelistic Christian witness* for being there, day after day, week after week, continually broadcasting the Good News all across this nation and around the world. In my life, this expression of Christian evangelism was as the hand of Jesus reaching out to me and it has been a continuous lifeline of support and enrichment through many hard times.

This aspect of Christendom takes a lot of criticism, but the tele-ministries that truly carry His commissioned witness, amid their own struggles and victories, are valuable beyond measure in reaching out to repenting sinners as well as supporting millions of Christians in their daily lives, some of whom rely heavily on these tele-ministries. I just want to add my own small voice of support to this invaluable aspect of the great Christian commission.

My Life's Calling Today

In His time, the Lord called me out in a very powerful way to share my testimony with the Christian community through a layman's witnessing ministry. Viewing the New Age Movement now with Christian eyes, I am appalled at how quickly it is growing and how it plays a major role in the end times rise of the Antichrist forces.

In unraveling the story of my New Age seduction and bondage from a reborn Christian's perspective, I have been able to penetratingly discern how Satan is perpetrating his "tricks of the trade" today on millions of unsuspecting people. As a Christian, I can draw from 15 years of (dead) past experiences — having lived the "inside story" of the New Age — to expose the New Age for the gilded abomination and glittery bondage that it is. This is my calling, my burden, and my joy today.

The Holy Spirit has shown the way for this witnessing ministry by opening doors in wonderful ways. Sharing my testimony with Christians all around the country through radio, TV, churches, conferences, and other Christian platforms, continues to be an exciting and challenging way to serve the Lord and His Church. I sincerely hope that I can continue to add my voice along with other Christians in exposing the strategies, deceits, and ploys of Satan's New Age Movement that pose such a powerfully rising threat to Christendom today and tomorrow.

The New Age Movement is not going to die down. In fact, it has really only *just begun* to hit its stride during the late 1980s. In the years ahead, the New Age will be escalating into a major worldwide force to be reckoned with as Satan uses it as a tool to give rise to the Antichrist forces. Stay tuned. By keeping up with current trends in the New Age, many of these forces' movements and strategies lay exposed, and Christians may be forewarned and forearmed regarding the lurking dangers of tomorrow's impending titanic world events.

Yes, the New Age Movement will be growing stronger in the years ahead, *but* it has a number of Achilles' heels that can be pierced by the sword of the Spirit to great advantage toward protection of the Church-Body as well as maximizing the harvest that Jesus will reap when He returns in the near future.

In concert with every Christian who holds to the testimony of Jesus, I longingly await His personal and visible Second Coming and the Rapture of the Church-Bride. When Jesus defeats the abominable Antichrist and his sons of iniquity after their short, one-world-order season, His millennial victory will reign supreme forevermore.

Notes

1. Billy Graham, *Approaching Hoofbeats: The Four Horsemen of the Apocalypse* (Waco, TX: Word Books, 1983), p. 93.
2. Ephesians 6:12.
3. See chapter 9, "How Do New Agers View Christians?" for more on this subject.
4. Matthew 13:42.
5. Jude 1:3.
6. See chapter 9, "How do New Agers View Christians?" for more information on this subject.
7. In this example, I should point out that when the factor of what scientists call "artificial intelligence" comes into the picture of advanced computer technology and robotics, this issue takes on an *entirely* different complexion. For example, if the "mark of the beast" is, as some Christian theologians say, a tiny computer chip implanted in the forehead or wrist, then the choice of using this computer technology or not definitely would be a spiritually based decision.
8. See bibliography for a list of Christian books critiquing the New Age.
9. See chapter 10, "Perspectives on Helping Others to Get Out of New Age Involvements," for more information on this topic.
10. 2 Thessalonians 2:11.
11. Revelation 20:15.

FOUR

CHE NEW AGE MOVEMENC: A FORMER INSIDER'S VIEW

Let me tell you what the New Age Movement is really like, from the perspective of one who has lived it, breathed it, and worshipped it for 15 years. By holding up the serpent's original temptation to partake of the forbidden fruit, the New Age Movement has seduced many millions of people into accepting the promises of personal godhood, unlimited power, and immortality through reincarnation. Quite the temptation. However, there is a dark underside to the movement's banner cries of love, light, peace, and universal brotherhood that needs to be exposed for what it truly is.

Introduction: What Is the New Age Movement?

Essentially, it is a Satan-controlled, modern-day mass revival of occult-based philosophies and practices in both obvious and cleverly disguised forms. In effect, it is an end- times "plague of the spirit" propagating the "powerful delusion that they should believe the lie."[1] It is nothing more than a glitteringly seductive, broad road leading only to eventual destruction.

The New Age is actually not anything new at all. It always has been active throughout history in numerous and widespread Western occult traditions and Eastern mystical religions. Over the last three decades, however, an enormous and unprecedented massive revival of occult-based practices has been taking place, some of it disguised as being non-occult in nature. To many peoples' surprise, New Age philosophy and practices have crept into the very fabric of American society in both subtle and profound ways. The magnitude and momentum of this movement is to such an extent that it poses one of the fastest-growing threats to Christianity today, especially in the years ahead as the end times unfold.

What do most people think of when they hear the term New Age? Shirley MacLaine? Harmonic Convergence? Reincarnation? Crystal power? Channeling? Psychic readers? In fact these are only a part of a very broad spectrum of different New Age forms, strategies, and practices. To make matters all the more difficult, the term New Age is sometimes not even used when something is actually New Age at the core. The attempt to answer the sometimes slippery complexities of the question, "What, exactly, is the New Age Movement?" will be the recurring theme to be explored from many angles throughout the rest of this book.

The New Age Explosion

The New Age Movement needs to be understood as one of the fastest-growing uprisings of the end-times powerful delusion occurring in the world today. In fact, it has expanded with explosive diversification in the last three decades to a much greater extent than many realize. Today's rapid growth of the New Age phenomenon is nothing less than a major branch of the prophesied latter-day rise of the Antichrist forces. It is in this context that the most penetrating insights into the greatest deceptions and dangers of the movement are seen.

Bible prophecy warns:

"For false Christs and false prophets will arise and will show great signs and wonders, so as to mislead, if possible, even the elect. Behold, I have told you in advance" (Matt. 24:24, 25).

Due to its deep and inextricable involvements in Scripturally forbidden practices[2] — like divination, witchcraft, sorcery, mediumship, spiritism, and numerous others — the New Age opens the gates for the adversary and his demonic legions to unleash an end times Pandora's box of unrighteousness. In effect, the movement acts as a rapidly enlarging breeding ground for the seeding, propagation, and unleashing of a *plaque of the spirit*. The massive releasing of ghouls and demons in the movies, Ghostbusters and Poltergeist, the New Age acts in a very similar way in opening the gateways for Satan's demons.

Dave Hunt, in his excellent book, *America: The Sorcerer's Apprentice*, comments on this theme:

"Today's world confronts a strange and growing paradox that could very well mark a pivotal point in human history. Even as the scientific and technological advancement which ushered in the space age is accelerating at an exponential rate, we are witnessing far and away the greatest occult explosion of all time."[3]

One thing is certain: "the winds spreading the seeds of sorcery have reached gale proportions."[4]

The words of a leading New Age spokesman, Marilyn Ferguson, author of the landmark New Age manifesto, *The Aquarian Conspiracy: Personal and Social Transformation in the 1980's*, speak to the magnitude of the forces in motion:

"Broader than reform, deeper than revolution, this benign conspiracy for a new human agenda has triggered the most rapid cultural realignment in history. This great shuddering, irrevocable shift overtaking us is not a new political, religious, philosophical system. It is a new mind—the ascendence of a startling worldview."[5]

Further elaborating on the magnitude of this "benign conspiracy," Ferguson's book states:

"This network—the Aquarian Conspiracy—has already enlisted the minds, hearts, and resources of some of our most advanced thinkers, including Nobel laureate scientists, philosophers, statesmen, celebrities, and steadily growing numbers from every corner of American society.

"... [the] network is working to create a different kind of society based on a vastly enlarged concept of human potential [and] ... shows us how the technologies for expanding and transforming personal consciousness, once the secret of an elite, are now generating massive change in every cultural institution—medicine, politics, business, education, religions, and the family.

"Will our present turmoil lead to a worldwide breakdown of society—or to a breakthrough to the next step of human evolution? The answer may depend in large measure on the influence of the Aquarian Conspiracy."[6]

The roots of the Movement go deep, much deeper than they would appear at first glance. In a tempestuous world and a society filled with millions of restless people thirsting for answers and spiritual fulfillment, it offers a huge array of tempting alternatives to the Christian faith—"the faith once for all delivered to the saints."[7] The New Age offers multitudes of age-old, occult-based temptations re-packaged in the glossy modernized guise of a new, improved New Age.

The influences of this phenomenon are much more pervasive in our society than it might appear on the surface. To cite just a few indicators and examples:

• A University of Chicago poll showed that 67 percent of Americans now believe in the supernatural; and 42 percent believe they have been in contact with the dead.

• The Christian film, "Gods of the New Age," asserts an estimate of 60-million Americans as being involved in one aspect of the New Age or another.

• Twenty-three percent of Americans believe in reincarnation.[8]

• Forty million Americans believe in astrology, and there are 1-billion astrology believers worldwide.[9]

• *Forbes Magazine* estimates that the (obviously) New Age market does $3.43 billion in business each year.

• Business corporations (including numerous Fortune 500 companies) spend $4 billion on management and employee programs that subtly but distinctly are based on New Age philosophies and practices. In some cases, employees are required to undergo these programs if they want to keep their jobs.

• A 1978 Gallup poll indicated 10-million Americans to be engaged in some form of Eastern mysticism. (Note: Eastern mysticism is only *one* of many branches of the New Age Movement.)

• The best-selling book, *Jonathan Livingston Seagull*, is reported by the author, Richard Bach, to have been channeled by a spirit, and which is totally based on New Age philosophy, has sold over 25-million copies and met with tremendous popular appeal. This is only one of many examples of subtle intrusion into mass public exposure of New Age ideas in a way not explicitly labeled New Age.

• The philosophy of "The Force" so graphically depicted in the "Star Wars" trilogy is a veritable primer of the New Age gospel, exposing millions of young minds in a subtle, entertaining way to the New Age hero-image of the Jedi Knight.

• There are over 200,000 registered witches in America. Untold numbers are unregistered.

• The use of psychics by lawyers and police departments has become much more commonplace today than at any time before.

• The B. Dalton Booksellers chain reported a 95-percent sales increase of New Age books during the week after Shirley MacLaine's mini-series, "Out on a Limb," and sales continue to rise steadily.

• Robert Muller, former assistant secretary general of the United Nations, has written a book, *The New Genesis: Shaping a Global Spirituality*, calling for a globalistic "New Order" based on many aspects of New Age philosophy.

• Jean Houston, Ph.D., one of the most renowned New Age leaders, reports having led a three-day intensive workshop for 150 high-ranking government officials, and other workshops included top-level corporate businessmen and government officials.[10]

• Fifty-two publishing houses have formed the New Age Publishing and Retail Alliance, whose slogan is "A Consciousness Whose Time Has Come." In all, New Age books account for approximately $1-billion publishing dollars per year.

• Professor Carl Raschke, of the University of Denver, a New Age critic, calls this movement the "most powerful social force in the country today." He adds: "If you look at it carefully you see that it represents a complete rejection of Judeo-Christian and bedrock American values."[11]

These examples are but the tip of the iceberg. Clearly, this fast-rising movement demands serious attention.

An End Times Force to Contend With

We live today in a time of revolutionary stirrings and worldwide shakings:

The realm of orthodox science and technology is making many awesome, world-shaking advances.

Profound worldwide socio-political changes are in motion.

National and international economic forces are shifting.

Global ecological deterioration plus the increased frequency of natural disasters have become facts of planetary life.

Many other deep-seated worldwide changes are astir.

The Biblically prophesied end-times stage is set.

Commenting on the New Age uprising, John Ankerberg and John Weldon state in their book, *The Facts of the New Age Movement*:

"Thus the stage has been set for a revival of spiritism that could dwarf earlier eras. Some have asserted that channeling will one day be 'bigger than fundamentalism.' Regardless, spirit contact has become in many quarters a socially acceptable practice—and the spirits have served notice that they intend to influence our future."[12]

Yes, the spirits have indeed served notice in many ways. A prime example being Lazaris, by far the most influential spirit being channeled in the late 1980s, who has stated this point clearly: "Those who hide behind their masks of fear and confusion hope this thing called the New Age will pass. However, that which is truly new in this age of rising consciousness will be the bridge to the future and the hope of humanity."[13]

The New Age makes no real attempt to hide its fundamental underlying agenda—*its* "bridge to the future and the hope of humanity." This agenda is nothing less than the complete revolutionizing of the very foundations of not only America but the entire world. Such a plan calls for the total restructuring of planetary civilization into an enlightened One-World Federation in which national boundaries and sovereignty are secondary, and "planetary citizenship" in the "global village" is the order of the day. This innovative orthodox science bearing many new advances combined with a "Universal Oneness" philosophy (a neo-New Age worldview) is to offer a world in desperate need, a grand solution to profound global problems. Apparent world peace and unprecedented opportunities for "actualizing the human god-potential" (i.e., New Age higher consciousness) are to be unveiled. Herein lies the Antichrist's last temptation, offered to all the world.

What does the New Age Movement hold for the future?

One view is that it is an occult revival that will die down or level out in due course.

Another view is that it will be rather insignificant relative to other national and international factors.

But it also could very well be something else—a major tool of the adversary's latter day deception that has really only *just begun* to hit its stride. It could certainly be a platform upon which the Antichrist will rise to world domination.

Dave Hunt, in *America: The Sorcerer's New Apprentice*, shares some sobering thoughts to consider:

"The last time anything approaching this mass flight from reason to mysticism occurred was in the 1920s and 30s. It was very likely this great occult resurgence in Western Europe, and particularly in Austria and Germany, which helped to set the stage for Germany's acceptance of Nazism. Some historians, in fact, have referred to Hitler as the 'Occult Messiah.'"

"... Something of great significance is occurring, and it must be taken seriously. The last revival of occultism played into Adolf Hitler's hands, and the eventual victims numbered in the millions. One can only wonder where the current and far more pervasive renaissance of such occultism will lead."[14]

In effect, the New Age is one of several major gateways for the adversary to unleash his plans and forces for global domination. The Antichrist comes bearing an innovative orthodox science in one hand and a Universal Oneness (neo-New Age) philosophy in the other, seated on a politico-economic throne of worldly power. A One-World Order, headed by the ultimate wolf in sheep's clothing, offers a desperate world many miracles, gifts, and wonders in the name of peace, love, planetary healing and universal brotherhood.

What used to be as obvious as an orange-robed Hare Krishna devotee or a blissed-out hippie may come today as a man in a three-piece suit or laboratory coat.

The New Age as "Spiritual Humanism"

This movement can actually best be understood as a broad spectrum of non-Christian philosophies and practices that can be categorized as *NEW AGE SPIRITUAL HUMANISM*. The cornerstone of this humanism is the belief that man is divine in nature, and is therefore essentially "God" or an enlightened "God-man."

New Age man, believing himself to be divinely perfect and ultimately all-powerful, sets himself up on a cosmic throne. This highly touted god-man claims to have inherently unlimited powers to command and manipulate the universe according to his sovereign will. Man is elevated to divinity, deity, and sovereignty—the essence of the blasphemy of New Age spiritual humanism that seeks to exalt sinful man to godhood and to displace Jesus Christ as King of Kings and Lord of Lords.

The New Age school of thought offers myriad substitutes and counterfeits for the Chief Cornerstone.[15] Different from the atheist/agnostic orientation of secular humanism in many fundamental ways, New Age spiritual humanism presents *a spiritually based set of belief-system alternatives* to the Christian faith.

Just as secular humanism offers its own type of anti-religious deceits to certain types of people, so does spiritual humanism offer *spiritually based counterfeits* to an entirely different strata of people in our society, people who hunger for and search for spiritual meaning, truth, and fulfillment in their lives.

Secular humanism denies Deity and exalts man's own intellectual, creative, and moral powers as the way to find true meaning in life. On the other hand, *spiritual humanism* affirms Deity (though a distinctly different Deity concept than Christian theology) that casts man in the role of a higher race of cosmic gods, with correspondingly grandiose god-power—the ultimate "power trip."

Secular humanism puts man on an earthbound throne of scientific rationalism, self-generated truth, and self-created destiny; *spiritual humanism* assigns man to a throne that spans the heavens and the earth in a divine heritage of universal lordship, omnipotence, and self-created glory.

In *The New Age Rage*, Robert L. Burrows amplifies this topic:

"Ironically, New Age spiritually echoes, and is a logical extension of, the secularism it repudiates. Both deny the reality of the Creator, and both see humanity as the final arbiter of truth and value. New Age spirituality simply heightens secularism's mistakes by inflating humanity's significance, yielding what Brooks Alexander dubs 'cosmic humanism.'"[16]

In *Unmasking the New Age,* Douglas Groothuis further clarifies this important philosophical point: "The old-fashioned secular humanist ... said, 'There is no Deity. Long live humanity.' The new transpersonal or cosmic humanist says, 'There is no Deity but humanity.' God is pulled into the human breast. Scientific prowess and rationality as the crowning human achievements are outstripped by psychic abilities and unlimited potentials."[17]

However, the falseness and deep-seated dangers of the forces of secular humanism are well documented in Christian literature. What this book seeks to do is to help expose and define the often-underestimated grave dangers that New Age spiritual humanism, in tandem with secular humanism, poses as the Antichrist forces magnify their plans today and tomorrow.

Surveying the Landscape of Spiritual Humanism

The New Age is an extremely difficult movement to define with anything other than generalized statements. In many ways it is as difficult as trying to represent the broad spectrum represented by the term Christianity. Even as all Christians are united in their faith in Jesus Christ, there are very diverse, oftentimes conflicting views between Baptist Christians, Greek Orthodox Christians, Catholic Christians, Pentecostal Christians, etc. So, too, there are at least as many different sectarian schools of New Age thought.

There are no centralized organizations controlling all doctrines, activities, or agendas. No single committee, council, or organization dictates the doctrines and agenda, or controls all activities. The landmark manifesto, *The Aquarian Conspiracy,* terms it "a leaderless but powerful network." This characteristic has allowed room for an immense variety of philosophies and phenomena to flourish via all manner of diverse individuals and organizations.[18]

In any given large city, there are hundreds to thousands of informal and professional groups, businesses, organizations, classes, teachers, New Age professionals, psychics, etc. Even in most smaller cities and towns across America there are loose networks, organizations, and businesses of New Agers. What the movement touts as its Network has indeed spread throughout the land, and into every available socio-cultural niche.

The New Age spectrum runs the full gamut of types of people and areas of society involved. What used to be an arena composed of gurus, witches, and weirdos is now flooded with virtually every type of person in society. Furthermore, the New Age has so many faces and directions to its overall agenda that it has infiltrated into every facet of American society in both obvious and very subtle, deeply underlying ways. From religion, business, and politics to music, education, and science the New Age has wended and wormed its way into the very cornerstones of Western civilization—more so than many people realize.

Let us explore this further: New Age spiritual humanism is primarily born of a deep-seated disillusionment or dissatisfaction with any or all of a variety of orthodox mainstream Western values and institutions. This attitude increased primarily in the youth and *avant garde* of the late 1950s and the 1960s, but throughout the 1970s and 1980s a much more across-the-board, society-wide trend toward rejecting some or all of mainstream Western values and institutions strongly surged.

This was born of an intense searching for new alternatives to the problems and challenges of human existence and spiritual fulfillment. For more and more people there was a perception that Western society just did not provide adequate answers or fulfillment on personal, interpersonal, societal, and global scales. Commenting on the undercurrents of mood and thought of the ninety thousand people attending a 1978 "Festival for Mind and Body," columnist Bernard Levin wrote:

"What the world lives by at the moment just will not do. Nor will it; nor do very many people suppose any longer that it will. Countries like ours are full of people who have all the material comforts they desire, yet lead lives of quiet (and at times noisy) desperation, understanding nothing but the fact that there is a hole inside them and that however much food and drink they pour into it, however many motorcars and television sets they stuff it with, however many well-balanced children and loyal friends they parade around the edges of it ... it *aches*.

"Those who attended the festival were seeking something—not certainty, but understanding: understanding of themselves."[19]

Searching for a New Age Worldview

This grass roots swell of discontent finds millions of all varieties of people searching and experimenting in new directions for peace, wholeness, and happiness. Those people looking in New Age directions find an eclectic grab-bag of opportunities drawing from the *foundational sources of the New Age spectrum*:

- Ancient and modern occult traditions.
- Eastern and Western mystical religions.
- Neopaganism—natural religions and goddess worship.

- New Age-based psychologies.
- And modernized sorcery.

Furthermore, a host of contemporary innovations and eclectic syntheses have blended many of these elements together into countless New Age hybrids. American drive, ingenuity, and entrepreneurial skills have instilled tremendous vigor to the New Age agenda.

These searching people, reaching out for new answers, new alternatives, new directions, seized upon every facet of human experience to remold according to sets of New Age principles. The spectrum of issues and activities addressed is indicative of why the New Age is so widespread today in every corner of American (and Western) culture. These areas include: religion and spirituality; government and politics; education; environmental issues; women's rights; psychology; art; music; health care; science and technology; diet; child care; human potential; creativity; sports; economics; social change; interpersonal relationships; marriage and family; brain-mind research; and many others.

What is important to note here is that the New Age Movement is not just confined to obviously occult, cultic, or otherwise fringe elements of society. Rather, New Age thought encompasses all aspects of human experience. In essence, it is an attempt to revolutionize every facet of life on personal, interpersonal, societal, and global scales. There is no aspect of the human experience or societal issues that New Age spiritual humanism does not attempt to remold into non-Bible-based counterfeit solutions and alternatives. It is what spokesperson Marilyn Ferguson calls the "new mind—the ascendance of a startling worldview."

Whatever the issue, whatever aspect of the human experience being questioned, spiritual humanism attempts to creatively draw upon other cultures and ancient traditions and combine them with contemporary innovations to remold the subject area into a more enlightened, less limiting, more advanced, and more fulfilling format. Essentially, the New Age takes all that the Bible states about human nature, principles for living a righteous and fulfilling life, and the Way to salvation, and attempts to redesign everything according to supposedly superior concepts. It's a matter of taking the Creator's perfect design for man as revealed in the Bible and trying to create something better and more perfect.

Therefore, in reevaluating the area of marriage and family, for example, spiritual humanism rejects the Bible's revealed wisdom as old-fashioned or unevolved or just not my thing. Instead, it explores a multitude of open-ended do-it-yourself possibilities that appear attractive and viable to the new mind of New Age man. Indeed, there is not just one perfect New Age model for revolutionizing marriage and family, but an entire spectrum of different options are outlined for each person to choose from according to his or her own personal preference.

There's a basic credo that says "create your own reality according to what feels right for you." For example, whether a person chooses to be homosexual, bisexual, monogamous, polygamous or whatever is OK as long as "It's right for me" or "It's done with love and no one's hurt." This is a kind of relativistic, human-founded ethics (or design-your-own ethics). In effect, New Age persons pick and choose from the multitudes of options in each area of life according to their own personal preferences. Here you pick your own truth, your own morals, and your own wisdom. The absolute moral standards and eternal principles of wisdom revealed in the Holy Bible are either selectively picked through *à la carte* or they are tossed out the window completely.

The Alternative New Age Menu

The New Age menu encompasses the practical, the socially acceptable, the *avant garde*, the routine, the down-to-earth, the adventurous, the bizarre—all types and forms appealing to the spectrum of humanity's tastes and interests. To provide an idea of the multiplicity of New Age topics, here's part of the table of contents from one of the most successful New Age media ventures, San Francisco's "New Dimensions Radio": "Self-Help," "Consciousness, Personal Growth, and Personal Transformation," "Body Awareness," "Holistic Health and Wellness," "Visionary Futures," "Practical Philosophy," "Moving into Space," "Appropriate Energy and Technology," "Medicine People and Healing Visions," "Right Living," "Evolutionary Economics," "Psychology Tomorrow," "Birthing, Babies, and Beyond," "Shamans, Sorcerers, Wizards, and Other Wonders," "Myths to Live By," and "The Spiritual Quest."

Also, here are some week-long topics from a vacation seminar center: "Inspired Poetics," "Writing for Enlightenment and Profit," "Learn to Relax," "Green Politics," "Dreams and Your Personal Mythology," "Massage and Acupressure: Healing from the Heart," " New Approaches to Birth, Sex, and Death," "Communication Skills: Talk (and Listen) Straight from the Heart," and "Personal Spirituality and Social Responsibility."

It's easy to see from these short lists that any number of the topics sound positive, unflaky, and even sometimes socially responsible. Mixed in with the obviously occult (like "Shamans, Sorcerers, Wizards, and Other Wonders") are topics that sound like something a concerned, thinking person might want to explore. What is not so obvious is that each subject area is a New Age version of economics, interpersonal psychology, space travel, poetics, self-help, spirituality, etc. Even further, sometimes the way that the subject is presented is not blatantly New Age but instead a quite subtle and implicit expression of the spiritual humanistic agenda. For the unwary, spiritual humanistic views sometimes can be assimilated without even realizing it.

It's not hard to begin seeing how the extensive branching of the New Age Movement has opened doors at every turn of human experience, at every angle of human issues. Few stones are left unturned in its quest to revolutionize the world and every individual in it.

Two Major Schools of New Age Thought

Let's explore a brief overview of two overlapping but different major schools of New Age thought:

In *The New Age Journal*, an article on "What is the New Age?" in the Jan./Feb. 1988 issue generally defines *the first viewpoint* of New Age thought as *"Consciousness Renaissance."*

"In its broadest sense, new age thinking can be characterized as a form of utopianism, the desire to create a better society, a 'new age' in which humanity lives in harmony with itself, nature, and the cosmos.

"... unlike the biblical "Second Coming" or most other millenarian visions, the new age being discussed today by a number of philosophers, scientists, and social critics will not result from a future upheaval brought about solely by God. Rather, they say society is now in the midst of the transformation, a change potentially as sweeping as the Renaissance or the Protestant Reformation. What's more, it is occurring in society from the inside out, as more and more people begin to question traditional assumptions about life, the future of the planet, and the nature of reality."[20]

Consciousness Renaissance sees humankind currently experiencing the beginning of a new spiritual and socio-political awakening, a modern-day super-Renaissance destined to lead man into a new era of enlightened spiritual humanism. Spurning the thought of man needing divine intervention to assist in the creation of a global utopia, this perspective sees the awakening of "unlimited human god-potential" as the means by which "heaven on earth" will manifest. In essence, as man achieves higher states of "god-consciousness" through New Age practices, heaven will dawn on Earth only through the dawning of man's enlightened "higher consciousness."

As a leading spokesman of this position, David Spangler, writes: "... The essence of new age thinking is the process of seeing the heaven that is right here on earth every day, a process ... called 're-naming the sacred.'

"... To rename the sacred is to have a different view of the universe. ... It is to re-expand those boundaries we have placed around God, even to redefine the nature of divinity. It is to look at the objects, people, and events in our lives and to say, 'You are sacred.'"[21]

What this school of thought basically asserts is that by elevating man's consciousness, the "heaven" that always has been here on Earth is then perceived. The veils of man's limited thinking are then lifted and, lo and behold, heaven was here on Earth all along. Man is divine and perfect, the world is divine and perfect, and the cosmos is divine and perfect. Man has simply been blind to this eternal fact because he has been veiled by a limited consciousness, a state of ignorance that needs to be overcome by awakening into cosmic enlightenment.

The *second major branch* of New Age thought can be termed *"Quantum Leap of Consciousness."* A quote in literature from a New Age center in Florida typifies this school of thought: "We are on the brink of a new age, a whole new world. In the twinkling of an eye, mankind's awareness, our collective consciousness, is going to make an instantaneous quantum leap into the heavens. Everything will change in a flash of divine Light. Get ready. Your heavenly heritage awaits. Come on in; the water's fine ... He who hesitates is lost. ... He who chooses life is found."[22]

In this theory, humanity now has reached a critical phase of individual and collective evolutionary growth. When sufficient momentum is generated by enough people having developed "higher consciousness," then the entire world will be ready to make a collective quantum leap into a higher dimension of the heavenly realm. Earth and humanity will literally leap in a flash of light into the heavens above.

In contrast to the Consciousness Renaissance view, this Quantum Leap of Consciousness model is directly tied to some form of divine intervention. Though there are a rich variety of concepts about the nature and form of this divine intervention, essentially a sovereign and omnipotent celestial force is said to deliver Earth into the heavens above. Various groups attribute this intervention to different sources.

Examples include "highly evolved extraterrestrials," a "Council of Ascended Masters," an "Enlightened World Teacher," or some other all-powerful "divine" being(s). Earth and humanity are to be pulled up to the next major notch on the evolutionary ladder, thereafter to be governed benevolently by the intervening celestial force(s).

Man's task right now, according to this view, is to help generate enough people with higher consciousness in order to meet the requirements for intervention to occur. It's like meeting a quota before the next stage of the job can begin.

The distortions of Scriptural prophecies are abundant; for example, many who believe in the Quantum Leap of Consciousness hold that the false prophets, earthquakes, plagues, wars, famines, etc. prophesied in the Bible will be magically bypassed by enough people meditating for peace, thereby avoiding this kind of "man-created negative thinking." Furthermore, this school of thought maintains that some other "World Teacher" or "Council of Ascended Masters" will have divine authority in the New Age, not Christ.

Another variation on this skewed theme is that it is not the personal and visible Jesus who returns, but rather "Christ consciousness" that descends into the minds of all earthly inhabitants. Yet others believe that the world will be delivered via extraterrestrials' intervention during a time of enormous, out-of-control world tumult.

From the article, "What is the New Age?" this tension between the two perspectives is highlighted: "Some new age fundamentalists do predict that a literal apocalypse is imminent and that it will be brought about by mystical, extraterrestrial, or cosmic forces. But for many others, the new age has become a metaphor for the unprecedented changes now occurring in many aspects of daily life, a process of rapid personal and social transformation ..."[23]

Many of the Consciousness Renaissance camp try to distance themselves somewhat from what they regard as the flakier side of the New Age—UFO telepathic communications, crystal power, glorification of channeling, and the like. These folk tend to focus more on integrating increasingly socially acceptable New Age values into personal and societal life. This is the side of the New Age that has made especially strong inroads into areas such as the corporate business world, psychology, entertainment media, education, health care, and science (among others).

In terms of value-system and practical-level infiltration into mainstream American culture, this aspect of the New Age has proven the more successful of the two schools of thought due to its subtler humanistic approach.

Though there is much overlapping between these two major philosophies, the Quantum Leap of Consciousness viewpoint is much more predisposed to the metaphysical-occult end of the spectrum. In particular, the predominant themes lie much more towards mediumship, spiritism, witchcraft, psychic powers, and sorceries in myriad shapes and forms. One of the primary dangers from this branch of the New Age is its major contribution to the historically unprecedented unleashing of demonic forces into the world today.

What Type of People Are Attracted to the New Age Spectrum?

No longer is the New Age the sole province of gurus, hippies, witches, psychic readers, mediums, fortune-tellers, and all the other popular associations with New Age. Today, people involved in one aspect of the New Age spectrum or another cut across all boundaries, come in all forms, and from all walks of life.

Marilyn Ferguson, in *The Aquarian Conspiracy*, comments on the incredibly wide range of conspirators.

"The Aquarian Conspirators range across all levels of income and education, from the humblest to the highest. There are schoolteachers and office workers, famous scientists, government officials and lawmakers, artists and millionaires, taxi drivers and celebrities, leaders in medicine, education, law, psychology. Some are open in their advocacy, and their names may be familiar. Others are quiet about their involvement, believing they can be more effective if they are not identified with ideas that have all too often been misunderstood."[24]

Here are some primary categories of people who often are attracted to the movement. As you will see in this quick overview, it cuts into every level of American culture.

1) Socio-cultural rebels who have a profound disillusionment with every level of Western culture, and feel a powerful need to search out ancient and contemporary countercultural alternatives. This kind of person can come in any kind of guise, from an organic farmer to a corporate business executive.

2) Regular folks looking for answers to the many challenges and problems of human life, as well as sometimes looking for new excitement and adventure. People looking for answers to such diverse things as stress, psychological blocks, interpersonal communications problems, sexual dissatisfaction, weight reduction, and many others sometimes unknowingly can be introduced to New Age ideas and techniques.

3) A significant number of people have carried the lineages of mystery schools, goddess worship cults, witchcraft, esoteric elite circles, and other such metaphysical-occult traditions and schools throughout the centuries. There always have been New Agers continuously active throughout history.

4) People who turn away from the Christian faith due to rebellion, apathy, curiosity, lukewarm faith, backsliding, serious personal problems that cloud judgment, or who are unwary.

5) People who are prone to trying new fads, trends, what's hot—those who like to experiment, adventure, and dabble in new and exciting things.

6) Teenagers and young adults who are finding themselves, rebelling from authority, experimenting with new things, checking out powerful experiences, going along with peer pressure, or trying to find truth along misguided directions.

7) People who are bored and have a lot of extra time on their hands sometimes wind up dabbling and experimenting with various options on the New Age menu.

8) People who are lonely and become involved in New Age circles to find acceptance and companionship.

9) People who are spiritually, psychologically, and/or physically sick and who delve into New Age alternatives claiming to provide relief, healing, and fulfillment.

10) People looking for personal power and control over themselves, others, and/or universal forces.

The New Age has an enticement for every weakness in natural man.

Different Pictures of the New Age Spectrum

Now, let me give you several snapshots of the New Age spectrum from different perspectives. The purpose here is not to give a complete and exhaustive overview of the New Age; rather, it is intended more as a helpful introduction toward understanding the multifaceted nature of the movement as the reader continues through the chapters ahead.

Examples of the New Age Spectrum

Yoga; est seminars (now called The Forum); Transcendental Meditation; developing psychic powers; subliminal cassette tapes for self-improvement; "writing your own ticket with God" ("create your own reality" seminars); "tapping into the powers of your Higher Self" seminars; pendulums, dowsing rods, and the I Ching; astrology; contacting spirit guides techniques; neopagan nature religions; consulting psychic readers; dabbling with Ouija boards; and LSD and other psychedelic drugs.

Some Dangers of the New Age

Deep self-delusion; rejection of Christ Jesus; false happiness and contentment; demonic possession; physical/mental/emotional breakdowns; love of untruth and abomination; family disintegration; making wrong life-decisions; more frustration and discontent in life; committing immoral acts; performing scripturally forbidden practices; and, judgment into the lake of fire.

Examples of Obvious New Age Phenomenon

Ouija boards; astrology; yoga; past life regressions; crystal power; Shirley MacLaine; spoon-bending with mind power; fire-walking; out-of-body experiences; astral traveling; psychic readings; pyramid power; channeling; spirit guides; tarot cards; and witchcraft paraphernalia.

Examples of Sometimes Not-So-Obvious New Age Phenomenon

Some types of guided mental-visualization exercises; some mental-power development techniques; subliminal programming cassette tapes and videos; hypnosis; some types of holistic health care; *Hatha Yoga* classes at the local YMCA; meditation techniques subtly based on Eastern mystical philosophies; "Dungeons and Dragons"; "trans-personal psychology"; "humanistic psychology"; world peace meditation events; brain-drive machines; re-birthing techniques; and some children's cartoons and toys.

Examples of Some of Today's "Hottest" New Age Phenomenon

Channeling; crystal power; contacting your "Higher Self"; going to geographical "vortexes" (occult "power spots"); goddess worship; world peace meditations; psychic readings; self-empowerment seminars; occult-based success and prosperity seminars; interpersonal development and sex workshops; and, telepathically contacting UFOs.

Thus, in this chapter we see that far from being a tempest in a teapot, the winds of New Age spiritual humanism are blowing through grass-roots America with alarmingly increasing force. This mounting threat to American society and the Church is not based on simplistic strategies but is instead a complex, multi-level phenomenon which is an end-times force whose prophesied time has come.

Notes

1. 2 Thessalonians 2:11.
2. Deuteronomy 18:9-12.
3. Dave Hunt, *America: The Sorcerer's New Apprentice* (Eugene, OR: Harvest House Publishers, 1988), p. 9.
4. Ibid., p. 86.
5. Marilyn Ferguson, *The Aquarian Conspiracy* (Los Angeles: J. P. Tarcher, Inc., 1980), p. 23.
6. Ibid., from the book jacket.

7. Jude 1:3.
8. From the film "Gods of the New Age."
9. John Ankerberg and John Weldon, *The Facts on Astrology* (Eugene, OR: Harvest House Publishers, 1988), p. 8.
10. Dave Hunt and T. A. McMahon, *The Seduction of Christianity* (Eugene, OR: Harvest House Publishers, 1985), p. 76.
11. Quoted from *Dark Secrets of the New Age*, by Texe Marrs (Westchester, IL: Crossway Books, 1987), p. 32.
12. John Ankerberg and John Weldon, *The Fact on the New Age Movement* (Eugene, OR: Harvest House Publishers, 1988), p. 16.
13. Editors of *Body, Mind, and Spirit, The New Age Catalogue* (Doubleday: New York, 1988).
14. Hunt, *America: The Sorcerer's New Apprentice*, pp. 10, 25.
15. Ephesians 2:20.
16. Karen Hoyt, *The New Age Rage* (Old Tappan, NJ: Fleming H. Revell Company, 1987), p. 46.
17. Douglas Groothuis, *Unmasking the New Age* (Downers Grove, IL: Intervarsity Press, 1986), p. 81.
18. See the appendices for extensive lists of some of these abundant New Age phenomena.
19. Ferguson, *The Aquarian Conspiracy*, p. 40.
20. Joseph Adolph, "What is the New Age?" *New Age Journal*, Winter 1988, p. 9.
21. Ibid., pp. 10-11.
22. From promotional material from "The Center for New Age Light."
23. Joseph Adolph, (op. cit.), p. 9.
24. Ferguson, *The Aquarian Conspiracy*, p. 24.

FIVE

NEW AGE SORCERIES AND IDOLATRIES: A PANDORA'S BOX OF FORBIDDEN PRACTICES

hus says the Lord, your redeemer, and the one who formed you from the womb,
'I, the Lord, am the maker of all things,
Stretching out the heavens by Myself,
And spreading out the earth all alone,
Causing the omens of boasters to fail,
Making fools out of diviners,
Causing wise men to draw back,
And turning their knowledge into foolishness,
Confirming the word of His servant,
And performing the purpose of His messengers"
(Isa. 44:24, 25).

"You cannot drink the cup of the Lord and the cup of demons; you cannot partake of the table of the Lord and the table of demons.

"Or do we provoke the Lord to jealousy? We are not stronger than He, are we?" (I Cor. 10:21, 22).

Up until recent times, the better part of occult phenomena, especially the innermost secrets and most powerful practices, were kept relatively hidden from the masses by the elite of the various worldwide esoteric traditions. While a basic body of teachings was available to the average "man on the street," the higher levels of teachings were reserved for the privileged inner circles of occult societies.

In the last three decades, though, an unparalleled revealing of the higher echelons of elite occult secrets has occurred. One of the rallying cries of the New Age is that what was in the old age reserved for the privileged few is now available to the entire planetary populace, so that each and every individual may awaken his "god-powers" toward paving the way for the Aquarian Age of planetary enlightenment. What before was known only by inner circle esoteric initiates is now readily available in neighborhood bookstores and weekend public seminars. The secrets of yesterday are the common knowledge of today.

What I ignored as being "restrictive" and "limiting to my spiritual growth" when I was a teenager and young adult just starting to delve into Oriental mysticism and yoga has a tremendous amount of Divine wisdom behind it. This is to say, using my own standards of man's "wisdom" and sloughing off Divine wisdom that appeared to be "odd," "uncool," and "unnecessarily limiting," I walked into a lion's den that Satan makes to appear as a heavenly utopia of New Age higher consciousness.

Dangers of New Age Involvement

The forbidden fruit of the New Age appears so glowingly golden, so delightfully compelling, so promising of peace, healing, and higher truths—yet underneath all the layers of gilded power and distorted truth is a rotten core of Satanic bondage. People may enjoy a host of apparent benefits—amazing out-of-body experiences, sometimes accurate psychic readings, apparently effective healings, temporary relief from some problems, etc.—but eventually the rotten core creeps more and more into the person's life. It is then that the demonic tentacles tighten their grip, the New Ager's addiction to occult activities intensifies, and a harvest of dark fruit starts to corrode a person's life from the inside out.

All this rarely occurs overnight, though instantaneous full demonic possession is always a possibility in occult dealings. In most cases, it is only after regular, habitual indulgences in New Age practices that the most severe dangers manifest. However, as pointed out earlier in this chapter, the very first dabbling in any New Age activity often sets a demonic hook into a person's life in subtle but insistent ways.

Some of the dangers of New Age involvement include:

• A short-term rush of energy and peace into one's life followed by a fall-off into anxiety, disorientation, depression, and a driving desire for another occult experience to alleviate the inner emptiness.

- A severe fall-off in job performance, family relations, and other responsibilities as the person becomes more self-absorbed, distracted, and moody.
- A change in personality marked by a hyper-happy, starry-eyed, blissfully enthusiastic attitude. This floating on a New Age cloud nine mentality can sometimes last for months, but usually ends with disappointment, frustration, and sometimes disillusionment, or seeking out yet another New Age high.
- A progressively absorbing addiction to seeking the advice of psychic readers and channels to gain ego-strokes, security about the future, self-glorification, answers to problems, etc. This can be as addictive as any drug, and sometimes more expensive.
- An absorption into some grand vision quest—like preparing for a UFO beam-up or discovering an ancient artifact of world-importance in Peru or some other planet-shaking event—to the extent of totally ignoring the rest of one's life (job, family, mortgage, etc.) as it disintegrates.
- An awakening of the *kundalini* ("serpent power" said in the occult to lay dormant at the base of the spine) through occult practices can lead to many severe problems including: mental/emotional upheavals and breakdown, intense involuntary body spasms, severe brain and perceptual distortions, and sometimes even psychosis and insanity.
- An abrupt intrusion of a demon-spirit into one's life leading to various kinds of possession and control.
- An erosion of Biblical morals into a more lax and liberal viewpoint that opens the way to committing sins such as adultery, fornication, and spiritism.
- An overload of occult energy into one's system, resulting in a type of "circuit overload"—severe hyper-tension and anxiety, mental and emotional disorders, deep depression, rapid breakdown of physical health, and others.
- An increasing hardening of the heart and dulling of the ear to the Good News of Jesus—this becomes particularly ingrained the more one delves into the New Age.

There are many other disorders, breakdowns, personality aberrations, delusions, and types of possession but this should suffice to demonstrate the manifest dangers a person risks with any type of dabbling or habitual involvement in the New Age.

Becoming involved in occult snares is a classic catch-22 situation. Those who are deluded are not aware that they are in fact deluded. Anything shown to the contrary is regarded by the New Ager as a delusion.

Spiritism: The Root of New Age Evil

"But the Spirit explicitly says that in later times some will fall away from the faith, paying attention to deceitful spirits and doctrines of demons" (I Tim. 4:1).

In one form or another, to one degree or another, the influence of "spiritual wickedness in heavenly places"[1] lies at the root of all occult evils. Satan's demons work their charms both directly and indirectly, overtly and extremely subtly.

In *The Facts on the New Age Movement*, John Ankerberg and John Weldon state: "To put it simply, the teachings of the New Age are the teachings of spirits. What the New Age teaches and believes is what the spirit world has revealed and wishes men to believe ... the New Age teachings and practices are not simply the enlightened discoveries of men, but more precisely the deliberately revealed teachings of the spirits that men have adopted and utilized. They merely appear to be enlightened teachings because the spirits use psychological principles and spiritual language; they speak of God and love; and they satisfy many of the genuine desires of fallen men. ... The spirits are coming out of the closet in force, in numerous disguises, doing all they can to spread the teachings of the New Age."[2]

Sometimes the workings of spirits are quite obvious—like the phenomenon of "trance channeling" where the medium allows a spirit-entity to occupy his body and completely take it over for a time. In other cases, where a person has an inner spirit guide or wise friend with which he communicates, again we have the activity of spirits feeding people information and invisible influences. Ouija boards and automatic writing, as well, are a specific way of asking for spirits' direct input.

In other ways, the influence of unclean spirits is much more subtle. For example, the use of pendulums (for divination), astrology, tea leaf reading, runes, fortune-telling, and palmistry all use a defined method as a focal point for discerning specific types of information through occult means. Especially in the more subtle spiritistically based New Age practices, it can be difficult-to-impossible to outwardly discern whether the practitioner is receiving influences from spirits.

Some astrologers, for example, would deny categorically that they are in contact with any spirits whatsoever in rendering a person's astrological chart interpretation. Such astrologers may perceive themselves as simply using their own intuition or psychic abilities or even confining themselves to solely rational input. However, the crucial point here is no matter what the astrologer's (or palmist's or pendulum user's) perception is of what he is doing, because of the *occult method* he is using there is an open invitation to demons to subtly weave their works, oftentimes in invisible, devious ways.

On still another level, there are scores of other occultic avenues that are less obviously forbidden, but must be understood as spiritistic in nature in order to be aware of their horrific dangers. For example, the use of psychedelic drugs in the New Age to achieve "higher states of enlightened consciousness" is not obviously spiritistic in nature, but it *is* just that. In short, psychedelics are often a type of metaphysical doorway to spirit contacts and demonically counterfeited domains of glittery darkness.

Though the Bible does not specifically prohibit the use of LSD or "magic mushrooms" or peyote buttons, the fact is the *function and actual effects* of these drugs is often to open doorways in the mind to possible "other spirit influences." This makes the practice "implicit spiritism." This category of Bible-prohibited practices—implicitly forbidden—means that even though the Bible does not name something outright as forbidden, the actual *function* of the practice is directly occult in nature, and therefore definitely comes under the category of scripturally forbidden practices.

Other examples to be further discussed in this chapter include: occult breathing exercises, telepathic UFO contacts, occult sex practices, past life regression sessions, "create your own reality" practices, out-of-body experiences, and numerous others that are all implicitly forbidden.

In one way or another all the other listed categories of Bible-prohibited practices—like casting spells, witchcraft, walking through fire, necromancy, and idolatry—and their implicit counterparts rely directly on the rulers, authorities, and powers of darkness.[3]

Altered States of Consciousness (ASC): Open Windows to Spirit Contacts and Influences

One of the most powerful strategies in Satan's New Age trickeries is the use of a large variety of altered states of consciousness to induce contact and interaction with demon-spirits and their many-faceted powers. In the great majority of cases, ASCs are thought by New Agers to be absolutely healthy means to open oneself to positive, benign, and beneficial spiritual and psychological influences. It is thought that an integral part of developing one's unlimited human potential is learning how to put oneself into various types of higher states of consciousness, that is, ASCs.

The basic idea is that there are thousands and thousands of different levels of higher consciousness available to man, each level accessing a different type of universal experience and corresponding benefit.

It is said that man's evolutionary imperative is to claim these aspects of his unlimited divine heritage in order to grow into a more evolved, more advanced human being—the New Age god-man of unlimited consciousness abilities. There are a host of supposed positive benefits, including:

- Contacting higher sources of universal wisdom.
- Releasing psychological traumas.
- Getting in touch with one's intuition and creative powers.
- Developing a variety of psychic powers.
- Reducing stress.
- Contacting spirit guides.
- Creating health, prosperity, and happiness.
- Having fun.
- Becoming more centered and together.
- Programming the subconscious with positive attitudes.
- Exploring the higher heavenly realms.
- And many others.

An altered state of consciousness basically can be defined as a trance or trance-like state of mind, normally induced by specific techniques, rituals, or other sorts of volitional efforts. In most ASCs the person is in a deeply relaxed, very passive, receptive, non-rational state in which he is opening himself to psychological and/or spiritual higher consciousness experiences. ASCs can occur with eyes open or closed. The primary problem is that the person indulging is opening a door in the mind that weakens the rational, critical faculties as hypnotically mesmerizing influences increase vulnerability to many sorts of undesirable influences. At the core, ASCs are like occult windows to the New Age beyond.

The recurring theme in inducing ASCs is *relaxed passivity* and *decreased rational, analytical faculties* in a trance-type state.

Instructions for entering an ASC often include:

- "Let go and surrender."
- "Allow your body to feel like it's dissolving into infinity."
- "Release all rational analysis and let it all flow."
- "Visualize yourself as a perfect being of light."
- "Feel like you're floating into another dimension."
- "See yourself spiralling upwards into the spirit realms."
- "Let go of your body and float upwards."
- "Just flow through any feelings of fear, alarm, or suspicion."
- "Feel your body becoming warm and tingling all over as you release yourself into deeper and deeper relaxation."

- "Just allow any thoughts or emotions to arise, surrender to them, and let them flow through you."

Instructions such as these and many other variations lead the participant step-by-step into taking down his guard, relaxing into a deep state of passivity and vulnerability, and surrendering to higher forces, energies, and experiences.

There are many associated tools and methods used for inducing ASCs, including:

- Mystical New Age music.
- Looking into a mirror for extended periods.
- Guided creative visualization.
- Hypnosis.
- Swirling, psychedelic light-shows.
- Repetitious drum beating.
- Repetitious chanting.
- Occult breathing techniques.
- New Age deep relaxation exercises.
- Psychedelic drugs.
- Yoga positions.
- Gazing at esoteric geometric figures.
- Metaphysical sex practices.
- Brain-relaxation machines.
- Self-hypnosis.
- All types of New Age meditation.
- Subliminal cassette and video tapes.
- Twirling occult dances and repetitious body movements.
- Crystal power techniques.
- Multitudes of others.

In effect, by opening up forbidden doors, the participant creates a breach through which demons can infiltrate, often in quite subtle ways.

Channeling

"We want to talk to you of love. We want to blend with you—we want to blend our energy with yours so we can touch each other—so we can work together."—Lazaris, an internationally famous spirit-entity channeled by Jack Pursell.

"We are here to merge, to blend with your human egos, to help your race become the central guidance system of a vast new being."—Angels, channeled by popular New Age leader Ken Carey.

Channeling is indeed a blending, a merging, a touching, between humans and disincarnate spirits. However, behind the oh-so-friendly and wise facade are demons who touch to deceive, blend to invade, and merge to possess. They come with an olive branch of peace, love, and universal brotherhood in one hand, and a smoking gun concealed behind their back in the other.

Channeling, both by high-priced, internationally renowned mediums and by the many thousands of regional and grass-roots mediums, is the single most influential phenomenon on the New Age scene today. A virtual avalanche of seminars, consultation sessions, books, cassette tapes, and videos has cascaded into every corner of the New Age Movement, infusing it with an entirely new level of vigor, upgraded philosophies, and powers of deceit. Millions of people today are fashioning their lives on the ideas of some exalted, evolutionarily superior spirit-entity. The repercussions go much deeper, as increasing numbers of health care professionals, psychologists, philosophers, educators, and other influential people subtly integrate these concepts into their respective professional fields.

Channeling started to become really hot around 1982-85, coinciding with the beginning of the "Shirley MacLaine era," and its exponential rise to the present day height shows no sign of let-up. If anything, it is accelerating today even faster along its ascent to fame, power, influence, and glory.

Commenting on this, Christian authors John Ankerberg and John Weldon write: "Thus the stage has been set for a revival of spiritism that could dwarf earlier eras."[4]

In my years as a New Ager, I went to many channeling sessions, and have heard the alluring words of high cosmic wisdom of multitudes of spirits claiming to be an "Ascended Master," a spirit-God, an extraterrestrial visitor, a dolphin, the Council of Twelve, and others of this unholy host of creative demonic tricksters.

On stage, the medium goes into a trance and often twitches involuntarily as the spirit takes over the body and the medium relinquishes control. In many cases, virtually a total change of posture, overall demeanor, voice tone, speech style, and general bearing occurs as the spirit's presence manifests itself through the medium's body. Often there is a perceptible tingling, buzzing, electric sensations and high-pitched ear ringing experienced by many in attendance as the spirit starts to assert its powers of subliminal persuasion and hypnotic charms.

The audience is spellbound as the veil between heaven and Earth ostensibly is parted, and the gods from above are about to impart their celestial dewdrops to the elite privileged in attendance. Using an almost invariably highly dramatic, glib style, the spirit proceeds to dispense exalted proclamations and predictions, sometimes accompanied by miracles (and promises of miracles) of many bedazzling varieties.

While the disguised demon is seeding an outpouring of New Age thoughts into peoples' minds, there is much more going on than meets the eye.

Carl Raschke, professor of religion at the University of Denver, comments, "I'm convinced there is some kind of mass hypnosis going on."[5]

This is exactly the case. Through speech cadence, orchestrated body and hand movements, voice inflections, and invisible demonic powers that fill the room, the spirit weaves a hypnotic web of rainbow-gilded infiltration. Not only do the participants take in false information but, more deeply, they absorb the permeating influences of the demon's formidable powers into the heart, mind, soul, and spirit. Often, a type of open-eyed trance-state overtakes the listeners with a sense of relaxation, pleasant tingling sensations, and rapt fascination with the goings-on.

Acquiring Familiar Spirits

Familiar spirits operate in a somewhat different manner than those involved in trance channeling, though they all work toward the same ends. While trance channeling involves the spirit fully inhabiting the medium's body while the medium is absent, familiar spirits function more like counselors or inner friends who communicate invisibly with the person during an altered state of consciousness.

In this case, the person usually employs some form of step-by-step ASC induction technique to get into a deeply relaxed, receptive, (and vulnerable) state of mind. At this point, the familiar spirit is contacted, and some form of inter-communication occurs.

The manner of intercommunication is as unique as the individual. But, usually there is a mental imaging (or visualization) or some other type of volitional opening of the lines of intercommunication with inner guides, who present themselves in many ways including:

• A friend.
• A wise one.
• An inner counselor.
• A spirit guide.
• An inner council.
• An inner healer.
• A master.
• The Higher Self.

- An Ascended Master.
- A friendly extraterrestrial.
- A power animal.
- A dolphin deva.
- An archetype.
- A council of Masters.
- An angel of light.
- A crystal helper.
- A bodiless sphere of light.
- A spark of Universal Intelligence.
- And a creative array of others.

The practice of engaging familiar spirits is one of the most diverse, pervasive, and influential New Age methods in use today. In terms of mainstream societal infiltration, some types of familiar spirit practices have made the deepest New Age inroads of all. Such practices have made deep advances in the areas of psychology, inner healing, success/motivation techniques, creativity enhancement methods, mind-power schools of thought, stress management, creative visualization techniques, intuition building, and others. A great degree of discernment is necessary here. Too many people acquire familiar spirits without even realizing that this is what's actually happening.

Essentially, any type of method that establishes an inner helper of one sort or another, and accesses it during any type of ASC is a familiar spirit practice that should be avoided like the plague that it is.

Once a spirit helper of one variety or another is acquired, the individual indeed has acquired something—a deceiving, parasitic influence. It is not uncommon for information or influences received via the inner helper actually to prove helpful in some real but relative way, as it did for me. But like a parasite that offers a few presents and promises in order to "set the hook" into the victim, the familiar spirit gives short-term rewards but long-term victimization.

Mystical Out-of-Body Experiences

Some of the most seductive of all Satan's wiles are in mystical out-of-body experiences (OBE). Here are a few samples of such experiences:

An LSD user, in the book *The Varieties of Psychedelic Experiences*, by R. E. L. Masters, and Jean Houston, Ph.D., relates his experience: "Although consciousness of self seemed extinguished, I knew that the boundaries of my being now had been dissolved and that all other boundaries also were dissolved. All, including what had been myself, was an ever more rapid molecular whirling that then became something else, a pure and seething energy that was the whole of Being."[6]

Fritjof Capra, a foremost New Age scientist, details his seminal mystical experience for writing the landmark New Age book, *The Tao of Physics*: "I 'saw' cascades of energy coming down from outer space, in which particles were created and destroyed in rhythmic pulses; I 'saw' the atoms of the elements and those of my body participating in this cosmic dance; I felt its rhythm and I 'heard' its sound, and at that moment I *knew* this was the Dance of Shiva"[7] (note: Shiva is a Hindu deity of destruction and devouring).

Shirley MacLaine's televised dramatization of her hot tub mystical experience relates: "My whole body seemed to float. Slowly, slowly I *became* the water. ... I *felt* the inner connection of my breathing with the pulse of the energy around me. In fact, I was the air, the water, the darkness, the walls, the bubbles, the candle, the wet rocks under the water, and even the sound of the rushing river outside."[8]

The high gloss and glamour of attaining these often exquisitely beautiful altered states of consciousness is like an utterly seductive forbidden fruit promising enlightenment, infinite knowledge, and ultimate fulfillment.

I, myself, have explored these mystical terrains with considerable enthusiasm and vigor over my many years in the New Age Movement. Some of the most spectacular of Satan's counterfeit heavenly domains are accessed via such out-of-body experiences. A sort of high-tech gloss is painted over sheer darkness in these dazzling celestial principalities. But in fact, they are bedazzling to the point of *blinding* and *binding* the pilgrim to the underlying consuming darkness.

Crystal Power: A New Age Millstone

Crystals and gemstones have no power or light in and of themselves — they are neutral and inert objects. In the context of mind-power-based and other types of New Age techniques there are some types of unusual effects experienced subjectively, sometimes powerfully so. These effects scientifically are not measurable, and therefore subject to all sorts of wild metaphysical theories, speculations, and fantasies, serving only as yet another powerful New Age delusionary influence.

Crystals have a long history of usage as power objects in the practices of witches, wizards, sorcerers, alchemists, shamans, and other occultic figures. When such power objects are applied in conjunction with occult practices, there is sometimes the subjective experience that the crystal is assisting in some ways in manipulating occult forces. Though it is not scientifically verifiable, this is the reason why crystals have such a long history in the occult and why so many millions of New Agers today are in such a craze about crystal power.

Seeing from the eyes of a Christian now, I realize that if Jesus had wanted us to use crystals for healing or spiritual reasons, surely He would have brought up the subject clearly in His teachings. The New Testament does *not* show the apostle Peter, Paul, or John holding a crystal to their third eye to pray or to tune into Universal Intelligence or for any other purposes whatsoever.

Crystal power applications in the New Age invariably are involved with scripturally forbidden practices, either explicitly or implicitly. This is the ultimate and irrevocable flaw.

Instead of being crystals of light, they are actually yet another glossy New Age millstone.

Initiations

Initiations involve a ritual infusion of occult, mystical power into the recipient, who thereby receives various gifts, powers, and awakenings. Though there are innumerable varieties of initiations within the spectrum of New Age activities, all involve a direct interlinking of the individual with demonic powers and domains via the intermediary human initiator. By choosing to walk through this kind of door, the person undergoes a marriage of sorts with the principality of darkness that sponsors and controls each different type of initiation. Often, powerful experiences of apparent bliss, joy, and love accompany initiations. Profoundly altered states of consciousness and out-of-body experiences are also quite common.

In addition, it is not uncommon for certain types of psychic powers, worldly good fortune, inner feelings of peace and contentment, and other apparently positive effects to be received by the initiate. For such a person, all these apparently marvelous effects tend to give confirmation that they have undergone a profound growth step toward enlightenment.

I underwent several types of initiations, entering into them as enthusiastically as millions of others. Each initiation felt like a major spiritual breakthrough into new plateaus of higher consciousness and psychic powers, but I see so very clearly now that it was in reality being plugged into yet another of Satan's principalities, like an electric cord into a socket of dark power.

The UFO Issue

I was deeply involved in the UFO phenomenon. But because it is such a weird subject, I feel it inappropriate to comment at this point, and rather let the words of various Christian leaders and authorities speak for themselves, perhaps provoking the reader to curiosity and further thought:

Brooke Alexander, president of the respected (Christian) Spiritual Counterfeits Project, commented on the "John Ankerberg Show": "A lot of the characteristics that attend UFO 'close encounters' are also highly characteristic of demonic encounters ... more than anything else, the thing that we came to understand was that these UFOs are not extraterrestrial space vehicles, but they are extra-dimensional beings."[9]

Dave Hunt, noted Christian author and New Age critic, reports the research of the renowned astrophysicist and computer scientist, Jacques Vallee, Ph.D., on the "John Ankerberg Show": "... a very brilliant man who has just done logical, scientific research for 20 some years on the subject. He says four things about UFOs. He says, 'Number one, they're real. ... Number two,' he says, 'They're not physical.' ... 'Number three,' he says, 'They're messengers of deception' ... 'Number four. ... They are psychologically programming, setting up the human race, for some ultimate delusion that is too horrible even to imagine as yet.'"[10]

In *Confronting the New Age*, Christian author Douglas Groothuis reports, "Those supposedly contacted by the UFOs often display traits common in other kinds of occult phenomena such as a trance state, automatic writing, peering into crystals, the poltergeist effect, levitation, psychic control, psychic healing and out-of-body experiences."[11]

Billy Graham, in his book *Angels: God's Secret Agents*, comments: "Some Christian writers have speculated that UFOs could very well be a part of God's angelic host who preside over the physical affairs of universal creation. While we cannot assert such a view with certainty, many people are now seeking some type of supernatural explanation for these phenomena. Nothing can hide the fact, however, that these unexplained events are occurring with greater frequency around the entire world and in unexpected places."

Zola Levitt, Jewish Christian authority, in a taped lecture, "UFOs: What on Earth is Happening?" states:

"We think the UFOs represent demon activity come out in the open in the end times."[12]

It is most interesting that so many conservatively sided, Bible-believing Christian authorities are willing to give serious comment on the subject of UFOs.

Whitley Strieber, famous novelist, has been the subject of national exposure in his best-selling books on his UFO encounters, *Communion* and *Transformation*. With no previous involvements in any metaphysical areas, formerly a staunch secular rationalist,

Strieber has gone through a radical change of beliefs and spiritual philosophy due to alleged direct encounters with extraterrestrials.

He reports that the visitors "have caused me to slough off my old view of the world like the dismal skin that it was and seek a completely new vision of this magnificent, mysterious, and fiercely alive universe."[13] He adds: "What ever the visitors are, I suspect they have been responsible for much paranormal phenomena, ranging from the appearance of gods, angels, fairies, ghosts, and miraculous beings to the landing of UFOs in the backyards of America. ...

"It should not be forgotten that the visitors—if I am right about them—represent the most powerful of all forces acting in human culture. They may be extraterrestrials managing the evolution of the human mind."[14]

As with me (when a New Ager) and so many *millions* of New Agers, contact with forces or entities identifying themselves as extraterrestrials, Strieber has undergone a radical higher consciousness transformation that propelled him into a New Age type of philosophy.

From the perspective of past, personal, first-hand involvement in the UFO phenomenon, now viewing it with the eyes of a Christian, I believe that this subject merits the most serious investigation, for it could hold a very real threat to the entire world in both expected and highly unexpected ways. From millions of New Agers' experiences, there is a profoundly potent force behind whatever the UFOs really are. That force is definitely demonic in nature and has extraordinary delusionary brainwashing effects on people. I believe that, whatever new information may be uncovered about this phenomenon in the years ahead, UFOs are *messengers of deception*, nothing else.

Former President Ronald Reagan made an interesting comment at the 42nd General Assembly of the United Nations on September 21, 1988:

"In our obsession with antagonisms of the moment, we often forget how much unites all the members of humanity. Perhaps we need some outside, universal threat to make us recognize this common bond. I occasionally think how quickly our differences worldwide would vanish if we were facing an alien threat from outside this world."

Could this be a major worldwide issue of the future? We shall see.

Astrology

This scripturally prohibited practice of divining the influence of stars and planets (and their various interrelationships) on human affairs and terrestrial events is one of the more popular and seemingly benign phenomena. Every day, in newspapers circulated in every city, astrology holds out an open invitation to the curious, the dabblers, and the believers.

Thousands of professional and semi-professional astrologers offer their services through an incredible variety of avenues, both in New Age circles and mainstream society. The temptation to dabble in astrology has been a doorway for many an unwary person leading into deeper involvement in the New Age.

I have come across numerous New Agers who swear by astrology for charting out their daily lives in every detail. During "Mercury retrograde" days, for example, they anxiously would minimize their daily routines in dread of the negative, downpulling effects of the planets. From the choosing of marriage partners to the planning of business ventures to the making of major life decisions, those involved in astrology essentially become slaves, or at least servants, of the stars, the planets, and the demons behind this type of divination. Instead of being more free, those who use astrology cuff themselves with yet another shackle.

Professional astrologers make sophisticated arguments for both the scientific and spiritual aspects of this discipline, and point to a host of apparent benefits and levels of accuracy. The bottom line, in response to any and all of their arguments, is that: 1) the Biblical faith of Jesus is not the chief cornerstone[15] of astrology, and 2) astrology is specifically forbidden in the Bible.[16]

Firewalking

This practice has been in existence throughout the centuries, and enjoyed a dramatic revival in the New Age during the early 1980s. The reader may be surprised to know that people actually do walk on searingly hot coals for significant periods of time, and (most) come through totally unscathed. Even National Geographic scientists have set up controlled circumstances to observe this phenomenon and, though they cannot yet agree on the scientific rationale, they have verified its factualness.

As supernatural as firewalking may seem, it is yet another entrapment scheme. Firewalking seminars always have specific ways of building up an altered state of consciousness of high intensity. Whipped up into a controlled high-trance frenzy, the participants dare to do the impossible. The reluctant and even the very fearful are swept along as the mass hypnotic force generated by the whole group reaches its peak, and the demons are freed to do their work. An extreme high is commonly experienced, which is, unfortunately, a combination of adrenaline rush plus demonic intrusion. The Bible specifically prohibits "passing through the fire."[17]

Occult Sex Practices

The allure of mystically enhanced super-sex is one of the New Age's hottest items. Under the guise of spiritual development a host of occult breathing practices, meditation techniques, *kundalini* awakening (serpent power), and intricate intercourse techniques are used in a wide variety of ways to generate occultic forces via sex. The experiences can induce a host of mystical and out-of-body experiences, as well as the intoxications of drinking the nectar of awakened serpent power.

Past Life Regressions

By inducing a deep trance state (an ASC) via meditation or hypnosis, a person searches the depths of his mind (referred to as the collective unconscious) to recall supposed past lives. From personal experience, I can report that such experiences can be quite richly detailed and vividly perceived. You actually can feel like you're in the body of some past incarnation of you, experiencing all the thoughts and sensations of that past incarnation.

The environmental landscape surrounding the past you can be incredibly detailed, whether it appears as Renaissance Europe, the Christian Crusades, or even sometimes alien planets and extraterrestrial spaceships. The apparent authenticity and depth of experience can be most convincing and invigorating. It seems that entirely new vistas of the multidimensional you are there for unendingly fascinating exploration and review.

I see now that such experiences are sophisticated fabrications perpetrated upon the unwary person by unclean spirits. As the individual leaves himself vulnerable during the trance-state (ASC), demons have free rein to create all kinds of fairy tales with the person experiencing it all in dramatic detail. Not only does each past life regression excursion open the person's mind to further levels of New Age brainwashing, the New Ager often comes out with severe identity problems. People actually start to believe that, for example, they are Cleopatra, Leonardo da Vinci, and John the Baptist all wrapped up in one big, multi-dimensional persona.

One of the most curious facts about this popular practice is that, almost invariably, the past lives are those of:

- Royalty.
- High priests and priestesses.
- Leading historical characters.
- Famous scientists.

- Super-advanced alien intelligences.
- Angelic beings in human form.
- Celestial super-beings.
- And all manner of other exalted, glorified figures.

Seldom have they been involved in normal, unremarkable past incarnations. How curious. You wouldn't believe the hyper-inflated spiritual ego-trips that come spewing out of the demonic dens marked "Past-Life Regressions: Come on in, and see the untold wonders and mysteries of you, glorious you!"

Psychic Powers: Clairvoyance, Telepathy, Precognition, Psychometry, Psychokinesis, Remote Viewing, and Others

Waving high the banner of awaken your unlimited divine god-potential, the development of a large spectrum of psychic powers is a major New Age directive. Psychic powers are supposed to be evidence of a superior, more "god-realized" person. While some who claim to have psychic powers are victims of their own wishful thinking or are merely shams, there are surprising numbers of those who have real psychic powers.

It is important not to shrug off the notion of psychic powers. The Bible is abundantly filled with references to the real powers of sorcerers, magicians, enchanters, and the like (though the almighty power of the Heavenly Father always proved superior and ultimately sovereign).[18] Also, the end-times prophecies point to "counterfeit miracles, signs and wonders,"[19] and "great signs and wonders"[20] that clearly foretell an end-time proliferation of superhuman powers.

Though much could be said on this subject, Dave Hunt provides some eye-raising observations in *America: The Sorcerer's New Apprentice*:

"... inside informants continue to insist that the United States government is taking psychic power seriously enough to spend millions on secret research, and that the Soviets are doing likewise. ... Representative Charles Rose (D-NC), a member of the House Select Committee on Intelligence, calls the possibility of 'psychic war' all too real."[21] And: "there are many serious researchers who are now convinced that psychic phenomena may well involve something potentially no less dangerous than atomic energy."[22]

I have seen and personally experienced too many demonstrations of psychic powers, many of them of the "false wonders" variety,[23] to discount the distinct possibility that they are real. The growing body of scientific verification points to the fact that this subject merits serious consideration.[24]

Once, I was in training using numerous advanced yoga methods to prepare literally to walk on water. Believe it or not, I was serious about this, and spent hours and hours building up the yogic *siddhis* (powers) toward the big event. But, I sank like a rock.

The other major problem is that psychic powers ultimately draw upon demonic principalities as their source of power. At no place in the Gospel does Jesus provide lessons on the development of psychic power. The power of the Holy Spirit alone, not man's, is all each of us needs. Anything beyond this not only is superfluous but also ultimately *deadly*.

The following are definitions of some psychic powers:

- Remote viewing: the ability to psychically see distant locations and occurrences.
- Levitation: defying the law of gravity.
- Clairvoyance: the general ability to see the future, remote happenings, "auras," ghosts, etc.
- Telepathy: the ability to communicate thoughts directly from one mind to another, without need of speech.
- Psychometry: the ability to take an object and psychically trace its past history, every event that has happened to it, and every person who has come into contact with it. Another type of psychometry can take a map or an object from a piece of land, and psychically "see" the geographical characteristics of the land at a distance.
- Psychokinesis: mind over matter — the ability of the mind to physically influence matter.
- Precognition: the ability to foresee events before they happen via psychic means.

Yoga

The aim of the many kinds of yoga schools of thought is for the individual to be absorbed into a state of Universal Oneness-Bliss, like a drop of water dissolving into a great cosmic sea. Individual identity is lost, as a type of self-less Nirvana is attained. Self becomes "God" — the root of New Age heresy.

In order to do this, the different yoga traditions all have systematic disciplines for awakening the *kundalini*-serpent power that is said to reside dormantly at the base of the spine. Through long, diligent hours of emptying the mind or endlessly repeating *mantras* (Hindu deity-names) in meditation, a progressive evolutionary ladder is said to be climbed over thousands of reincarnations. Along the way, a spectrum of *siddhis* (psychic powers) are acquired that help the yogi to master space, time, and matter with powers of the mind.

Extended fasting, strict vegetarian diet, *Hatha Yoga*, chanting, and diverse prescribed physical purification exercises (like slipping a length of cloth down the throat to the stomach, and pulling it back up again) all are combined into a highly disciplined regimen.

From having delved seriously into the mysterious world of yoga myself, several observations come to mind, from a Christian perspective:

1) There are extreme dangers involved in awakening the *kundalini* practices. I have observed numerous New Agers experiencing the subtle and extreme casualties—mental and emotional disruptions, involuntary physical movements (from uncontrollable spasms to incessant quivering), nervous system burn-out, outrageous ego-inflations, sexual obsessions, intense delusionary states, hallucinations, and other quite undesirable side-effects.

Several times through these years my mind felt like it was racing uncontrollably, like a wind-swept wildfire. Nothing could stop it, and a few times I felt like I was teetering on the brink of insanity. For several months after such an incident, I would treat certain advanced practices with extreme caution, but I didn't do the smart thing, and stop totally.

2) The extensive *yogic* practices easily can take the better part of a day, depending on how serious the yoga practitioner is. There is so much focus on *self*-development that there is little or no time spent on serving and caring for others. *Yoga* often leads into a self-absorbed type of meditative narcissism.

3) Invariably, different schools of yoga have gurus positioned at the top of the hierarchical religious ladder, claiming to function as the necessary interconnection between "God" and the yoga aspirants, who must bow to the personage and will of the guru. Obviously, the guru is a type of false christ, attempting to take the place of Jesus as the only Way (Jn. 14:6).

4) *Hatha Yoga*—the pretzel and stretching exercises—is being offered with alarming frequency through such bedrock institutions as YMCAs, colleges, continuing education college classes, high school phys-ed classes, and in other areas of society. Often it is thought that *Hatha Yoga* is benign and somehow disassociated from the rest of the total Yoga system. This is a potentially dangerous fallacy, for *Hatha Yoga* is part and parcel of the whole of yoga, with many of the same dangers.

In addition, *Hatha Yoga* also functions as a door through which the curious sometimes walk to explore the other aspects of the New Age.

Create Your Own Reality: The "Health, Wealth, and Godhood" Doctrine

One of the loudest trumpet calls in the New Age Movement is CREATE YOUR OWN REALITY.

The myriad variations on this trumpeting theme include:

- Vision your life perfect.
- You are god and can create all things.
- By my power, all things are created by me.
- Write your own ticket with God.
- Mind power creates all success.
- By my faith and power, I create all things.
- Thought power controls all reality.
- My powers of godhood manipulate all universal energies.
- Psychic powers are man's divine heritage.
- And my thoughts and words are binding on the powers of the cosmos.

The New Age teaches faith in man. Jesus teaches faith in Him.

The New Age teaches power to man. The Bible teaches the almighty power of the Most High.

The New Age teaches "I am in control." The Holy Bible teaches "I can do all things through Him who strengthens me" (Phil. 4:13).

Power-by-me vs. power-by-the-Lord is a fundamental dividing line between the New Age and Christianity.

The New Age uses decrees, creative visualizations, *mantras*, repeated affirmations, and occult invocations to create its own reality. New Age man steps on the pedestal of "godhood" and seeks to command the universe according to his beck and call.

Jesus says: "Whoever exalts himself shall be humbled; and whoever humbles himself shall be exalted" (Matt. 23:12).

Pantheistic Worship Practices

In a neo-paganistic revival, New Agers bow to the god they think is contained in every aspect of creation. Stars are god, trees are god, planet Earth is god, dolphins are god, everything is god. They worship creation rather than the Transcendent Creator.

This fundamental flaw leads to countless pantheistic errors. For example, sun worship and nature worship practices are rampant. All kinds of ceremonies and rituals are performed for invoking the spirits of trees, animals, birds, plants, lakes, rivers, mother earth, whales, and the like for purposes of healing, consciousness expansion, and communion and co-participation with the powers of the universe.

Pantheism makes an idol out of creation and its various parts and is a direct violation of the second commandment.

Divination Practices

Examples of some divination practices include:

- Tarot cards (a set of occult symbolic cards).
- *I Ching* (an ancient Chinese "Book of Changes").
- Rune stones (an ancient Nordic technique using stones with hieroglyphics inscribed on them).
- Palmistry (divining personal knowledge from the palm).
- Dowsing (using pendulums, wands, angle rods, etc.).
- "Star + Gate" (a new New Age divination "game").
- "The way of *Cartouche*" (an Egyptian divination tradition).
- Astrology (already discussed before).
- Reading tea leaves (attempting to divine meaning from patterns of remnant tea leaves).
- Ouija boards (see below).

Sometimes such divination techniques can appear to be accurate, but any such relative effectiveness ultimately is flawed. By using a Biblically prohibited practice the person opens up subtle or overt demonic doorways.

One of the main dangers of such practices is that the more a person uses them, the more deeply involved he becomes.

In my personal experiences with *I Ching* and using pendulums to divine questions about the status of my life and for making life-decisions, I found a momentum was evoked that made me want to use the techniques more and more often.

In the beginning, I used the practices sparingly and only for important issues. Later on, I found myself using them with increasing frequency for smaller and smaller issues. A growing dependence on them arose before I realized what was happening. At times I would feel compelled to consult these divination methods 20-30 times every day, sometimes for the most minute decisions. After a time, I simply quit the practice because of the obvious dependence.

Divination may look harmless to some, but it most certainly acts as a subtle snare to further involvements in occult dependencies.

Aura Readings

Some New Agers claim to have clairvoyant super-sight that allows them to view rainbow colors that are said to radiate around each individual. Different color-patterns and levels of brightness and dimness are said to indicate facts about the person on physical, mental, emotional, and spiritual levels.

Ouija Boards

This occult tool is likely one of the most dabbled-with of all. Looking to be fun, different, an interesting experience, just something to do, a mysterious adventure, and so many others reasons, people, young and old, have played with this seemingly innocent game. To many a person's great surprise, some invisible force actually will start to move the ouija indicator with a volition of its own. The very act of choosing to use the ouija board and the utilizing of the board opens a potential demonic "window" into the situation.

Though this does not happen every time, this game is no game at all; it is really a matter of playing with occult fire. This is a potent technique for demonic familiar spirits to entice the curious, ensnare the dabbler, and possess the habitual user.

Automatic Writing

This is another form of channeling in which the medium goes into a light-to-deep trance and allows a spirit to take over the arms and hands only in order to write down information. Innumerable volumes of New Age books have been written in this way, with the medium sometimes being totally unknowledgable in the subject matter.

Ruth Montgomery, formerly a highly influential Washington syndicated columnist, quit her prestigious job when a council of spirits started to write voluminously via automatic writing through her. She has written numerous landmark books in this way, and is known to many as "The Herald of the New Age."

Talismans/Amulets

Talismans are believed to be power objects that attract and emit different kinds of occult energy. When applied directly in an occult-based ritual or related New Age activities, there is sometimes the subjective experience of these occult tools acting to help manipulate the cosmic forces. Orthodox science finds no hard evidence to confirm or verify such observations or claims. On the other hand, centuries of occultists — including alchemists, wizards, witches, sorcerers, shamans, and medicine men — consistently have used occult tools as an integral part of their tools of the trade.

Examples of talismans and amulets include:

- *Ankhs* (an ancient Egyptian occult symbol).
- *Scarabs* (beetle figures — another Egyptian symbol).
- *Crystal skulls* (a figure of a human skull carved out of quartz crystal or other precious stone).
- *Crystal wands* (for "energy focusing and amplification").
- *Kachina dolls* (American Indian idols).
- *Fetishes* (feathers, crystals, special dried plants, and other items tied together in a bundle).
- *Medicine pouches* (a collection of different talismans, supposed to be the wearer's power focus).

Talismans fall under the same category as crystals — they are inert objects but, when combined with occult practices, they apparently can be instrumental in producing various subjectively experienced, but unmeasureable, effects.

The Dolphin Movement

The New Age really has gone ga-ga on this one. Quite popular is the belief that dolphins are repositories of virtual libraries of information from super-advanced ancient civilizations (like Atlantis), and can communicate this knowledge telepathically to those tuned in on the New Age wavelength.

Another well-liked view is that dolphins are also beacons of contact with UFO intelligences and can relay intergalactic communications through to their New Age friends. Some even believe that dolphins are a superior life-form to humans.

On one occasion I was teaching a seminar at an upscale hotel in Los Angeles. Coming back from a break I heard an incredibly piercing series of high-pitched noises that sounded like someone was being choked to death, or at least two cats having quite a battle. When I realized that this was coming from *my* conference room, I flipped. There was a growing crowd of businessmen from another conference room gathering around the door, peering in.

I ran in, expecting to see the room in shambles and somebody seriously hurt. Instead it turned out to be a New Ager's exceptionally loud, off-key imitation of a dolphin. (She thought she was a dolphin in a previous life and practices her dolphin cries for a couple of hours every day.) Life in the New Age was not dull.

"Dreamwork"

Here's an ad which appears for "Creative Dreaming": "Plan dreams in advance, control them while they are happening, recall them with startling clarity after awakening and banish nightmares forever!"

Dreamwork is an enduring area of New Age interest and over a thousand books on the subject teach how to develop a type of psychic power over dreams and how to contact higher dimensions and spirit-beings while asleep. This area is actually a type of occult meditation transferred over into the sleep state.

I used some of these techniques and found them leading to experiences very similar to out-of-body experiences and occult meditational experiences.

Occult Breathing Exercises

There are any number of ways to perform special breathing exercises to induce altered states of consciousness. In yoga, this is called *pranayama*—carefully controlled breathing cycles used to regulate consciousness. Some of these exercises are done very slowly over 15-30 minutes and calm the mind into a state of meditative emptiness.

Some other varieties involve a dramatic display of huffing and puffing to awaken the *kundalini*-serpent power. Recently Stanley Krippner, Ph.D., one authority, developed a state-of-the-art holotropic breathing technique which is designed to induce psychedelic experiences without the use of psychedelics.

Whatever the technique, such breathing exercises are just another line dangling tempting bait to the unwary as well as the seasoned New Age veteran.

Psychic Readings

If people want to waste their hard-earned money and also clog their minds with all sorts of ego-tempting clutter, psychic readings are just the thing. The domain of shams, clever people-readers, half-baked psychic abilities, full-blown psychic powers, as well as potent demonizers, psychic readings and fortune telling are a highly popular hotbed of demons' dens.

For the curiosity seekers who are looking for a relaxing afternoon's recreational diversion or just something new to explore, entry into these dens costs not only money but also a price exacted at Satan's toll booth.

For veteran New Agers these psychic three-ring circuses are yet another playground in which to romp and gleefully absorb layer after layer of psychic drivel and gilded rainbow follies.

Other names by which psychic readings present themselves include:

- Life Readings.
- Reading the *Akaschic* Records of Your Life.
- Whole Person Insights.
- Identity Readings.
- Intuitive Personality Profiles.
- Shamanic Counseling.
- Transpersonal Counseling.
- And Readings for Life Success.

Conclusion

After my extensive excursions through many Biblically forbidden New Age doors in pursuit of truth and fulfillment, I came up empty. The rainbows of light crumbled into dust, leaving only the face of consuming darkness, which was there all along but was cunningly hidden. Would that I had obeyed my Heavenly Father's commands instead of following my own well-rationalized desires — the lesson I learned is that simple.

Notes

1. Ephesians 6:12.
2. Ankerberg, op. cit., pp. 18-19.
3. Ephesians 6:12.
4. Ibid., p. 16.
5. Carl Raschke, as quoted in *Time*, December 15, 1986, "And Now, the 35,000-Year-Old Man," by Cristina Garcia.
6. R. E. L. Masters and Jean Houston, Ph.D., *The Varieties of Psychedelic Experiences* (New York, NY: Dell Publishing Co.), p. 308.
7. Ferguson, op. cit., p. 374.
8. Shirley MacLaine, *Out On a Limb*, (New York, NY: Bantam Books, 1983), p. 268.
9. Brooks Alexander, as quoted in *The New Age and the Church* (Chattanooga, TN: The John Ankerberg Evangelistic Association, 1988), p. 16.
10. Ibid., Dave Hunt being quoted.
11. Groothuis, *Confronting the New Age* (op. cit.), p. 30.
12. Zola Levitt, cassette tape: "UFOs — What on Earth is Happening?"
13. Whitley Strieber, *Transformation: The Breakthrough* (New York, NY: Beach Tree Books, 1988), frontispiece.
14. Ibid., p. 21.
15. Ephesians 2:20.
16. Deuteronomy 18:10-12.
17. Deuteronomy 18:10.

18. For example, see Acts 8:9-13 and Acts 13:6-12.
19. 2 Thessalonians 2:9 (NIV).
20. Matthew 24:24.
21. Hunt, op. cit., p. 194.
22. Ibid., p. 68.
23. Matthew 24:24.
24. *Psychic Discoveries Behind the Iron Curtain*, by Shroeder and Ostrander, *Beyond Biofeedback*, by Elmer and Alyce Green, *Remote Viewing*, by R. Targ, and others.

SIX

BEHIND THE "RAINBOW-COLORED GLASSES": AN INSIDE LOOK AT THE LANDSCAPE AND PEOPLE OF THE NEW AGE

*B*eware of the false prophets, who
come to you in sheep's clothing, but inwardly are ravenous wolves. ...
A good tree cannot produce bad fruit, nor can a bad tree produce
good fruit. Every tree that does not bear good fruit is cut down and
thrown into the fire. So then, you will know them by their fruits"
(Matt. 7:15, 18-20).

I have been on the other side of the New Age "rainbow-colored
glasses."[1] I have walked the highways and byways of the New Age
landscape; and have broken bread with pilgrims of all varieties. It is
a completely different world.

What lay behind the rainbow-colored glasses of the New Age is in
some cases as alien a landscape as if you suddenly woke up one morning on Pluto. In many ways the truth of the people and landscape is
as bizarre as the boldest science fiction.

What was "home" to me for 15 years is one of the biggest lies
going. In the midst of the New Age world, the glittery veils of false
luminosity completely enfold one's perceptions, feelings, thoughts,
and attitudes. Satan has created a host of convincing counterfeit New

Age landscapes, each of them custom designed to prey upon the many weaknesses of natural man.

Once the rainbow-colored glasses have become part of a person's daily wardrobe, it is the mind, heart, and soul that become woven about with what appears to be the light of the rainbow, but is in reality false webs of glowing darkness. Once a person crosses through the rainbowed threshold of Satan's innumerable New Age doorways and becomes a citizen of this world, the "glasses" that promise to liberate and unveil cosmic mysteries are "shades of darkness" that only *blind* the person to the very light he seeks.

The blind lead the blind in a New Age world lit by flawed prisms of Satan's own devious works. Thinking to become wise, they become fools; seeking after golden treasures, they find only fool's gold; following the serpents path, they become harlots.

Observing the New Age Scenery

Now let me paint some profiles and pictures of different aspects of New Agedom in order to highlight its profiles and pretensions as well as its bad fruits and abominations.

The grass is *definitely not* greener on the other side of the fence. It only appears so sometimes until you look at it more closely. To disarm any allures of the New Age, both obvious and subtle, can be an edifying endeavor. A Christian needs to have a general awareness of what makes New Agers "tick," as well as their dark fruit. This means he will be forewarned and forearmed that much the more.

The manner in which I am viewing the New Age in this section is from a somewhat sociological perspective. It's not so much looking at specific individuals involved, it's viewing it more as a diverse subcultural spectrum of people and activities marked by certain discernible patterns, trends, and general characteristics. Just like a profile of all American citizens portrays generalized characteristics, strengths and weaknesses, so too a profile of the large New Age spectrum of people and activities will highlight its broad landscape.

By liberating themselves to "create their own reality," New Agers cast aside the absolute moral principles revealed in Scripture. Bible-based ethics are regarded as either old-fashioned limited thinking or only one of several options for choosing one's own reality.

The extensive and clever rationales for the immoral aspects of their behavior are a subject of voluminous proportions. New Age ethical relativism allows a person to pick and choose from many alternatives on any given ethical subject. It's like custom-designing your own system of morals. Furthermore, a positive virtue in New Age thinking is benign acceptance (or even encouragement) of what each person has chosen for himself. So whether a person is, for example, pro-abortion, or a homosexual or whatever, he is regarded as acceptable and righteous. In such thinking, ethics are essentially a matter of personal opinion. Scripture-based ethics are ignored, rejected, or distorted.

Whatever the rationale used, rejecting or distorting the fullness of the Bible's Divine wisdom inevitably will lead to straying into the manifold ways of sin. The iniquities and bad fruit that inevitably result are found in abundance.

Family Structure Devaluation and Breakdown

One of the most pervasive and indicative breakdowns in the New Age house is a manifest devaluation of the cornerstone importance of the family unit. This subject is one of the most underemphasized and underrepresented aspects of New Age thought. While there are untold thousands of classes, seminars, books, etc. on individual development, couples' interactions, and general group dynamics, there is a relative void of emphasis on the subject of family.

What in Christianity is a commonly understood subject of foundational importance is to the New Age a subject of widespread disinterest and apathy.

The enormous amount of self-centeredness among New Agers plus a severe breakdown of morals leaves many families broken, dismantled, or ignored to an alarming degree. There is simply a lack of interest in putting the right effort and the high degree of prioritization needed to build a cohesive, love-based family unit that is so important an aspect of our Father's plan for His people.

I often came across New Age parents who either didn't live with their children or who had left them. Often the parents did so out of preference, not necessity. When one is so busy exploring his own glorious potential, kids just get in the way. This is usually done rather casually, as if it were a healthy, viable option for those seeking enlightenment.

It was also clear that New Age parents whose children did live with them commonly placed a lower priority on their children and the time and effort needed to raise them. Subtle and overt neglect of children, while the parents cater first and foremost to their own desires, is a widespread phenomenon in the New Age.

These children often are exposed to many types of immoral ethics and confused behavior.

This should be one of the first clear indicators that the New Age house (hold) is built on a foundation of sand.

Men Becoming Feminine and Women Becoming Masculine

The ideal of androgyny—that is, unisex—is widely held. No matter what gender a person is, the New Age pictures humans as being composed of two equal principles of male and female. A spiritual-psychological goal here is to balance the male and female side of each person. In effect, a man needs to "get in touch" with the feminine side of himself; and vice versa for a woman.

By going through various New Age psycho-spiritual transformational techniques, a man is taught to think and act with more feminine qualities; and a woman, with more masculine qualities.

The overall effect is predictable—more feminine males and more masculine females.

While still a New Ager, it was hard not to notice this pervasive ideal and trend. There is significant peer pressure in many contexts to conform to this "try-to-be-more-androgynous" goal.

When males start acting more like females, and females acting more like males, the results are simply not balanced nor in alignment with God's creative design. Instead, as it so often does, the New Age tries to improve what it perceives as old-fashioned, unevolved Bible-based male-female roles that actually are based on Divine wisdom.

Metaphysical Branches of Feminism

In league with the mix-up of male and female identities and roles, the New Age is ripe ground for significant aspects of the feminist movement (though definitely not all its spectrum). In fact, there is a major emphasis on the rise of the goddess and the awakening of the universal feminine principle in much of the New Age. Goddess worship, female shamanism, female-dominated witchcraft activities, and female-oriented nature worship are some of the most powerfully rising forces in the New Age today.

Homosexuality

The metaphysically inclined homosexual community finds a good deal of benign or encouraging acceptance in the New Age. Homosexuality is broadly accepted as a viable, positive option for people who feel that this is their own truth. Many New Age-oriented psychologies treat homosexuality as a moral life-option to be assisted and furthered toward its growth potential.

In many circles, to state an opinion about the inappropriateness or immoral aspects of homosexuality is generally thought to be intolerant, biased, negative thinking.

Whether a person is homosexual, bisexual, or heterosexual is all quite relative in their "enlightened" ethics. It doesn't matter as long as the option is "right" for the person.

Is it any wonder that the family unit fares so poorly in the New Age?

Free-Thinking Sexual Ethics

Sexual conduct is also a choose your own reality venue. Modesty dictates a generalized, non-explicit approach here. But New Agers have a well-developed system for rationalizing promiscuous sex.

Waiting to have sexual intercourse until marriage is quite rare. The belief that sex should only take place in marriage (between a man and woman) is considered old-fashioned and even "limiting your potential. Concerning ethics, sex outside marriage is exceedingly permissive, morally accepted, and justified as such in many ways. Within marriage, one of the more common excuses for committing adultery is the concept of an "open relationship" in which married mates are free to explore their potential by having sexual relations with others as they desire. Immoral sex is justified as something done as an expression of love. The principle here is "as long as what you do is done with love and doesn't harm anyone, it's okay."

"*Karma*," as well, is a widely used excuse for sexual dalliances. If two people have some *karma* left over from past lives together, they think, "now's a good time to work out that *karma*." It is a common practice to attend weekend seminars or week-long workshops, not just to receive knowledge but also to find new casual sex partners. The sexual undercurrent at many New Age events is pervasive, even if it is glossed over with mannerisms that put a more enlightened mask on the same old sinful desires of natural man.

Social Nudity

Though not practiced by all New Agers, social nudity is a commonly accepted practice. The acceptance of yourself and your body, by yourself and others is a major rationale. To reveal your whole body is a sign of self-acceptance and positive confidence in this way of thinking. To be unwilling to expose yourself is considered a "blockage" or "limitation" to be overcome.

Group saunas, jacuzzis, hot tub baths, sexually oriented workshops, lake swimming, and sweat lodge rituals are some of the many activities in which social nudity is a commonly accepted occurrence.

The rationale for this immoral behavior is, for the most part, a smokescreen that covers the workings of sexual titillation and temptation. Social nudity is often a prelude to immoral sexual behavior.

Thus we see another prime example of how the New Age espouses high-sounding ideals that justify and encourage the immoral appetites of natural man.

Divorce

The stability of marriage in the New Age is in a terrible state. The combination of the above-mentioned ethical imbalances and a relatively casual acceptance of divorce makes for an unsettling situation.

One might think that for all the time and energy spent by New Agers in self-development, higher consciousness, and interpersonal interactions, they would provide a superior demonstration of the marriage institution. Unfortunately, it is just the opposite. With a general breakdown in sexual morals, a confusion of male-female identities, and attempts to create marriage alternatives to the Biblical model, all combine toward a severe erosion of marriage stability and well-being. Not only are New Age-based marriages often unstable and unfulfilling, but their divorce rate is unusually high.

Through the doctrine of *karma*, it is exceedingly easy for New Agers to justify divorce by such excuses as: "We must have worked through all our *karma* together — now it's time to move on to another *karmic* relationship" or "We can work through our problems in another lifetime" or any number of other creative justifications that try to put a positive face and a more casual light on the serious issue of divorce.

Abortion

Abortion frequently is regarded as a viable, responsible alternative. While having to resort to abortion many times is regretted, the regret is superficial and does not provoke the voice of conscience enough to refrain from this horrendous murdering of innocents.

With all the problems in New Age marriages, the permissive sexual dalliances, and the devaluation of the family unit, the option of abortion arises with a commonness that New Agers would generally deny.

Unwanted pregnancies both in and outside of marriage are commonly (though not always) treated as inconveniences to the lifestyle and self-development goals. Again, the doctrine of *karma* and reincarnation provides easy justification. For if a soul is immortal and continuously reincarnates,then abortion is no problem because that soul simply will recycle itself into another body at some later time, no harm done.

Some New Age philosophies even go so far as to say that perhaps the soul of the unborn chose to incarnate into a situation where it would experience abortion, due to some past life *karma*; therefore, the parent is doing the right thing.

When any philosophy can be molded to justify the murder of innocents and live to smile about it, that should be all that's needed to know about its claim to ultimate truth and enlightenment.

Drug Use

Although not all New Agers use illegal drugs, hallucinogenic drugs such as LSD, hashish, psilocybin mushrooms, mescaline, *peyote*, and many others indeed are utilized widely as consciousness expanders. Drug use of this nature is commonplace, and it is widely agreed to be a *bona fide* tool to self-actualization.

Patently few in the New Age have even an inkling that these types of hallucinogenic drugs lead directly into some of Satan's more powerful and sophisticated snares.

Because of the emphasis on health, the use of drugs such as heroin, crack, and cocaine is not that widespread.

Commentary

For all its self-proclaimed, leading-edge superiority and evolutionary status, the New Age house though sometimes cleverly designed and eye-pleasing on the outside, has as its foundation ethical free-thinking which produces obvious and extensive decay and degeneration. From a distance the New Age sometimes appears as a luminous castle, but upon closer inspection the gilded outer walls try to veil the odor and ugliness of unholiness and bad fruit that lays inside.

Though it is highly common and unpopular to do so, a small number of New Agers are starting to voice concerns about the sad state of affairs.

John White, author of 13 books, writes in an article, "If This Is the New Age, I'll Take Budweiser!": "I've clipped articles from daily newspapers that indicate an appalling lack of discrimination and integrity in some New Agers, and an even more appalling lack of ethics, compassion and just plain common sense among those who are supposed to be at the forefront of spiritual growth and the demonstration of higher consciousness. It's getting pretty bad out there, folks. Sometimes, I just want to throw up my hands in exasperation."[2]

"Me! Me! Me!": The New Age Chorus

If there is one singular trend and characteristic of the movement as a whole, it would have to be the monumental self-centeredness, self-glorification, and selfishness. It is a prime trademark of the New Age.

Is it any wonder that this is so in a philosophy that exalts man as a divinely perfect being, proclaiming him actually to be a "god" having all universal forces at his fingertips? There is a narcissistic fervor, even a fever of sorts, that has infected the New Age community with especial vigor. Something happens to a person when he starts believing that he is an all-powerful god.

A basic New Age axiom is: to discover yourself is to discover the entire universe, for you and the cosmos are one.

Leaders tell eager followers: "Just remember that you are God, and act accordingly." In this logic, it follows naturally that the highest form of love is self-love, and through loving oneself, one comes to love all creation.

A famous guru *Swami* Muktananda, takes this to its logical conclusion: "Kneel to your own self. Honor and worship your own being. God dwells within you as You!"[3]

The logical and practical consequences of these kinds of teachings bear incredibly narcissistic fruit. Can you imagine a world with billions of little gods around creating their own personal kingdoms according to their own will, kneeling to the altar of themselves? This is heaven?

The New Age is obsessed with the quest for self-empowerment — that is, the regaining of one's innate god-powers and applying them to create one's own reality as easily as molding silly putty. What happens so often is that the desires of natural man for glory, attention, power, and control are unleashed and given free rein as they are wrapped in all manner of clever rainbow ribbons of light, peace, and love.

Even before I was converted to the Christian faith, it was hard to overlook the deeply ingrained self-centeredness exhibited by so many New Agers. It seemed as if almost everyone wanted to get, get, get with little or no thought to giving without thought of return. I started to imagine little cartoons in my mind of New Agers, warming up for their next seminar, intoning in front of a mirror — "me, me, me ... I, I, I ... my, my, my."

New Agers are so busy preening themselves, admiring their multi-dimensional god-personality, and strutting it about for others to admire, they do indeed create a new person — a poor, sinful natural man adorned with glorious self-imaginings but who is in reality an emperor with no clothes.

I rarely have seen health, wealth, and godhood practices used for anybody except oneself.

A typical morning's 15-minute ritual of visualizing and affirming one's desires is much more likely to be "$100,000, a house, and a jeep" than any thought for the welfare and needs of others. The self perches on a self-created throne chanting "me-$100,000, me-house, me-jeep" into a universe of multi-mirrored narcissism that is supposed to respond to the will-power of the person's every wish.

Likewise with spirit-channeling, a paid session with a channeler or a psychic reader is more like a psychic ego-massage than anything else. The theme almost invariably is "focus on the glories, wonders, problems, and desires of me." After 30-60 minutes of learning how magnificently evolved one is, how many important people one has been in past lives, how world-shakingly important one is today, and the fortunes, adventures, and soul mates one will come upon shortly, the person leaves with a wonderful sense of "me-wonderful-me."

The self loves to focus on the self—this is only natural to natural man. The mediums, psychics, spiritists (and the demons behind their activities) know this all too well and play it to the hilt ("that'll be $100, please").

In scanning over the entire New Age spectrum of activities one of the most glaring deficiencies is the virtual void of free-giving service activities. In a movement obsessed with one's own self, there is little or no thought for ministering to the needs of others in this world—the poor, the uneducated, those in crisis, those needing spiritual support, the hungry, and the many others in desperate need.

When a person puts on the rainbow-colored glasses of the New Age, somehow the world starts to revolve around the axis of self, and a hardening of heart and a deafening of the ear to the screams of suffering so pervasive in our world occurs.

I have combed through 60-page New Age networking newspapers from major cities involving ads and articles covering hundreds of projects and offerings. If there are one or two non-fee-based service activities or organizations listed, then that's a lot for that issue.

Virtually nothing is given freely without thought of return in this movement. Everything has a price. Enlightenment has a price; healing has a price; love has a price; and truth has a price.

Christians can be pleased with the great numbers of vital outreach, missionary, ministering, and witnessing activities throughout the entire world.

For me, personally, this was a breath of fresh air after becoming disillusioned with the high-priced love and light that supports the New Age. Comparing the extent of service-based activities between Christendom and the New Age is like the difference between Mt. McKinley and a gopher's mound.

Here's a letter to the editor in the Sept./Oct. 1988 issue of the New Age magazine *Body, Mind, and Spirit* that speaks to this point with simple eloquence: "Do any of your readers care about anyone but themselves? Maybe if they went out and did more for other people they would be less concerned about their own problems and how to fix them. But then, of course, you'd be out of business. B. J. Cleveland, OH"

Hearts, Hugs, and Hilarity

One of the most disarming aspects of the New Age scene is the friendly, smiling face filled with words of peace, togetherness, and love that is so often a high profile aspect of gatherings.

Sugar-coated truths and practices are parlayed to the gullible, ignorant, and naive who revel in the candied sweetness of hearts, hugs, and hilarity. Just like candy, there's a "sugar rush" to the gatherings, pumping people up with words of self-glorification, adding a good dose of gaiety and laughter, and a large portion of togetherness, hugs, and back-patting. Hence you have a recipe for one successful event.

Somehow, there's an unspoken, underlying assumption in the midst of all this that if there's a feeling of warmth, togetherness, smiles, gaiety, and starry-eyed hugs and kisses, then this must be the true way of light and love. Playing on the human needs for a sense of acceptance, love, attention, and excitement, the demons and natural human weaknesses prey on the openness of the human heart and mind with hearts, hugs, and hilarity.

It's much easier to insert untruth and subtle webs into natural man when he is relaxed, open, and feeling good. New Agers have absolutely no idea this is what's really happening, so effective is this disarming strategy. The masquerading, smiling faces of the demonic legions come with an olive branch in an outstretched hand and a sugary drug-brew of hearts, hugs, and hilarity in the other.

It's one of the oldest tricks in Satan's book—the embrace that suffocates.

Flakes a-Flocking in the New Age Cuckoo's Nest

The New Age has some of the most bizarre, flaky, out-of-touch people you'll ever meet. It seems to attract an inordinately high percentage of people with incredibly creative and vigorous flakiness. Even when I was involved in the movement, as the years went by it was getting harder and harder to stomach. It would require an entire book to begin to describe the antics, identity problems, grand delusions, and cosmic glory quests that pass as normal behavior in many New Age circles.

This flakiness is found in all types of people. I've had conversations, for example, with M.D.s, Ph.D.s, dentists, chiropractors, teachers, and other highly educated professional people. Some of the conversations would develop nicely until the person brought up the idea, for example, that he or she was an alien being from the Sirius star system here on Earth to develop a revolutionary technological breakthrough, or that they have been doing past life regressions and finding out that they have been Moses, Cleopatra, Renoir, Edison, and Michelangelo in their past lives. Or that they have been in telepathic contact with UFO aliens and are going to be beamed up to the spaceship shortly to experience the "33rd-Ray Master Initiation."

The words of the apostle Paul are appropriate here:

"For the time will come when they will not endure sound doctrine; but wanting to have their ears tickled, they will accumulate for themselves teachers in accordance to their own desires; and will turn away their ears from the truth, and will turn aside to myths."[4]

One of the primary ingredients that makes the New Age world go round is the element of HIGH DRAMA. Nothing else so well titillates, fascinates, stimulates, and motivates as drama. It may take the form of a psychological catharsis, an interpersonal "peak experience," a healing crisis, an anticipated UFO "beam-up," a hypnotically induced look into past lives, quests for lost Atlantean treasures, pilgrimages to planetary "power points," looking for a crystal originating from planet Venus, a channeled spirit revealing universal mysteries, hankering after "miracle-healers," firewalking, the Harmonic Convergence, or psychic spoon-bending.

However boring or unfulfilling a person's life may be, it needn't be so anymore. There's always a fresh variety of the latest drama-experiences to be had on the menu. Once a person has found his personal favorites, there's always more to be had, one leading to the next, dramas within dramas within dramas.

Here's a menu of some dramas:

Initiations are all the rage. Initiations into this mystery school, initiations into that light-worker brotherhood;

- Initiations into shamanic powers.
- Initiations into white magic practices.
- Initiations into UFO contacts.
- Initiations into secret societies of wisdom and knowledge.
- Initiations into higher *yogic* states of consciousness.
- Initiations into Eastern meditation traditions.
- Initiations into metaphysical healing traditions.
- Initiations into acquiring spirit guides.
- Initiations into nature religion rites.
- Initiations into just about anything you could think of, and a lot more.

If you want to go chasing UFOs in secluded areas where only a few select people know where it will be, it's on the menu.

All sorts of "transformational vacations" are offered to the more up-scale clientele including trips to the pyramids and tombs of Egypt with special initiations at each occult site.

Trips to see the famed "psychic healers" of the Philippine Islands and Brazil, with special rituals and healing performed for the vacationers, also are available as well as to Hindu shrines and temples in India and crystal-power cruise ship vacations to the Caribbean Islands.

You also can take pilgrimages to vortex power spots: particular areas, like Sedona, Arizona and Mt. Shasta, California and many others, that are supposed to be sites of pre-historical, super-advanced civilizations and are thought to be big "interdimensional windows" to the beyond. It's great for UFO-chasers, too.

Then there are the more-than-plentiful supply of psychic readers, mediums, and spiritists who are ready to clog the mind with a wide assortment of fantasies, visions, myths, tales, and advice guaranteed to spice up a person's life with all the drama he cares to ingest.

There inevitably is a solid selection of workshops involving one aspect or another of sex. From *tantric yoga* to erotic massage to *taoist* sexual secrets to interpersonal exploration, a host of sex-theme classes and seminars cater to singles, unmarried couples, and married couples who engage in subtle-to-explicit sexual practices in a group setting. Such gatherings also provide ample opportunity to seek out new *karmic* partners for the next round of musical bedrooms, for those desiring such.

Personal Identity Problems

Some of the identities that New Agers assume as part of their multi-dimensional personas are truly amazing. From partaking of such things as past life regressions, channeling, psychic readings, and the like, an impressive array of identities can be collected—like building a cosmic resume of sorts. Identities from past lives plus exalted, cosmically proportioned present-day life-identities are as common as weeds. Understand, this is considered part and parcel of everyday thinking, widely accepted as normal.

Here are a few examples of *New Age identity problems*:

• Thinking that you're a "walk-in"—this is where a highly advanced celestial being or master comes into an adult body and possesses it, as the original soul is displaced. Such a walk-in is supposed to be here on Earth on a crucial mission to enlighten the human masses.

• A "star seed"—many believe that the Earth is not their true "home," and that some other far-distant galaxy is their real point of origin. These more "highly evolved" intergalactic intelligences have deigned to incarnate in lowly human bodies on Earth in order to teach humankind of higher knowledge and wisdom. You would be surprised at how pervasive this kind of identity is.

• Some people think that they are angels from the heavens who have taken on human form, and who have supernatural, miraculous powers to bestow upon humans, when they are prepared properly to receive them.

• Many New Agers do not feel that their transformation into full New Age-iness is complete without changing their mystical name. People actually present themselves as *"Gurudev,"* "Sanat Ananda," "Helios" (a sun god), "Angel Fire Ecstasy," "Crystal Moonriver," "White Eagle," "Dancing Brook," "Angelica Starseed," and an unending array of creative new identities.

The belief in reincarnation is exceptionally fertile ground for sprouting false identities, such as believing that one is a:

- Reincarnated priestess of the magical mysteries of the Isis cult (goddess worship).
- Reincarnated Atlantean scientist who dabbled too far in superadvanced crystal technologies and blew up the entire civilization.
- Reincarnation of Leonardo da Vinci, Michelangelo, and Einstein in past lives, who is today a merged super-genius of all three.
- Reincarnation of Merlin the magician, Alexander the Great, and Genghis Khan—a modern day Gorbachev.
- The 23rd reincarnation of the royal lineage of ancient Egypt.

The sometimes rather extensive religious hierarchies in the New Age hold a plentitude of identities to assume, such esoteric hierarchical positions as:

- High priestess of the secret gnostic mysteries.
- Shaman power-woman of the Crystal-Moon lineage.
- 3rd level Eck: just below 4th Eck state of initiated consciousness level and just above 2nd Eck state of consciousness (whatever that means).
- Holder of the Masonic keys of knowledge and initiation.
- Crystal Queen-goddess of nature religion rites.
- 3rd level Reiki master (metaphysical healing).
- 1st level Initiate of Great Pyramid mysteries.
- Communication contact agent for the Ashtar Space Command.

Channels, Channels, Everywhere

As we've seen already, channeling is hot on the New Age scene. The demonic agents and the sly, slick mediums and psychic readers feed people what they want to hear—advice on problems, projections of success for the future, the glories of self.

As a result, people often naively or willingly choose to believe the tripe, hype, and malarkey doled out by demon-used harlots, psychic cons, and just regular cons.

Here are some examples of enlightened sugar-coated lies and deceptions:

- Money and success are *just around the corner.*
- A magnificent love partner is *just around the corner.*
- You'll be beamed up to the spacecraft, *just around the corner.*
- Your problems will be solved, *just around the corner.*
- You are an incredible musical genius—a combination of Bach, Beethoven, Mozart, and Jimi Hendrix.
- You are the great king of past Egyptian centuries come back to lead the select of humanity into the ancient mysteries of Hyperborea.
- You are a holy angel sent by the solar Council of Twelve to instruct the humans of planet Earth as to the Knowledge of Universal Unity.
- You are going to come into a lot of money shortly which will solve all your problems and fuel your manifesting of a world-shaking Rainbow Temple of Human Enlightenment.
- You will find a lost cave in the foothills of the Sierra Nevadas which will contain the Lemurian Emerald Tablets.
- Your path leads to the opening of the hidden Door of Entry into the inner chambers of Mt. Shasta.
- You will be given the powers of a god-warrior, to ride the winds and rule the plains.
- You are to be the one to re-invent an ancient Atlantean crystal holographic super-computer.
- You were one of the great Illumined Ones who measured and crafted the Great Pyramid from your master Command Space vehicle.

All I can do is shrug my shoulders and ask you: "Can you believe that people really do believe this kind of stuff?" I used to believe, and even taught some of it. Satan's delusions are so profound that even rational, intelligent people get wrapped up in the New Age and start believing these things before they know it.

Without the foundation of Scripture and Jesus, the human mind (with Satan's pervasive influences) concocts brilliant worlds of delusion and even brainwashing. People actually live in a metaphysical world of beliefs that are sometimes as elaborate as a science fiction novel. Satan can spin some pretty fancy yarns on the willing or naive human mind.

If I never again meet a person who introduces himself as "Zeta, High Commander of the Ashtar Space Command Vehicle," it will not be too soon.

Canòieò Thrills anò Primrose-Path Aòòictions

So much of New Age behavior can be understood as different types of addiction. While the New Age highs feel good for a while, there's inevitably a coming down with a corresponding feeling of emptiness and the desire for yet another dose. With each new fix, they're one step deeper into addiction.

Although it felt marvelous for a time, at home at night, alone, there's still a feeling of gnawing emptiness.

The demonically manipulated altered states of consciousness can be like a skyrocketing roller coaster experience, and when the ride is over there's still no lasting inner peace.

The profound interpersonal transformational processes experienced in weekend seminars carry a person over for a few days, but towards the end of the week or month the person is right back where they started—empty and inwardly crying out for something to fill the void.

Seminars are filled with seminar junkies who regularly frequent the latest "hot" leader's lectures or the newest miracle technique or the new, improved, magic bullet cure.

Many a lonely person chronically attends interpersonal and sexually oriented workshops to be lavished with attention, to meet a new sex partner, to feel a sense of self-acceptance, to fill the inner cold void with outer warmth.

Yet, like a hamster relentlessly running on its exercise wheel, the New Ager gets nowhere fast. In a day, a week, a month the seekers are right back where they started. Unless they seek after Christ, the addiction cycle rolls merrily along, much to the amusement of Satan and the bank accounts of those who cater to this addicted clientele.

To further provide New Agers with techniques so that they can satiate their addiction on their own, hordes of people are going to seminars to learn how to channel and do psychic readings for themselves. The banner cry is "we're all gods; we're all-knowing; we're all our own channels."

Now, you don't have to pay the extravagant fees of the professional channels and psychics. The self-made channel can tune in to the charming supernatural antics of masquerading demons any time of day or night, no charge. Except one's soul.

The many-faceted addictions hold the golden carrot always just beyond the grasp, beckoning the seeker to take one more step down the rainbow-staircase, even as Satan's flawed mirroring makes the person think he's stepping up into the heavens. Down is up and up is down in this demon-orchestrated house of mirrors.

New Age Leaders: A Brood of Vipers

Some New Age leaders and teachers propagate wrong but well-intentioned views and practices. They are blind to the faith of Christ and thereby commit all manner of false teaching and acts, thinking that they are truly beneficial to others. Though constituting a relatively small portion of the leadership ranks, these people are sincere even as they are deluded and well-intentioned.

On the other hand, the majority of leaders and teachers are not so naive. They know to one degree or another that they have sold out to some force or principle that provides energy, power, and influence for the asking and gives more in the obeying. This higher force or principle is, of course, the Enemy and his myriad masquerading demons. So it is no surprise that they all deny the true faith of Christ.

The worst leaders are aware of the manipulative occult, psychological, and sensationalistic "tricks of the trade" that they pull on their audiences. They know the things people want to hear and therefore pander to their egos and conspire to strategies insuring their continuing patronage.

The most extreme 1) ensnare willing submissives to exploit, 2) harlot themselves to demons for power, fame, and money, 3) calculatingly exploit human weaknesses of all types, and 4) perform all manner of other grossly manipulative and cutthroat practices to further their own vested interests.

What's interesting is that a substantial number of these leaders often appear to be the most light-filled. Satan is shrewd enough to pick and choose from the pool of people to find those with intelligence, sophistication, cunning, and other desired qualities. Those who receive Satan's call respond by prostituting themselves into greater magnitudes of possessed puppetry.

Look to the cream of the leaders, and there you will see some of Satan's finest handicraft. To one degree or another, these leaders know that they have sold their souls in return for the fame, power, and money they enjoy. Many of them consciously have the eyes of a predator and enchanter, applying Satan's dazzling peace, light, and love to disarmingly weave their webs, work their charms, and reel in the unwary.

Others, especially the mediums and psychic readers, have prostituted themselves to the drug-like power of darkness and are so controlled, so possessed that they're just going along for the ride, with demons holding the reins.

I can tell you from personal experience that the all-loving peacemaker image that most leaders exude when they're on stage is a mask that disappears after the event. I naively assumed when first coming into the national New Age scene as a rising author and lecturer that the high-sounding love and cooperation ideals spouted out by the leaders were actually real.

Very soon, as the new kid on the block, I found out quite the contrary. There is incredible cutthroat competition, back stabbing, rumor-creating, and just plain meanness behind the scenes. Also, many leaders employ magic, psychic abilities, channeled demonic forces, and other tricks of the occult trade to attack and undermine their competitors. Rather than being an association of colleagues demonstrating a model of enlightened cooperation for others to emulate, all too many act the hypocrite.

The Big Business of the New Age: The Bandwagon Effect

Especially in the last two decades, there has been an explosive rise of any and every imaginable sort of New Age product, seminar, therapy, book, cassette tape, video tape, paraphernalia, psychic, channel, holistic healer, and myriad other business-based offerings. According to *Forbes Magazine* (June 1, 1987), the general market has increased to $3.43-billion. This market shows no sign of let-up, and continues to skyrocket.

The quartz crystal market is a prime example. Starting in 1984-85, quartz crystals started to become a fast-rising trend. In a matter of a few years, the New Age had become such an influential part of the worldwide crystal market that the price for this common mineral rose at least 3-10 times (depending on the type of crystal). The number of crystal teachers, merchants, seminars, books, etc. also rose astronomically—the "bandwagon effect" was in full swing.

Wherever there's money to be made, a drove of New Agers will be found hungrily exploiting every possible angle towards their own vested interests. The New Age has indeed become a big business, and this has had profound repercussions affecting every corner of the subculture.

In a philosophy that puts such high value on cooperation and non-competitiveness, the New Age market is one of the most competitive, cutthroat markets around. There are incredible pressures in this market to flatter and aggrandize self-absorbed New Age egos as well as offering the newest, quickest way to self-actualization, enlightenment, desire fulfillment, problem-solving, and the like.

The pervasively self-centered audience generates intense pressures affecting what New Age businesses offer as well as how they offer them. Without appeasing the cries for "faster and faster," "easier and easier," "slicker and slicker," "me, my, and I," a business simply does not stand a very good chance of survival.

The same business dictum that dominates virtually all forms of business predominates in the New Age: Give the people what they want, or you don't survive.

So, spirituality, packaged into rainbow-ribboned, price-tagged boxes of "instant enlightenment," "you, glorious you," "you, glorious god," "push-button fulfillment," "instant desire gratification," etc., have become a perfectly reflective mirroring of the serious flaws and self-centered predispositions of the audience in general.

Go to any event—world peace meditations, expos, seminars, small, grass-roots gatherings, etc.—and you inevitably will find an array of people hawking their wares with a New Age smiling face that tries to belie the underlying vested self-interest. By voicing high ideals of sharing, networking, and loving concern for others, the merchants disguise their primary survival and profit motives. The bandwagon effect has, in the last 5-7 years produced an extremely saturated market that, in turn, has redoubled the underlying self-centered motives.

On this subject, author John White notes:

"There's an incredible amount of nonsense and exploitation occurring today in the name of higher consciousness. I'm talking about the spiritual materialists—the crass hustlers who slickly package New Age activities, goods and services. They tout them as the ultimate experience in the spiritual supermarket and then sell them at inflated prices. And the bogus psychotechnologies they devise are endless: meditation hats, enlightenment meters, cosmic stress alert monitors, golden brainfood pills, superionized vitamin XYZ, holistic haircuts, transpersonal tea, biosolar alphafeedback jewelry—you name it and someone will sell you a dozen, wholesale. ..."[5]

As White points out, there has been an incredible explosion of "supercharged," "cosmically activated," "leading edge" devices and goods that are trumpeted as modern-day breakthroughs guaranteed to bolster your enlightenment quotient, turn your brain into a supercomputer, instantly dissolve personal neuroses and fears, keep you in a state of stress-reduced alpha-bliss from now to eternity, and anything else that appeals to the desires and fancies of the audience that hungers for such things.

It's getting pretty thick in the New Age. A combination of purely quack ideas, plus multiple variations on the "pet rock" theme, and even considerable numbers of items that do indeed manipulate occult forces is absolutely saturating the market with a dizzying array of consumer options.

At best, this spiritual materialism is accepted as common practice and not to be discouraged, lest the boat be rocked. The movement has no real respect or understanding of the sanctity of holiness. It is rife with its own myriad versions of the thronging merchants clogging the temple courtyard. The New Age does little to nothing to rid itself of this crass infestation. If it did, business would suffer for the sake of apparent sanctity — and apparently they aren't willing to pay that kind of price.

Speaking of price, the New Age puts a premium price on its most powerful philosophies and practices offered by its acknowledged leaders. The pay scale for acquiring the highest levels of truth revolves around the principle that the more famous the leader, the higher the price able to be extracted from pilgrims. Hardly a single leader strays from this principle of success. Weekend workshops or seminars offered by top-line leaders regularly cost $250-$400 for the privilege of being packed like sardines to lap up the golden dewdrops of high-priced wisdom with others of this privileged few.

In New Age success philosophy, since everything in the cosmos is "God" (pantheistic monism), then money is also an expression of "God." It is a widely held dictum that: "Money is God in action." Furthermore, success philosophy states that the more attuned a person is to the "Universal Mind," the more the universe will demonstrate this level of enlightenment by mirroring more "god-money in action." That is, the more enlightened a person is, the more money and success will naturally occur in his life.

The equating of Deity to money and degree of worldly success is, of course, a rank abomination. This is one of the logical flaws of the "All is One" philosophy that produces all manner of bad fruit. For, as Christ Jesus said, "No man can serve two masters; for either he will hate the one and love the other, or he will hold to one and despise the other. You cannot serve God and mammon" (Matt. 6:24).

Further, the concept of free-giving service is not only severely lacking in New Age circles due to self-centeredness and spiritual materialism, but it is also denounced by some leading New Age philosophies.

Lazaris, for example, one of the most famous spirits being channeled today, comments on this subject:

"Therefore, if we did workshops for nothing, if we did other things for nothing, we would be robbing people because we would be giving them the idea that what we have to offer is worth nothing. And, therefore, they would not avail themselves of the opportunity to listen and that would be a great injustice to them."[6]

Virtually everything has a price attached. If you want some "love" in a healing session, that will be $50; if you want the highest wisdom around, that'll be $300; if you want to experience the greatest "light," you must pay the price-tag. To give truth free-of-charge is, as Lazaris teaches, an "injustice and robbery." Evidently Jesus was not aware of this.

Obviously, the New Age has gone full circle in its warped materialistic concepts of light and love. Somehow, amid the rush for self-deification the cornerstone Christian truth that "It is more blessed to give than to receive" (Acts 20:35) is forgotten, ignored, or even denounced.

About the closest thing a person ever gets to a free-giving service is an event listing "love donation: $25." That is, if you don't have $25 worth of hard cash "love" to give at the door, you don't get in. In all the hubbub, the call to humble ministering to others without thought of return is a long-forgotten echo.

On the other hand, the command of Christ to His disciples stands today as a cornerstone to all who follow His Way: "Heal the sick, raise the dead, cleanse the lepers, cast out demons; freely you received, freely give" (Matt. 10:8).

Conclusion

One of the tests given by the Lord to discern true from false — "ye shall know them by their fruits" — clearly shows the New Age for what it is: a radically flawed Satanic house of mirrors reflecting every weakness of sinful man in luminous rainbow-veiled delusions. The fruits of entering this alien landscape are as an apple, golden and eye-pleasing on the outside, but rotten and festering at the core.

Notes

1. The New Age Movement misappropriates the Biblical symbol of the rainbow. The use of the word "rainbow" in this book is applied in the New Age sense of a gilded gateway of false light and false hope.
2. John White, "If This Is the New Age, I'll Take Budweiser," *Psychic Guide*, March 1987, p. 39.
3. Quoted in Groothuis, *Unmasking the New Age* (op. cit.), p. 21.
4. 2 Timothy 4:3, 4.
5. John White, op. cit., p. 41.
6. Krysta Gibson, "Interview with Lazaris," *The New Times*, April 1987, p. 5.

SEVEN

WHAT'S HOT ON THE NEW AGE SCENE TODAY?

And when they say to you, 'Consult the mediums and the spiritists who whisper and mutter,' should not a people consult their God? Should they consult the dead on behalf of the living? To the law and to the testimony. If they do not speak according to this word, it is because they have no dawn" (Isa. 8:19, 20).

The New Age landscape has undergone significant changes in the latter 1980s. Coming into the "Shirley MacLaine era," the New Age took a quantum leap in national exposure and popularity. Not only has the New Age market experienced an explosive surge, but also the level of overall sophistication has added a shinier "polish" to many aspects of this phenomenon.

There also has been a new wave of demonic infiltration, both in terms of their scope and power as well as the sophistication of their wiles. Strong undercurrents are well under way toward using the mid-to-late 80s Shirley MacLaine era as a stepping stone to a next era of growth that well may eclipse all previous eras.

Taking note of "what's hot" today can provide some indicators about what to expect from the enemy's New Age directions in the near future and what the cunning wiles of Satan will conjure up from many unexpected directions.

Although some of this material has been dealt with earlier, I would like to review and in some cases expand certain themes since they are so pertinent to the New Age nightmare.

Channeling

This is by far the single greatest means by which demonic forces are tempting, deceiving, manipulating, and possessing people in alarming numbers and through diverse means. Not only are there fast-proliferating professional mediums who are attaining new heights of fame, fortune, and power but there is also a major trend toward teaching people how to channel and acquire familiar spirits for themselves.

Now it is not the few who channel, but the many who are taught systematic techniques to "open up" to the "higher self," "spirit guides," "ascended masters," "the wise ones," "psychic counselors," etc. Like a brushfire propelled by high winds, this trend is sweeping through the New Age subculture and mainstream society with frightening vigor.

Whether it is a New Ager channeling in trance or a businessman taking a coffee break to calm the mind and consult his inner guides (as taught in some business success seminars), this plague of the spirit is reaching all corners of the land.

Looking at this phenomenon from another vantage point, we see quite a few parallels to the movie, "Ghostbusters." The New Age is functioning as what the movie calls an "interdimensional cross-rip." That is, a supernatural gateway is opened, through which hordes of demons, ghouls, ghosts, etc. pour through into the earthly domains wreaking havoc. Though a gigantic marshmallow-man is not likely to come forth from the New Age, the basic idea of a massive unleashing of demonic forces is exactly what is happening through the New Age. The weird names of the movie's demons—Ghoser et. al.— even are paralleled in the New Age with all the strange-sounding spirits' names—Mafu, Ramtha, Zoosh, Bashar, Semjaza, and others.

This host of demons continues to give rise to all manner of false christs and false prophets, and it would not be all that surprising if many dramatic counterfeit miracles, signs, and wonders start to manifest with a new magnitude of power, high profile exposure, and numbers.

Nature Religions

Nature religions are increasing rapidly today. Neopaganism, especially American Indian mystical beliefs are extremely popular, particularly with regard to sorcerer's practices and magic rituals. Whereas before in history only the few occult elite had access to this kind of knowledge, now millions of sorcerer's apprentices are dabbling in and honing their skills with occult fire.

This branch of the New Age has made strong inroads into the ecology/environmental issues movement, the "Heal the Earth-Mother" trends, the World Peace Meditations, feminism, and the national New Age seminar circuit.

One can only wonder what Satan is grooming all of these modern-day sorcerers for.

Goddess Worship, Witchcraft, and New Age Feminism

The "rise of the Goddess, the Universal Female Principle, and the Universal Mother" has become a particularly potent rallying cry in the latter half of the 1980s. The New Age claim that "this male-dominated planet must undergo a radical restructuring through the rise to power of the Goddess-principle in order for the New Age to dawn," has fueled a furious fascination with goddess worship, female-dominated witchcraft, and New Age feminism.

The "power-woman" ideal has deluged the New Age with all types of female-dominated shamanism, witchcraft, sorcery, idolatry, goddess-channeling, and male-emasculating practices. Within these ranks are some of the most bitter, anger-filled female activists who readily employ sorcery against others. Being perceived as patriarchically imbalanced and female-suppressive, Christianity in particular is commonly belittled and reviled in many of these circles.

Initiations

Initiations into cosmic mysteries and powers are perennial best-sellers. Today you can be initiated into just about anything you can imagine (and then some) for the right price. The biggest trend here is to receive initiations in large groups from a leading authority at an outrageously high price.

In mid-1988, Lynn Andrews, author of the best-selling book series *Medicine Woman*, *Jaguar Woman*, *Star Woman*, and *Crystal Woman*, (and a forthcoming *Windhorse Woman*) has made a high-profile marketing campaign for her weekend workshop, "Into the Crystal Dreamtime: A Shamanic Initiation with Lynn Andrews."

This magical weekend, playing on the popularity of the "power-woman" ideal, can be had for the bargain price of $325.

Holistic Health

The holistic health movement has been making steady, vigorous growth into mainstream society's exposure, desensitization, and increasing acceptance. From the more obviously metaphysically oriented holistic health practices to ever-deeper subtle inroads into mainstream health care, the field of holistic health has been a primary carrier of Westernized occultism and Eastern philosophies into American culture. This trend has been steady over the last two decades and shows no sign of let-up.

Crystal Power

Crystals and gems for "healing, self-transformation, and accelerated enlightenment" are an incredible rage today. Whereas as late as 1980-83, crystal power was virtually unknown, it has skyrocketed astonishingly in just a few years. It is interesting to note that the rise of crystals has occurred at the same time as the new mid-to-late 80s wave of demonic forces.

Signs that this phenomenon has peaked are starting to be in evidence as of late 1988-early 1989. The crystal fever that struck so many millions still has solid momentum, but the heavy saturation of crystals in workshops, books, tapes, expos, metaphysical bookstores, rock shops, mineral shows, and other outlets is beginning to lose some of its glittery intrigue.

In my view, the crystals craze has peaked, yet in the years to come crystals will continue to be an integral component of many branches of the New Age. This stupendous surge effectively has spread the seeds of crystal power throughout the New Age landscape. Now, the initial frenzy is dying down somewhat and the seeds will be cultivated and pruned.

"Crystal power" has come to the New Age scene to stay, and it is very possible that some counterfeit miracles and wonders of sorts may develop from certain quarters of sophisticated crystal power research.

UFOs

UFO sightings and contacts have made deep inroads into the everyday fabric of much of the New Age. More than 75 percent of New Agers firmly believe in the existence of hosts of alien beings within and around planet Earth to assist in the birthing of the New Age. It is noteworthy to point out that the strong upsurge in this trend also parallels the crystal craze and the huge increases in channeling activities in the mid-to-late 80s.

With Shirley MacLaine using her powerful platform to do her part in UFO evangelism plus Whitley Strieber's national exposure through his best-selling books, *Communion* and *Transformation*, the UFO issue is spreading throughout all quarters of the New Age as well as mainstream society. HBO's special on UFOs, a nationally syndicated live special TV program in late 1988, and the popular movies about extraterrestrials (like "ET," "Batteries Not Included," "Close Encounters," "Cocoon I and II," and numerous others) all have brought this issue to the general public's attention in direct and indirect ways.

Overall, there is a powerful current rising today around this issue. There are many questions yet to be answered sufficiently and much serious scientific investigation is warranted before any concrete conclusions may be drawn. However, it is notable that the demonic power behind what New Agers call their "telepathic UFO contacts" and "channeling with the Space Brothers" is continuing to increase in power and magnitude. In fact, UFO "fever" is at an all-time high in many circles. Whatever Satan has in mind for the UFO phenomenon, (whether UFOs are "little green men from Mars" or explicit demonic activity or something else), it is an integral part of the powerful delusion of the end times.

World Peace Meditations

World peace meditations involving hundreds of millions of people around the world are one of the most potent rallying forces in the New Age today. Under the banner of meditating and praying for world peace, the New Age has made its broadest exposure around the globe.

On December 31, 1986, the "World Peace Meditation" is estimated to have involved 100-500 million people from 50-60 countries, cutting across religious, national, and cultural boundaries. It is important to note that these events are all part of the New Age agenda, regardless of attempts to put them in the context of an all-embracing spiritual ecumenism.

From current trends, it appears that the world peace meditation movement will become a global phenomenon that will eclipse the 100-500 million participants in the "World Peace Meditation" of Dec. 31, 1986 and the 1987 Harmonic Convergence by several orders of magnitude. World peace meditation activities still are exceptionally popular, and new ones are constantly in the works. In the future, more and more aspects of these types of events will not be so much an explicitly New Age phenomenon, but more an ecumenical effort inclusive of all religions, positive humanistic philosophies, and human-rights socio-political groups.

At best the World Peace Meditation movement promotes a flawed attempt at man-created world peace without Jesus as Lord; and, at worst, it is feeding perfectly into the Antichrist's plans for a false world peace under a one-world federation.

Dave Hunt makes a penetrating point in *Beyond Seduction*:

"We must beware not to encourage the deadly delusion that there is any hope for peace except through transformation of the human heart through Christ. Indeed, if the world were seemingly able to solve all of its problems without embracing the true gospel of our Lord Jesus Christ, that would be the greatest of all deceptions and precisely what Satan will seek to do through the Antichrist, whose world government will be a counterfeit of God's kingdom. Although they may not realize it, those who join, no matter how sincerely, in humanistic efforts to unite the world in a false peace are not furthering the cause of Christ, but in the long run the cause of the Antichrist."[1]

Brain-Drive Machines

Brain-altering machines are one of the latest "hot" trends in both the New Age and society at large. A bevy of new "brain-tech" devices that promise every sort of brain-mind improvement imaginable have been met with broad-scale, enthusiastic reception. Having such names as MC^2, Alpha-Stim, Bio-Pacer, Isis, Somatron, and Graham Potentializer, they are readily available, ranging in price from $300 to $6,000. One of the primary attractions to these devices is the stimulation of different types of psychedelic, relaxing, and pleasurable responses in the user.

These machines are the modern-day equivalent of hallucinogenic drugs, functioning like sugar-coated forms of LSD. Seemingly benign and non-threatening, they open up and manipulate the human brain-mind in ways that are potentially extremely harmful. They are also precursors to much more sophisticated brain-manipulation devices, computer-brain interface developments, bio-compatible computer chips, and high-tech subliminal advances. The high-tech aspect of the New World Order movement feeds right into trends paralleling Aldous Huxley's concept of the "Brave New World."

To give one example of startling high-tech developments that could very well add to the high-tech horrors on near-future horizons, consider this excerpt from *The Omni Book of Computers and Robots*, telling of a "biochip" that potentially could make every person in the world a super-genius.

"Almost unnoticed, the ultimate biological computer has reached the drawing boards. The bioprocessor will be a molecular lattice-work that can grow and reproduce. Capable of logic, reason, perhaps even feeling, its three-dimensional organic circuitry will not process data in the rigid, linear style of earlier computers, but networking-fashion, like the living brain. Small enough to mesh directly with the human nervous system, biochip implants may restore sight to the blind and hearing to the deaf, replace damaged spinal nerves, and give the human brain memory a number-crunching power to rival today's mightiest computers."[2]

Painless. Awesome. Tempting. (A candidate for the mark of the beast?)

Conclusion

Far and wide, across the land and sea, across more and more socio-cultural and religious boundaries, the New Age Movement forges ahead with accelerating momentum and diversification. *Caveat emptor* — let the buyer beware. The end-times watcher may see some pieces of the rising strategies of the Antichrist forces.

Watch out for Trojan horses of diverse kinds that will dot the global landscape in the years ahead — the prophesied counterfeit miracles, signs, and wonders are sure to come to pass.

Notes

1. Dave Hunt, *The Seduction of Christianity* (op. cit.), p. 249.
2. Owen Davies, editor, *The Omni Book of Computers and Robots* (New York, NY: Kensington Publishing Corp., 1984), pp. 89, 90.

EIGHT

A LOOK AT SOME OF THE SURPRISING INROADS THE NEW AGE HAS MADE IN MODERN-DAY SOCIETY

Examine everything carefully; hold fast to that which is good; abstain from every form of evil" (I Thess. 5:21, 22).

Satan, the master counterfeiter, works his cunning craft where'er holiness dwells not. Every crack, every crevice of unrighteousness is a window of opportunity through which to ply his trade. Today's world is riddled with such breaches by which the enemy applies leverage in opening up more and more chances to replace truth with untruth.

New Age spiritual humanism, in particular, is an increasingly powerful crowbar for opening up these cracks and crevices, and thus Satan's sleight of hand deftly places corroding lies that appear as the truth wherever vigilance is lacking. In today's times, the forces and influences of spiritual humanism have been and are continually being inserted into the very fabric of American society, to often surprising degrees. As this trend continues to gain momentum, it becomes increasingly important to be aware of this side of the enemy's attack.

To make matters worse, the times are past when the occult was "in the closet" on the fringes of society, being obviously bizarre and different from the norm, and therefore easy to discern and avoid. While many aspects of the New Age are indeed obvious and easy to see for what they truly are, there are just as many that have assumed deceptively "normal" and more socially acceptable guises.

This chapter seeks to paint a general picture of the sometimes alarming extent to which the New Age has made inroads in American society. As noted earlier the powerful forces of secular humanism work from one direction, spiritual humanism applies increasing pressure from the opposite direction, with "the faith that was once for all entrusted to the saints"[1] in the middle.

A Threefold Strategy: Diversification, Chameleon-like Re-Adaptation, and Enculturation

The overall strategy of societal infiltration is basically this:
• *Diversification*: Generate never-ending multitudes of diversified variations on the New Age theme.
• *Chameleon-like Re-adaptation*: Mutate a goodly portion of these variations into more widely acceptable, less obviously New Agey, and less bizarre and foreboding forms.
• *Enculturation*: Progressively saturate every aspect of society with these New Age phenomena so that, over time, inroads plus increasing social acceptability (even respectability) occur.

A Survey of Societal Inroads

The influences of spiritual humanism have become woven into a pluralistic society exploring for answers and fulfillment in diverse directions. The wide spectrum of New Age phenomena sifts into the socio-cultural landscape in bits and pieces, attitudes and opinions, shades and hues.

Desensitization is a matter of degree, a matter of regular exposure to New Age views so that they start to blend into the accepted socio-cultural picture. Enculturation is a matter of spiritual humanism integrating more and more into mainstream society. This trend is broader and wider than many realize.

Marilyn Ferguson remarks on the winds of stirrings blowing through America (and the globe):

"Human catalysts like the Aquarian Conspirators describe the new options—in classrooms, on TV, in print, in film, in art, in song, in scientific journals, on the lecture circuit, during coffee breaks, in government documents, at parties, and in new organizational policies and legislation.

"... Transformative ideas also appear in the guise of health books and sports manuals, in advice on diet, business management, self-assertion, stress, relationships, and self-improvement."[2]

In this chapter section, a collage of select comments, facts, and quotations serve to suggest the broad scope of the pervasive influences of spiritual humanism. Though definitely not exhaustive, they are indicative.

• The New Age has spawned a new breed of "visionary artists" who depict "higher dimensional realities" through their diverse styles. Such artwork is often lustrously beautiful, sometimes even breathtaking. It is so easy sometimes to mistake glamorous counterfeits for the true Kingdom of Heaven. You'll find depictions of such artwork cropping up in many common places—postcards, art books, science fiction book covers, posters, calendars, *Omni* magazine, futurist magazines, greeting cards, etc.

Probably the most successful of all artists in this genre is Gilbert Williams. His stunning renditions of utopian and mystical landscapes can be highly compelling. Williams' work has been featured several times in *Omni* magazine, has received innumerable artistic awards, adorned many a popular poster and greeting card, spawned two entire art books, and has reached into many other marketing avenues.

In the latter 1980s he has been collaborating with the most highly influential spirit being channeled—named "Lazaris." This demonic-spirit through its channel, Jack Pursell, has launched a nationally successful marketing array of video tapes, books, and calendars, most of which feature Gilbert Williams' beauteous visions of higher dimensional horizons.

Art, when masterfully manifested, can be a most powerful medium of communicating multi-level concepts, worldviews, insights, and realizations. Sadly, New Age visionary art often conveys the richness, texture, and luminosity of Satan's dazzling counterfeits. Both the mind and the heart can be titillated and intrigued.

• The publishing industry has contributed immensely to the propagation of the infinitely diverse variations of the New Age worldview. Basically, general trade publishers and New Age specialty publishers publish what people buy. Since the demand for "alternatives" has exploded in the last two decades or so, the vast field of books on various New Age-based themes has proliferated in both mainstream bookstore chains as well as local bookstores (both metaphysical and mixed-selection stores).

In the 1980s the New Age has become so big in the publishing field that it now commonly has its very own bookstore section. What used to be "Occult/Astrology" section now is branded "New Age

Philosophy." In addition, metaphysical specialty bookstores have mushroomed in cities large and small.

In the publishing world, the New Age Movement has arrived, to the tune of over 1-billion publishing dollars per year. New Age-based or-influenced books span beyond this one bookstore category into others, including: "Philosophy/Religion," "Psychology/Self-Help," "Health/Care/Medicine," and even "Science."

To have solid inroads into mainstream bookstore chains is a clear indication that spiritual humanism is a socio-cultural force that has gained a definite foothold in middle-America and a general influence whose time is at hand. In fact, 52 publishing firms have banded together to form a coalition called the "New Age Publishing & Retailing Alliance (NAPRA)." Their motto: "A Consciousness Whose Time Has Come."

The mainstream publishing mill is basically a neutral, filtering medium through which the buying audience determines what is published. New Age-based, New Age-influenced, and New Age-attitudinal books have made a major step into the mainstream niche. The public demands it.

• New Age magazines have multiplied and prospered over the last two decades. Four of them vie for top honors — *New Age Journal*, *Body, Mind & Spirit*, *East West Journal*, and *Fate*. *Fate* is a bit passé with many New Agers. *New Age Journal* has achieved a solid national standing — often being carried in national bookstore chains and grocery store magazine sections. *Body, Mind & Spirit* recently has changed its name from *Psychic Guide* and is making a strong bid for national prominence today. Millions of people read these magazines and their numerous counterparts.

To give an example of the reading fare of such magazines, the Nov./Dec. 1988 issue of *New Age Journal* featured these articles: "Astral Travel," "Outrageous Fortunes" ("Can America afford its ultra-rich?"), "Why Love Is Never Enough," ("Resolving interpersonal conflicts through cognitive therapy"), "Babies Remember Their Births" ("Birth memory may tell us much about new dimensions in human consciousness"), and "The Altruistic Personality" ("What leads ordinary men and women to risk their lives on behalf of others?").

• Dozens of media stars have joined the New Age bandwagon. Such star personalities include: Tina Turner, Richard Chamberlain, Marsha Mason, Helen Reddy, Linda Evans, Joyce DeWitt, Paul Horn, and others.

When media stars talk, people generally listen. Not that they necessarily have any degree of professional expertise in New Age disciplines, but the force of their testimony from their media stardom platform does have popular influence.

Shirley MacLaine is again a prime case in point. Before her New Age conversion, she had a number of best-selling autobiographical books. Her landmark book, *Out on a Limb*, (followed by *Dancing in the Light* and *It's all in the Playing*), is what some observers refer to as a "cross-over" book. Millions of middle-American fans bought a book detailing MacLaine's mind-boggling conversion story. This *New York Times* best-selling saga introduced the New Age agenda to millions of people who had not thought such thoughts beforehand. Even more so when her book became the (in)famous TV mini-series. In technicolor and in print, MacLaine evangelized a large chunk of American society. Many did not buy into it in the least, but many others were tantalized by these exotic new New Age frontiers. In fact, mainstream booksellers reported a 95-percent increase of sales in New Age/occult/metaphysical books during the two weeks after the miniseries.

John Denver is another prime case. Using his enormous stardom, he casts his "enlightened planetary oneness" voice towards "world peace, international brotherhood, and enlightened human rights." He is the director of a community in Colorado called "Windstar," at which a year-round schedule of New Age events is offered.

"Dynasty" star Linda Evans is yet another media New Age evangelist. She states in *Redbook* (May 1988):

"Only trust what feels right for you. But if it brings you more love and happiness, then what does it matter where it comes from?" Further: "For me, Ramtha [a famous channeled spirit] has been a great teacher."

New Age testimony through media stars opens many doors of potential curiosity and follow-up exploration.

• Political seats of authority often have kept arm's distance from occultists, yet it is not uncommon for there to be a direct-to-indirect alliance between the two. In the Bible, pagan kings often are seen having their kingdoms' most powerful occultists at their court command. It is not rare for the enormous amount of socio-political variables and forces pressuring the politician/king/potentate/etc. sometimes to resort to occult-based practices as a guiding and counseling voice and allied power.

Dave Hunt, author of *America: The Sorcerer's New Apprentice*, rightfully asserts:

"Though occultism was publicly treated as nonsense, however, secretly it has continued to be practiced in various forms even in the highest academic and government circles."[3]

• New Age music has become a category unto itself. There is even a Grammy award category for this particular musical genre. In national record-seller chains, "New Age Music" warrants a distinct niche for itself. Thousands of New Age musicians vie for a widening national market with diverse musical styles. There are even New Age radio stations popping up in some of the major cities.

However, not all that is generically categorized as New Age Music is necessarily demonic in nature. Though a significant chunk of music in this very generalized category is somewhat innocuous and entertaining, there is also a significant percentage in its ranks that promote and induce trance-states to higher consciousness. The repetitive, entrancing, floating quality of some of the New Age music genre can be potentially dangerous.

For myself, I feel it better to lean more towards the cautious and conservative side in discerning this realm of New Age music.

• Holistic Health is a broad field. It is also one of the most tricky and subtle conjunctions between a) the wholesome and healthy, and b) being based in New Age philosophy and practice. Quite honestly, being a former naturopathic doctor myself, the complexities of this important subject merit a full-length book to do the issues justice. While it is not the agenda of this book to cover such issues, two Christian-based books can be recommended for further reading: *New Age Medicine: A Christian Perspective on Holistic Health* (by Paul Reisser, M.D., Teri Reisser, and John Weldon) and *New Age Health Care: Holy or Holistic?* (by Dr. Jane Gumprecht).

For the most part, I see this field as being a mixture of positive and negative: three ingredients of wholesome and six ingredients of the New Age; nine ingredients of healthy and 20 of the New Age. In this trickily subtle holistic health field, discernment is at a premium.

From my own experience, over 70 percent of holistic health professionals have an underlying New Age-based philosophy. Many who have New Age roots do not advertise as such. It is best to ask any health care professional a number of informed spiritual and consumer questions before engaging in their services. Get to know your health-care professional(s), whether they be M.D.s, Ph.D.s, chiropractors, osteopaths, naturopaths, or otherwise.

A classic debate in point is the field of acupuncture. This discipline has met with success in both the holistic health field and even in increasing numbers of M.D. circles. Granted that it has a sufficient success ratio, *but* its philosophical foundations rest on a Chinese pantheistic system of Eastern mysticism and dragon- and serpent-power. Even if something works in a significant percentage of cases, that doesn't necessarily mean that it is righteous, holy, and true.

Biblical foundations of eternal truth must be congruent with any kind of health care system, holistic and otherwise. The informed Christian consumers may make educated determinations about their health care through Bible study, prayer, educated consumerism, and spiritual discernment.

• TV and movies propagate the New Age "gospel" in powerfully impacting ways. In one study, for example, a 3-week overview of movies on prime-time TV showed that 32 had occult or satanic themes. For me, a seemingly innocuous TV show "Kung Fu," was my direct window into New Age involvements. The hero-figure of the Eastern priest-mystic became my teenage hero-figure, and it was but a small step from there to naively exploring the exotic terrains of *Yoga*, meditation, and Eastern mysticism.

Numbers of New Age-influenced movies have hit the national scene. These include: "Dark Crystal," "Indiana Jones and the Temple of Doom," "Cocoon I & II," "Ghostbusters," "ET," "2001," "2010," "Brainstorm," "Altered States," "Batteries Not Included," "Jonathan Livingston Seagull," "Superman I" (with the green crystal), "Dune," "Poltergeist," and a host of others have introduced various aspects of the spiritual humanist worldview to the attention of the nation.

Movies have powerful desensitization potential. They can, for the unwary, introduce concepts, issues, and a worldview that can be taken on subtly by the individual over time with repeated exposure.

• Horror movies with occult themes are at the other extreme end of the occult-based spectrum. The 1980s trend toward the increasingly graphic and horrific is a turn toward the very worst. Such movies are ghastly tools of darkness pandering to the perversions of natural man, and creating a corresponding openness to the workings of unclean spirits in movie theatres and wherever else they are shown.

• Children's cartoons, toys, and games increasingly are infested with subtle-to-overt darkness. Though this subject may seem petty to some, the potential long-term effects on such impressionable young minds pose serious concerns. In his alarming book, *Turmoil in the Toy Box*, Christian author Phil Phillips points to the many-leveled threat that influences so many children today.

"A child's mind is corrupted in a subtle manner. With objects, so 'cute and innocent' as toys, childrens minds are being filled with images of sex, violence, and fear. This is *subtle deception*. It is formed, layer upon layer, until these evil and corrupt images are real to the child.

"... Occult symbols and violence guide a child's imagination into the world of Satan."[4]

Phillips exposes an eye-opening array of cartoons, toys and games that are polluting our children's minds in subtle but potentially profound ways. The New Age (as well as sex and violence) infiltrates into the very fabric of our youths' lives, if we are not vigilant.

• The corporate business world is not immune to the encroachments of spiritual humanist practices. In fact, a certain sector of the business world heartily embraces various mainstreamed versions of the New Age theme. A wide variety of self-improvement programs, management training, success/motivational seminars, and creativity enhancement programs based on New Age principles and practices, but which are re-packaged into de-religionised, Westernized forms, have proliferated.

In fact, 4-billion corporate dollars are spent each year for specialty firms—dubbed "The Corporate Transformers"—to train executives, managers, and other employees in the "new psychology and science" of becoming better selves who have higher productivity.

The Omni WholeMind Newsletter states:

"It's an unlikely romance: stodgy, authoritarian, rational Big Business and the mercurial, 'right-brain,' go-with-the-flow New Age. But today many Fortune 500 firms are having their right brains recharged, their alpha waves enhanced, their paradigms shifted, and their cultures 'transformed.' In California, the hotbed of transformation, over 50 percent of company owners surveyed by the magazine *California Business* said they used some form of 'consciousness-raising' technique to motivate employees."[5]

Such widespread corporate employee "transforming, motivating, and training," definitely are not confined to California—it's everywhere in the world of both big and small businesses. Here, New Age principles are presented by sophisticated teams of three-piece-suit "Corporate Transformers," many of whom would disavow any direct linkage with the New Age Movement. In thousands of cases, employees being processed through such programs are totally unaware of their New Age basis. But employees often are forced to take these programs, else their jobs hang in the balance.

In an article entitled, "New Age Big Brother," in *The WholeMind Newsletter*, a number of imperative points are brought out:

"'I feel very strongly that companies should not be in the business of changing their employees' belief systems,' says Richard Watring, personnel director of Budget-Rent-a-Car and self-appointed corporate-transformer watchdog. He says he has identified training courses that use everything from meditation and self-hypnosis to channeling. In some cases, the equivalent of a corporate cult may form, with its own private language, belief system, and thought policy.

"... Given the 'subtle influence that is exerted between a superior and a subordinate,' says Watring, 'even voluntary courses are, in fact, required.'"[6]

• The sports world, in its quest for excellence and pushing the limits of human potential, also has come to embrace a considerable amount of New Age influences. In the 1970s, for example, a highly popular groundbreaking book, *The Inner Game of Tennis*, by Timothy

Gallwey, strode onto the sports scene and offered a new mental approach to tennis, and sports in general.

Essentially, he repackaged a basic yoga approach of splitting the mind into two parts—an observer (Gallwey's "Self 1") and the actor ("Self 2"). Self 1 meditatively watches Self 2 go through all the motions and emotions of playing the sport. This is yoga meditation-in-action.

The national success that Gallwey met spawned a series of "The Inner Game ..." books by he and other authors. Talking to a ski instructor in the early 1980s, I was informed that the "Inner Game" approach had become that sport's orthodoxy in many circles.

It is not uncommon for serious athletes to try a host of New Age-based approaches, including psychologies, creative visualization exercises, meditation techniques, brain-drive machines, subliminal cassette tapes and videos, flotation tanks, and numerous others. Many such practices have highly accepted status. Books on such subjects abound.

• New Age-based psychologies have proliferated like weeds over the last 20 years. Some of them are labeled New Age, many are not. The "pop psychology" era of the 1970s provided exceptionally fertile socio-cultural soil for humanistic psychologies of both secular and New Age varieties to grow.

Well over half the books found in a bookstore under the category of "Psychology/Self-Help" have significant-to-total bases in the many New Age psychology variations. For example, the unwary consumer looking for a book on resolving emotional turmoil, feeling more happiness, or marital problem resolution easily can purchase a book based on New Age principles without realizing it, as it may not be labeled as such.

One of the founding fathers of modern-day New Age psychologies is Carl Jung. Through most of his world-renowned career he adamantly maintained that spirits had no independent existence. He wrote volumes of psychological thought based on the conviction that his many encounters with seemingly supernatural forces were a part of the "Collective Unconscious," a type of collective human mind-field containing all aspects of human experiences and psyche make-up. It was only at the end of his long career that he felt that he was being overpowered and possessed by forces beyond his control. He finally admitted that his invisible friend, named Philemon, was an independent spirit-entity:

"Philemon represented a force which was not myself. ... It was he who taught me psychic objectivity.

"... At times he seemed to me quite real, as if he were a living personality. I went walking up and down the garden with him, and to me he was what the Indians call a *guru*."[7]

Yes, Jung's source of inspiration and knowledge was an acquired familiar spirit, who was the behind-the-scenes author of Jung's "Depth Psychology." Here, at the very source of a huge percentage of New Age-based psychologies, we see the clever work of deceiving demons.

• In the field of education (kindergarten through high school), spiritual humanism is making some significant inroads, though less so than in some other areas. From one perspective, we can see in education how secular humanism and New Age spiritual humanism can work in tandem, even as different as their philosophies are.

Many Christian authors have alerted the Christian community to the powerful effect that secular humanistic "Values Clarification" teachings is having in schoolrooms across the nation. Here, the absolute moral values set forth in the Bible are cast aside as being merely one value-system option among many others. Students studying Values Clarification learn to use their own personal feelings about right and wrong, truth and untruth as moral guidelines. Using the self-perceptions of natural man as a gauge of moral conduct and worldview leaves the door wide open for self-justification of non-Bible-based attitudes and actions.

Values Clarification also opens the door wide for New Age spiritual humanism as being a viable, justifiable option, if such views "feel right" to the pupil. In this way, secular humanism creates a philosophical opening through which spiritual humanism may stride unhindered.

Also on the education front, a fast-growing New Age-oriented "Confluent Education" view is coming to the fore. Originated by Dr. Beverly Galyean, this strain of thought is meeting with increasing acceptance in educational and psychological circles.

As well, there are increasing reports of teachers who take it upon themselves to introduce students to New Age ideas and practices. *Child Abuse in the Classroom* is one book among others detailing these subtle-to-serious encroachments.

Personally, I recall quite a few private conversations with teachers who would boast of how they were using their position to inset various enlightened New Age ideas into their curriculum, and how easy they found this task to be in many cases. Parents, beware!

• Even in influential positions at the United Nations, the New Age agenda has taken root. A prime case in point is the former assistant secretary general of the U.N. Robert Muller, author of *New Genesis: Shaping a Global Spirituality*. In this work, he calls for "A Bimillennium Celebration of Life, the advent of an Era of Peace, a Golden Age, and the First Millennium of World Harmony and Human Happiness."

Further, "... we must join our Hindu brethren and call henceforth our planet 'Brahma' or the Planet of God."[8] (Brahma is the name of a major Hindu deity, one amongst the pantheon of other pantheistic deities.) His globalistic agenda and call for a One World Religion dovetail perfectly with the New Age agenda.

Conclusion

Though much more could be written on this subject, hopefully insight is given to the scope and magnitude of New Age inroads.

As a concluding thought, let me reiterate the comments of New Age spokesperson Marilyn Ferguson, as she offers insight into the scope of spiritual humanism:

"The Aquarian Conspirators range across all levels of income and education, from the humblest to the highest. There are schoolteachers and office workers, famous scientists, government officials and lawmakers, artists and millionaires, taxi drivers and celebrities, leaders in medicine, education, law, psychology. Some are open in their advocacy, and their names may be familiar. Others are quiet about their involvement, believing they can be more effective if they are not identified with ideas that have all too often been misunderstood."[9]

Notes

1. Jude 1:3.
2. Ferguson, op. cit., p. 35.
3. Hunt, *America: The Sorcerer's New Apprentice* (op. cit.), p. 27.
4. Phil Phillips, *Turmoil in the Toy Box* (Lancaster, PA: Starburst Publishers, 1986), p. 23.
5. Judith Hooper, op. cit., p. 1.
6. Marjorie Costello, "New Age Big Brother," *WholeMind Newsletter*, May 1988.
7. C. G. Jung, *Memories, Dreams, Reflections* (Pantheon Books, 1963), p. 183.
8. Robert Muller, *New Genesis: Shaping a Global Spirituality* (New York: Image Books, 1984), p. 186.
9. Ferguson, op. cit., pp. 23, 24.

NINE

HOW DO NEW AGERS VIEW CHRISTIANS?

I see the beginning of a new barbarism ... which tomorrow will be called a 'new culture' . . . Nazism was a primitive, brutal, and absurd expression of it. But it was a first draft of the so-called scientific or pre-scientific morality that is being prepared for us in the radiant future."

—Nobel prize-winning scientist Erwin Chargaff, called the "Father of Bioengineering"

"There has not been and there will not be a place for the unfit. The fit will lead, and if the unfit are not coming along there is no place for them. ...

"In the Age of Enlightenment there is no place for ignorant people.

"Nature will not allow ignorance to prevail. It just can't. Non-existence of the unfit has been the law of nature."

—Transcendental Meditation (TM) *guru* Maharishi Mahesh *Yogi*

How do New Agers view Christians? Answering this is one of the most revealing of all questions posed about the oh-so-loving-and-peaceful New Age Movement. For herein is the real face behind the luminously enlightened outer face of the New Age. Even unknown to most New Agers, this real face is that of devouring darkness—the face of the Enemy and his demons.

It helps for Christians to have a general awareness of what the New Age subculture thinks of them, if only more fully to understand the vast differences. This is especially relevant for those Christians who may be involved in some aspect of the New Age and want to get out of it. It is also relevant for Christians who may come into contact with New Agers, whether in the context of casual business acquaintances, school teachers, or otherwise. Perhaps most importantly, it is significant to understand the New Age subculture in end-times terms for, in truth, the horrific face of the Antichrist and his sinister plans lurk behind its false facade of light, love, and peace.

Orthodox Christianity Viewed as a Distorted Old-Age Relic

In general, Biblical Christianity is blithely dismissed by New Agers as a limited, exclusivistic, narrow-minded relic of an old age now past in this modern New Age era. It is astounding how little serious consideration is given by the New Agers to the profound theological differences that stand between them and Christianity. With a knowing smile and a few superficial clichés, they repudiate Christianity as antiquated, limited, and distorted as to merit little-to-no serious, open-minded thought or investigation.

To many New Agers, the first and foremost issue revolves around Christians' absolute conviction that Jesus is the one and only begotten Son, the Lord of Lords, and unique personal Savior. From a New Age perspective, this type of view limits the role of the many other alleged "saviors" and "enlightened teachers" — like Buddha, Mohammed, Gandhi, famous gurus, etc. — that are seen to be just as valid as Jesus (and sometimes even superior to Him).

New Agers see many ways to salvation; Christians proclaim that there is only one Way — Jesus Christ.

The New Age sees this Christian conviction as narrow-mindedly exclusive and needlessly biased. What New Agers don't realize is that this so-called "narrow-mindedness is due to the Christian realization that salvation lies only through the "narrow gate" — "For the gate is small, and the way is narrow that leads to life, and few are those who find it" (Matt. 7:14).

The New Age broad-minded thinking that seeks to embrace its many purported "enlightened masters, saviors, and avatars" is in reality the "broad" way "that leads to destruction, and many are those who enter by it" (Matt. 7:13).

Generally, New Agers perceive themselves as *THE* leading-edge force of a massive, worldwide, evolutionary awakening — an unparalleled super-Renaissance. Everyone who is not awakening to this higher consciousness is thought of as one of the "masses who sleep in ignorance of their true divine heritage." The self-perception is that they, the vanguard of a New Era of human destiny, are the superior forerunners to lead the less enlightened by the hand into the fast-approaching "Aquarian Golden Age." Christians are viewed as "evolutionarily backward" people—spiritual kindergartners who can be most ignorant and obstinate.

What is so lamentable is that this pervasive New Age SPIRITUAL SUPERIORITY COMPLEX completely *blinds* them from seeing the true Light of the world. The Enemy makes sure to weave into their delusion an aversion and close-minded sense of superiority to the Good News—the only Truth that can set them free from Satan's gilded bondage. The superiority complex is also a veil that can blind them to injustice, cruelty, and even murder.

Generally, these people simply avoid or ignore reborn Christians. Most references in seminars or casual conversation usually are passing comments or included in merely miscellaneous topics, just superficially brushing off Christian theology or making Christians the butt of belittling "limited-thinking" comments.

The most enlightened view in New Age circles generally tries to think compassionately of Christians as unawakened little children or slumbering, misguided laggards who may or may not wake up to see the light. Such a view holds that "if it's their *karma* to be cleansed from the Earth to reincarnate into another more appropriate, less evolved planet, then that is the perfection of divine order." Furthermore, there's no such thing as death in New Age philosophy. The soul is supposed to be immortal; therefore, there's no real death, just a "change of reincarnated form."

This kind of smug, blinded superiority complex leaves the way open for an array of potential horrors.

Four Categories of How New Agers View Christians

By and large there are four general categories of New Agers' perspectives on Christians.

The *first perspective* is that of relative apathy. The Christian community is simply not given much thought. Anything Christian is automatically not of interest and to be avoided whenever possible, lest it be irritating or needlessly inconveniencing.

If or when confronted with an unavoidable Christian witness, reactions are unpredictable, ranging from mild annoyance to outright hostility.

The *second perspective* is superior-minded benign tolerance. With the New Age dictum that "all spiritual paths ultimately lead to the same place," there must logically be an allowance for the relative validity of Christianity. There are, however, in this view, some paths that are more advanced than others; this is to say, some paths have progressed higher toward the spiritual mountaintop than others.

Here, New Agers believe that it is they who have achieved the higher plateaus of the spiritual mountain and can see much further and broader than those treading the other spiritual paths far below. From their self-created superiority perch, New Agers look far down the mountain to the less evolved paths of "limited perception" and "slumbering ignorance," which definitely include orthodox Christianity. However, if any Christian refuses to take the next step into the New World Order under the Antichrist when it comes, then such a person well may rationalize that "it will be their choice and their *karma* to go to a more suitable planet of less evolved souls."

The *third perspective* is that of subtle-to-severe irritation. As I learned during my year of witnessing to the New Age subculture, Satan plants seeds of aversion, close-mindedness, and irritation in his webs of delusion. New Agers are sometimes caught by surprise at their agitated response to the simple witness of Christ, who died for mankind's sins so that all may be alive-in-Christ and raised up with Him.[1] There is something about the Good News that goes against the New Age "grain." They don't understand this about themselves, and generally clamp their minds shut while sometimes also finding themselves disturbed. At this point, most try to avoid any further exposure, and take the next available opportunity to exit the situation. In few but significant numbers, the irritation factor can unleash a stronger, more confrontative and combative response.

The *fourth perspective* is that of conscious, active opposition to the Body of Christ. This involves a significant minority of the New Age spectrum mostly composed of witches, shamanic practitioners, satanists, and power-woman feminist activists who have some type of abiding Satan-inspired grudge against Christianity. For the most part, this continuing, active opposition is waged via attempts to cast spells, perform magic rituals, applying negative "mind-power" techniques, plus other occult tricks of the trade.

Sometimes, such individuals will secretively plant occult power objects on the grounds of a church or other sacred location. Some even attend church services and other Christian gatherings to try to disrupt such events by waging invisible spiritual warfare while sometimes outwardly appearing to be at-ease and non-disruptive. Such bad-seed activists are sometimes cunning, persistent, and powerful. For Christians to be alert to the potential of such activities happening in their midst can aid in being forearmed with the "full armor of God, that you may be able to stand firm against the schemes of the devil."[2] Of course, the power of Christian prayer, prevails in spiritual warfare.

END-TIMES NEW AGE DANGERS ARISING

The overall New Age agenda has definite plans for a planetary "purification" process as the world transitions into the fullness of a "Golden New World Era" inhabited by a superior race of god-men. Herein lies a grossly distorted "separating the wheat from the chaff" scenario. Most New Age prophecy foresees a millennial transition time during which those who accept the message and mark of the "New World Order" become a part of the greatly proclaimed New Age. But there will be others resistantly lagging behind who oppose it. The ones seen as "evolutionary laggards" (i.e., the remaining Christian saints who persevere,[3] and all other resisters) who raise a ruckus in active opposition to the rise of the New Age" (i.e., the Antichrist forces) are to be "compassionately cleansed" from the face of the New World and "relegated to other reincarnational bodies in other less-evolved planetary schools."

In effect, as the Antichrist forces come to greater world power, a revamped and upgraded New Age-based philosophy is to be applied toward "purifying" the planetary populace of those who are not "ready" to make the next step into becoming a superior race of god-men.

This should ignite memories of Hitler's blood "sacrifice" of the Jewish people.

Occult Roots of Nazism and Its Plans for a New World Era

One of the most overlooked facts of history is the occultic foundation of the Nazi regime. A number of excellent books have been written on this startling subject,[4] all clearly demonstrating that Hitler, many of the top German brass, and the Nazi SS were heavily involved in highly sophisticated occultism. Hitler's stunning rise to power is much more explicable in light of this fact.

Hitler's primary mentor, Dietrich Eckhart, was the high priest of the Thule Society, a powerful secret European occult society dating back many centuries. Much of this occult society's philosophy was based on the belief that the Germanic race was a descendant of an ancient race of gods called the Hyperboreans.

In following this lineage back to its roots, there were supposedly universal secrets to be found, and the keys to revive the descendants of this "master race" of "supermen" once again in a new millennium. Hitler called this new world era the Third Reich, "The Thousand Year Reich." In initiating Hitler into the innermost levels of the

Thule Society, Dietrich Eckhart unleashed what he perceived as a sovereign occult force. He wrote:

"Follow Hitler! He will dance, but it is I who have called the tune. We have given him the means of communication with Them.

"Do not mourn for me: I shall have influenced history more than any other German."[5]

Intimates and large crowds of people were overwhelmed by the superhuman, magnetic charisma of Hitler. Many of the top German brass came to realize that Hitler was being manipulated by overriding invisible forces they referred to as the "Unknown Superiors."

Herman Rauschning, Governor of Danzig, and a close confidant of Hitler, observed:

"One cannot help thinking of him as a medium ... beyond any doubt, Hitler was possessed by forces outside himself ... of which the individual named Hitler was only the temporary vehicle."[6]

Heinrich Himmler, head of the dreaded SS was profoundly steeped in occultism. He ruled over these elite troops who were all bloodsworn to their deep occult ties and the rise of the millennial Third Reich. In actuality, the SS, also called the "Black Order," was an elite band of black magicians who utilized sophisticated occult rituals and techniques as a secret basis of their power and influence. Many expeditions were sent to India and Tibet to find the lost keys to their Aryan Superman past. In fact, when Berlin was overrun by the Allies, they were surprised to find the corpses of over 1,000 Tibetans.

A clear picture of the massive unleashing and use of monumental demonic forces comes forth from documented research. An occult revival in Europe, particularly Austria and Germany, arose in the 1920s and 1930s, which served as a wave of momentum leading into the skyrocketing of a bumbling, 2nd- to 3rd-rate intellectual—Hitler—into a position that rocked the four corners of the Earth.

Hitler's ultimate goal was to forge a new step in human evolutionary development—to create a superhuman god-man species under a one-world government, headed by one supreme god-man. In order to attain this goal, a blood sacrifice of the Jews was thought to be necessary to "cleanse" German blood, thereby restoring genetic purity and resultant superiority. This "new man" was intended to be a race of Aryan gods.

Hitler is recorded as ecstatically pronouncing:

"The new man is living amongst us now! He is here! Isn't that enough for you?

"I will tell you a secret. I have seen the new man. He is intrepid and cruel."[7]

So, the basic themes of creating a millennial new world and a superior race of god-men founded on occult philosophy, requiring a "cleansing of inferior racial stock" highlighted the Nazi regime. This attempt failed. But the demonic forces in back of the attempt live on. Hitler's Nazism was but a crude, primitive dress rehearsal for the slick, sanitized, and sophisticated plans of the False Messiah.

How the New Age Can Justify Killing

By being able to self-righteously justify various types of killing, New Age philosophy opens the doors to potential logical Nazi extremes. Using its reincarnation- and *karma*-based philosophy, the New Age readily and easily can justify such acts as abortion, euthanasia, racial sterilization, and even murder. This philosophy asserts that the soul is immortal; therefore, there is really no such thing as death, only an endless "recycling" of the soul into body after reincarnational body—a belief that over half the world's population holds today.

In Shirley MacLaine's infamous book *Out On a Limb*, while looking at the wreckage of buses that had fallen off a Peruvian mountain road and pondering the possible meaning of such disasters, her mentor-friend David offers a classic response: "There's no real death anyway, so there are no victims." In this philosophy, suffering is an illusion, death is an illusion, victims are an illusion. By definition, whatever is, is right and perfect for all those involved.

Concerning abortion, for example, New Age rationalizations justify this act of the murdering of innocents as being totally acceptable and non-harmful, if the act is "*karmically* in balance." Among others, such rationalizations include:

• After abortion, the soul will be able to reincarnationally recycle into another fetus at a later time.

• The soul knew that the mother would abort and therefore chose to use the experience of the abortion as an evolutionary "learning experience."

• Death is an illusion, therefore there are no victims.

• The soul and the mother have a *karmic* relationship that can be "balanced" by the mother choosing to abort.

• If the mother receives "spiritual guidance" from her "Higher Self" or spirit guides that say that the abortion is okay, then the abortion is in "divine order."

• All the aborted soul needed was a short experience in the physical dimension to learn all it needed to learn.

• Plus many other creative variations on the reincarnation-*karma* theme.

The blatant immorality and ultimate inherent dangers of New Age philosophy are that it can, on its own terms, be a totally logical rationale for the killing of innocents and the justification of injustice of all varieties. This philosophy can go so far as even to justify outright murder. Here, the logic is: Since the soul is immortal, and therefore never really dies, it just keeps reincarnating. If, for example, two people have a past life involvement, where one person has murdered the other then in a future lifetime the two must come together and the *karma* balanced. The one who was murdered ultimately can be justified in a future lifetime in murdering the murderer so that the cosmic scales of *karma* are equalized. Such is New Age cosmic "justice."

In fact, this philosophy even could be used to make a claim that all those who committed mass murder at Jonestown have Jim Jones to thank for leading them through a valuable spiritual learning experience. Likewise, this warped view would assert that the Jews killed in the holocaust "chose" to undergo this experience either as payment of *karmic* debt or as a "soul-learning experience." The perversion of this philosophy can be molded to incredible extremes.

The extremes of secular humanism, as well, can work in concert with New Age spiritual humanism toward modern-day, neo-holocaust dangers. Sound unlikely? Not at all. A neo-holocaust is taking place in America *today*. It already has well outnumbered the 6-million Jews killed in Hitler's holocaust. Abortion clinics—more correctly called "neo-holocaust murder mills"—have slaughtered over 25-million innocents already. This legalized, sanitized, sterilized neo-holocaust run by professionals in lab coats and operating gowns should alert us all to the very real possibility that such horrors could be extended to other groups of people in the future. To murder innocents is the first huge step down the road toward justifying horrendous abuses of euthanasia.

Even if Roe vs. Wade, which legalized abortion, is overturned and jurisdiction turned over to states (as of this writing, the issue is still unresolved), there inevitably will be those states that will serve as abortion clinic havens. The outline of the problem may change, but the root core will live on.

The spirit of the Antichrist certainly is paving the way for even greater Nazi-like atrocities of the Antichrist himself in his false "New World Order."

A Perverse "Separating the Wheat from the Chaff"

In end-times terms, similar dangers potentially apply to all those who oppose the Antichrist's plans. Any philosophy that can logically justify murder, abortion, and the like, can be turned to rationalize the "cleansing" of all those who oppose it.

John Ankerberg and John Weldon comment on the ultimate logical flaw and potentially serious danger of New Age philosophy in *The Facts on the New Age Movement*:

"A thorough reading of New Age literature will show that some New Agers sanction the persecution of Christians. They do so on the basis of the need to remove those who may refuse to accept or attempt to 'prevent' a spiritual uniting of humanity.

"This is one of the darker aspects to the New Age, yet it is consistent with the overall world of the NAM [New Age Movement]. If true globalism—or world unity—is eventually to be a reality, then by definition all dissenting voices must either be converted, silenced, or removed. That, of course, is the 'rub,'—the New Age of love and harmony may have to be repressive for a time to usher in their version of peace on Earth."[8]

There are many examples of different New Age leaders and channeled spirits pointing to this time of "purification." Here are a few quotes from noted figures to supplement the earlier quotation on the weeding out of the "fit" from the "unfit" by the TM *Guru* Maharishi Mahesh *Yogi*.

Ruth Montgomery, former nationally syndicated political columnist turned leading New Age author, dubbed as being "The Herald of the New Age," has written:

"We are indeed on the threshold of a New Age, which the [spirit guides] guides say will be ushered in by a shift of the Earth on its axis at the close of this century.

"... The souls who helped to bring on the chaos of the present century will have passed into spirit to rethink their attitudes, and the new race will engage in peaceful pursuits and the uplifting of spirits."[9]

Jewish Christian leader Zola Levitt reports in his taped lecture, "UFOs: What on Earth is Happening?" that there is a popular "Berkeley Messiah" who has risen up as yet another New Age herald. This "messiah" states that he is the prime representative between Earth and "Masters" who coordinate the UFO hierarchy. The UFOs, this false messiah states, will intervene at a time of world tumult. At this point, the "Divine Plan" will be presented to the world by these intervening forces. The UFOs are to use "radiomagnetic rays" on Christians and all others who oppose the "New Order" in order to "cleanse the Earth of an element that holds back the evolutionary process for the rest of the world."[10]

A leading New Age channel and author, Ken Carey, in a new book released in late 1988 entitled *Return of the Bird Tribes* says:

"The Great Day of Purification has begun, a short but essential cycle of division that will gather those who promote fear and violence and separate them from this season of the world as chaff is separated from wheat at threshing."[11]

David Spangler, a long-time leading New Age spokesman, channels a spirit posing as "Limitless Love and Truth," which states:

"In revealing a New Age ... I can be a sword that divides and separates. You must be prepared to accept this and not resist it if such separation occurs."[12]

J. Randolph Price, New Age writer and primary inspirer and organizer of numerous large-scale World Peace Meditation events, asserts that those who deny "the divinity of all men" (i.e., man is a god) are of the "Antichrist." His spirit-guide, an "awakened one" called "Asher," has informed him that "Nature will soon enter her cleansing cycle" during which those of "lower vibratory rates" will be purified off the planet.

In effect, following this line of reasoning, those who oppose the coming "New World Order"—remaining Christians, Jews and any others who resist—are by definition of a "lower vibratory rate," and thereby are blocking the fullness of the New Age from happening. All resisters are seen as an anchor that holds the planet down so that it is not yet of a sufficient "higher vibratory rate" for the Golden Aquarian Age to fully dawn. Therefore, all those "ignorant, evolutionarily inferior souls of a lower vibratory rate must be compassionately transferred to another world of their own choosing that fits their lower spiritual level."

Furthermore, any persecution and woes experienced by "lower vibration people" also can be justified as the reaping of "bad collective *karma*."

New Age author Moira Timms, in her book, *Prophecies and Predictions*, distorts the meaning of the plagues of Revelation into being "special packages of *karma* visited upon the obstinate that they might awaken to their wrong attitudes."[13] The New Age attitude would be: "They chose to bring this on themselves. *Karma* is divine justice. We must not attempt to disrupt the workings of universal law. Those souls will use the situation as a positive, spiritual, learning experience. Who are we to oppose divine justice?" The blatant hatred of the Nazis for the Jews is re-wrapped into a New Age version of detached, compassionate concern for spiritual laggards.

New Age literature is filled with obvious and implicit targeting of specific types of people who resist the "New World Order," and uses "enlightened and compassionate" reasoning to justify the "purification" process. Using reincarnation-based logic, the "cleansing" process is said to be merely re-locating these laggard souls into other incarnations in less evolved worlds. The horrifying gas chambers of the Holocaust were a crude and obvious forerunner of a much slicker, glossier plan to round up dissidents and take them to "re-education centers of love and peace."

In essence, there is a time in the New Age agenda where it is a "holy duty" to "purify all oppositional elements that are holding back the fullness of the New World Order." When enlightened philosophy can justify mass murder as a holy duty, therein lies a gruesome danger. My bone marrow chills at the thought of smiling-faced New Agers, who have succumbed to the Antichrist's "powerful delusion" lovingly embracing those whom they are rounding up to send off to the "re-education centers."

"It'll be great." They will say, "You'll receive so much more love and light than you can possibly imagine. You'll find peace there, and you'll go with your own brethren to your very own 'new world.'"

Yes, Hitler's version of the Holocaust was a crude, barbaric, and absurd rehearsal for the slick and sophisticated plans of the Antichrist. If you would have told me this five or 10 years ago, I would have laughed uproariously. Such a notion would have seemed patently absurd. However, in view of the end-times rise of the New Age "plague of the spirit" and how it feeds into the plans of the Antichrist, New Age leaders and channeled demon-spirits are indeed laying out the basic agenda for a glowingly golden Age of Aquarius. Peace, love, and brotherhood are its mottos that cunningly conceal the devouring face of darkness that is behind it all.

Sadly, the people who are swept up in the Antichrist's powerful delusion will have little to no idea of the Neo-Holocaust that they are helping to perpetrate. Just as most New Agers today would scoff at these ideas, they are blinded to the fact that Satan is the author of this movement, serving his purposes alone in preparing the way for the False Messiah.

Douglas Groothuis, in *Confronting the New Age: How to Resist a Growing Religious Movement*, concludes on this subject:

"... the mixing of messianic and millennial enthusiasm, apocalyptic expectation, ethical relativism and occult intrigue makes for a very combustible compound. There is every possibility that if the people of God do not rise up in the Spirit's power ... it will assume an increasingly potent and sinister form marked by hostility toward its opponents."[14]

Dave Hunt, posing the question, "Are We in Any Real Danger?" writes:

"Something of great significance is occurring, and it must be taken seriously. The last revival of occultism played into Adolf Hitler's hands, and the eventual victims numbered in the millions. One can only wonder where the current and far more pervasive renaissance of such occultism will lead."[15]

Joseph Carr, who investigates the occult basis of the Nazi regime in *The Twisted Cross*, notes parallels between New Age philosophy and Nazi National Socialism:

"One cannot argue against the claim that the Nazi worldview and major elements of the New Age Movement worldview are identical. They should be, after all, for they both grew out of the same occultic root: theosophy. Their respective cosmogony, cosmology, and philosophies are identical."[16]

Further, he states that the New Age is "an Antichrist movement that could easily spawn another Adolf Hitler—and a holocaust that makes the killing of the Jews during World War II look like a minor action."[17]

Finally, in the classic book, *The Occult and the Third Reich*, a due forewarning is given:

"Those who induced Germany to embrace the swastika are not dead. They are still among us, just as they have been in every era, and doubtless will continue to be until the Apocalypse. National Socialism was for them but a means, and Hitler was but an instrument. The undertaking failed. What they are now trying to do is revive the myth using other means."[18]

Notes

1. Ephesians 2:5, 6.
2. Ephesians 6:11.
3. Revelation 14:12.
4. See *Hitler: The Occult Messiah, The Occult and the Third Reich, The Spear of Destiny*, and *The Twisted Cross*.
5. Dave Hunt, *Peace, Prosperity and the Coming Holocaust* (Eugene, OR: Harvest House Publishers, 1983), p. 140.
6. Gerald Suster, *Hitler: The Occult Messiah* (New York, NY: 1981), p. 120.
7. Hunt, *Peace, Prosperity, and the Coming Holocaust*, op. cit., p. 136.
8. Ankerberg and Weldon, op. cit., p. 23.
9. Ruth Montgomery, *Ruth Montgomery: Herald of the New Age* (New York, NY: Doubleday, 1986), p. 23.
10. Zola Levitt, from cassette tape—"UFOs: What on Earth Is Happening?"
11. Ken Carey, *Return of the Bird Tribes* (Uni-Sun), p. 62.
12. David Spangler, *Revelation: The Birth of a New Age* (Middleton, WI: Lorian Press, 1976), pp. 63-65.
13. Moira Timms, *Prophecies and Predictions* (Santa Cruz, CA: Unity Press, 1980), pp. 57, 58.
14. Groothuis, *Confronting the New Age* (op. cit.), p. 206.
15. Hunt, *America: The Sorcerer's New Apprentice* (op. cit.), p. 25.
16. Joseph Carr, *The Twisted Cross* (Lafayette, LA: Huntington House, Inc., 1985), p. 87. Quoted in *Dark Secrets of the New Age*, by Texe Marrs, p. 253.
17. Ibid., p. 276. Quoted in *Dark Secrets of the New Age*, by Texe Marrs, p. 253.
18. Jean-Michel Angebert, *The Occult and the Third Reich* (New York, NY: MacMillan Press, 1974), p. xvi.

TEN

PERSPECTIVES ON HELPING OTHERS GET OUT OF THE NEW AGE

And the Lord's bond-servant must not be quarrelsome, but be kind to all, able to teach, patient when wronged,

"With gentleness correcting those who are in opposition, if perhaps God may grant them repentance leading to the knowledge of the truth,

"And they may come to their senses and escape from the snare of the devil, having been held captive by him to do his will" (2 Tim. 2:24-26).

Three Categories of New Age Involvement

Now let's look at these three basic categories.

• *Occasional Dabblers*: People who knowingly or unknowingly taste of the forbidden fruit of the New Age on an occasional and casual basis. These are the ones who occasionally may consult a psychic, have their astrological horoscope charted, play with a ouija board, and other such seemingly innocent, sporadic flirtations with occult enticements.

Though people often seem to "get off easy," and sometimes do, more damage can come of such dabbling than a person is aware. Opening a Scripturally forbidden door is tempting trouble's way. Satan's spell is sometimes cast so subtly that a person does not even know what has happened. For far too many people, dabbling can be the proverbial "curiosity that killed the cat."

In my former days as a New Age leader and observer, I saw many people come to various types of events out of curiosity or just wanting to "check it out." It is all too easy for such unwary people to get caught up in the hype, dazzle, and allures of this phenomenon. As the end-times "powerful delusion" increases in magnitude and power, the dangers of dabbling are more than ever before.

• *Regular Experimenters*: People who regularly partake of any portion of the huge menu of New Age offerings. Such persons may go to a New Age-type event once a month or every two months. But the attraction to the razzle-dazzle is established, and by persistent involvements Satan's hook is progressively set and anchored. Regular experimentation is nothing else than buying into a rigged Satanic game and, for an overwhelming percentage of such people, leads into stage number three -"hard-core New Age-iness." There is a price to pay for every experimental adventure into New Age territory— and the cumulative toll that the Adversary exacts is the soul.

• *Hard-core New Age involvement*: Persons who have a self-identity and lifestyle founded upon the principles of New Age philosophy and activities. The New Age brainwashing has been deeply ingrained by habitual occult-based practices and a series of radical higher consciousness transformations. Such people are absolutely convinced that the New Age path contains the highest universal truths, above all other spiritual traditions.

Perspective on These Three Categories of People

People becoming involved to one degree or another in New Age activities cut across the entire spectrum. Rich, poor, and in between. Young, old, and middle-aged, and every other strata of occupation. Sometimes one's very own friends or family members are involved. The New Age is part and parcel of the American socio-cultural landscape, and its many different forms can entice the unwary as well as the willing.

For most dabblers, the Satanic hook is not yet set. The glossy allures do not yet hold full sway over the mind and heart. These are people that are most easily helped in turning away from New Age involvements, but the help is needed immediately.

For the regular experimenters, the task of helping them to see the wisdom in stopping further explorations is an order of magnitude higher than that of the dabbler. The experimenter often has a driving interest in the New Age and usually has had one or more significant experiences that tend to confirm the (dark) power of such practices as well as whetting their appetite for more of them.

Such individuals need earnest and timely assistance from Christian friends and relatives before the involvements take a stronger hold on their lives. Regular experimenters often are quite resistant to supportive Christian efforts, though a degree of openness to hearing (or re-hearing) the Good News is there. But it will close down sharply should they continue the path to becoming a hard-core New Ager. Fervent Christian supportive efforts are strongly needed to help these people.

Hard-core New Agers are far and away the most difficult to reach with the Good News. Brainwashing has set in, and the glittery rainbow-colored glasses of higher consciousness powerfully blind the individual to the Truth of Jesus. Aversion and irritation to the Good News in combination with the New Age superiority complex put up thick walls of resistance. Though nothing is impossible for the almighty power of the Lord, such hard-core New Agers are exceptionally difficult cases with which to work.

Less than a fraction of 1-percent of such people convert to the Christian faith. Though, perhaps with more Christian outreach efforts, on both individual and organizational levels, this can be changed.

A Few Thoughts on Christian Intercession on Behalf of Others Who Are Involved in the New Age

John Ankerberg and John Weldon, in *The Facts on the New Age Movement*, provide some insights:

"How can you deal with your friends who have joined the NAM? [New Age Movement] First you need to realize that you are not just dealing with man's philosophies which can be countered with human arguments. You are dealing with demonic deceptions that require prayer, patience, and the Word of God. These false philosophies and practices will have the devil's power behind them, which is why they cannot be effectively defeated by human means alone. Thus, you should meet these problems with earnest prayer, which "can accomplish much" (James 5:16), with patience and courage (Joshua 1:7; II Timothy 2:24-26), and with the power of the Holy Spirit and the Word of God. You also should love others and be careful to respect those who disagree with you, for in this way you will prove to the world you are truly a disciple of Christ (John 13:35; I Corinthians 10:24, 33; 13:13)."[1]

From my own personal experience, both in getting out of New Age involvements as well as helping others in this way, I wholeheartedly agree that prayer, patience, endurance, kindness, and love are powerful elements in Christian intercession on behalf of New Agers. It may take a long time, with much prayer, before the conviction of the Holy Spirit pierces through the delusions. Kindness, longsuffering compassion, and unconditional love for such people, even as they sin and blaspheme, is fertile soil from which much good may blossom.

When and as appropriate, the concerned Christian may offer to share various educational materials — books, pamphlets, cassette tapes, etc. — that compare and contrast the Christian faith and New Age philosophy from a Christian perspective.[2]

I would like to offer here a general outline for helping others to be extricated from the New Age Movement for Christians' consideration. Again, this is general and not meant to be totally comprehensive. Consult Christian leadership and appropriate informational materials for further assistance and guidance.

• The New Ager must come to the point of repentance, confessing sins to Jesus Christ in prayer, and making a commitment to renounce and release all things New Age. This is something that a New Ager will have to come to by his own choice, by the grace of the Lord. Further, the person needs to pray to Jesus for salvation and accept Him into his life as Lord and personal Savior.

• The individuals need to confess their acceptance of Jesus into their lives to Christian brethren.

• They should publicly profess this new commitment through the rite of baptism.

• Finding church leadership, counseling, and fellowship as soon as possible is of the utmost importance. Certain televangelist ministries can be most helpful for support and learning, but the personal contact on a local level is crucially important.

• Reading the Bible daily for inspiration, knowledge, and wisdom is necessary for Christian growth.

• Daily earnest prayer is a spiritual lifeline of renewal, correction, encouragement, strengthening of faith, inspiration, and guidance.

• It is imperative that the former New Ager get rid of all New Age paraphernalia. All crystals, jewelry, talismans, statues, pictures, artwork, gadgets, clothes, etc. that have any direct or indirect associations with the New Age must be cast out of one's life, home, and work-place. This needs to be done very soon after conversion. There is no room for sentimentality or straddling the fence here — a sharp sword of discernment and commitment to cutting all New Age ties is very important on this point.

From personal experience, and in helping others, I have found that a lot of subtle but significant New Age attachments crop up in this kind of personal housecleaning process. There is a strong tendency to want to keep just a couple of pieces of paraphernalia, with the thought that it won't hurt. However, it is precisely those objects that the person wants to keep that are their strongest psychological ties with their past. There can be no compromising.

The new Christian should re-evaluate all friendships and associations with New Age people and organizations. Especially with long-term friendships, this can be a most difficult task. Second Corinthians 6:14, 15 states:

"Do not be yoked together with unbelievers. For what do righteousness and wickedness have in common? Or what fellowship can light have with darkness? What harmony is there between Christ and Belial? What does a believer have in common with an unbeliever?" (NIV).

In my own and other former New Agers' experiences, a natural polarization arises in most friendships that hinged fundamentally on our Christian faith versus the friends who continued to cleave to New Age unholiness. It is important to know that New Agers, even well-intentioned, nice ones, can be unwitting vehicles through which demons can work their wiles on a newborn Christian, when vulnerability is especially high.

While I certainly do not recommend casting away such friends in contempt and hatred, 2 Corinthians 6:14, 15 does contain much wisdom and clear guidance in these matters. A graceful, loving, and firm bowing out of all New Age relationships is quite important, even as it can be a heart-rending experience.

• It is also important to begin supporting one's church and other Christian causes.

• A process of going through all one's possessions several times over a period of 6-8 months after conversion to Christianity is a high priority. It's amazing how many New Age-related artifacts, mementos, long-forgotten paraphernalia, artwork, diaries, cassette tapes, clothes, etc., the former New Ager likely will find. Search through everything kept in storage as well. "No compromising" is the order of the day. Though a person might think that doing such a process once will be enough, others' experience shows that doing it 2-3 times helps in weeding out subtler and subtler New Age-related articles as one grows in Christian faith and discernment.

• New Age-related habits, patterns of thought, and patterns of speech also must be weeded out. Especially if a person was in the New Age for a long time, it is astounding how deeply set New Age-iness can be. Through weeks and months, this is a process of continual self-examination to perceive where subtle "cue habits" and "cue words" lie. Such cue habits and cue words continue subtly to bring up mental and emotional past associations with the New Age that need to be conscientiously weeded out.

It can help to have a good Christian friend assist in pointing out such habits and speech patterns to the former New Ager in a kind, non-judgmental way. This can be a very long, tedious process, but a faith-building one as well.

• Reading Christian books critiquing the New Age can be most helpful in seeing the incredible web of multi-leveled darkness and deceptions as well as intellectually clarifying the distinctions between Christian theology and New Age philosophy.

• Keep in mind that Satan does not let go easily of those he has had in his grips, who have escaped by the Victory of Jesus. Even though a person is saved doesn't mean that the enemy will not vent his rage and send his demons of temptation, oppression, harassment, and the like against the newborn Christian who was formerly a New Ager.

From my own experiences, I can testify to the seemingly over-whelming force of demonic attacks that are sometimes in store for converted New Agers. Yet, believers are more than conquerors (Romans 8:37), and need not have any foreboding fear of Satan and his wiles. Proverbs 30:5 says: "He is a shield to those who put their trust in Him."

I would highly recommend that the new convert quickly learn the basic principles of spiritual warfare because, like it or not, that person may well be in the middle of such warfare for a season. The fundamental understanding of assertive spiritual warfare techniques with which to bind and rebuke Satan are basic survival skills. Among others, Johanna Michaelsen's excellent book, *The Beautiful Side of Evil* (Harvest House), has some fine chapters that would benefit converted former New Agers.

• Along these same lines, praying with other Christian believers and having such brethren continually pray on the former New Ager's behalf is crucial, especially during the first year or two of conversion.

• One last note to Christians helping former New Agers: Particularly for long-time New Agers, stepping into the Christian community can be a somewhat disorienting, anxiety-producing transition. There is often fear that Christians will stigmatize them for their past sins; or that if they slip up once or twice they will be judged as still being New Age and shunned or even ostracized. Former New Agers need a great deal of kindness and gentle but firm encouragement, for they have travelled very alien lands and often have to give up jobs, friends, and make other tremendously difficult adjustments in following through on their commitment to walking the Way of Jesus. Respect for them as intelligent, thinking individuals is also very important.

If I may speak out on behalf of former New Agers who have given their lives to Jesus as Lord and personal Savior, please treat such new converts with kindness, respect, and longsuffering compassion. These people have paid a very dear price for their past involvements in the New Age, and likely are being persecuted by past friends and associates as well as being demonically attacked. These converted Christians need a tremendous amount of support from Christian brethren—please treat them kindly. In my own experience of meeting with a loving hand of support, guidance, and love from so many Christian brethren, I have come more deeply to appreciate what Jesus said:

"Truly I say to you, to the extent that you did it to one of these brothers of Mine, even the least of them, you did it to Me" (Matthew 25:40).

[Please note: An excellent Christian ministry —Spiritual Counterfeits Project—has a telephone ministry called "Access" that provides callers with information on various aspects of cults and the New Age Movement. It also provides a referral service that directs callers to counselors across North America who are ready to assist people needing information or help. The access line is available Monday-Wednesday at (415) 540-5767(10 A.M.-4 P.M., Pacific Time.]

Notes

1. Ankerberg, op. cit., p. 27.
2. See Bibliography. Also, especially recommended in this regard are Douglas Groothuis' *Unmasking the New Age* and *The Facts on the New Age Movement*, by Ankerberg and Weldon.

ELEVEN

A CALL FOR MORE CHRISTIAN OUTREACH PROGRAMS TO THOSE IN THE NEW AGE MOVEMENT

he Lord is not slow about His promise, as some count slowness, but is patient toward you, not wishing for any to perish but for all to come to repentance" (II Pet. 3:9).

"It is not those who are healthy who need a physician, but those who are sick" (Matt. 9:12).

There are millions of people today caught up in the webs of Satan's New Age delusions. The momentum of new people exploring the New Age's many-faceted offerings is at an all-time high. The Biblically prophesied "powerful delusion" is at hand.

The heart-breaking paradox is that almost all New Agers sincerely believe they are on the path of truth, inner peace, and spiritual fulfillment. Few have any inkling whatsoever that Satan is the author and prince of the New Age. Ask New Agers if they believe in "God," and 90 percent plus will say yes. They truly believe that the guiding force in their lives is light, love, and peace.

The heart-rending truth of the matter is that New Agers are on "the way that is broad and leads to destruction, and many are those who enter by it."[1] How terrible to see that they are contributing to the rise of the Antichrist's false world peace, and how terribly aghast New Agers will be on the day of the Lord.

Such souls who are headed to hell need to be warned of the consequences of their actions, and desperately need the Christian witness.

After my conversion my first thoughts went out to the New Agers. In my 15 years of experience in the movement, I had only one short exposure to the Christian witness. Before conversion, I deliberately would avoid any direct contact with Biblical Christianity. For all those years, this was as easy as flipping the TV channel to another station. No Christian witness (except one) had intersected with my path.

When I converted to the Christian faith, I looked at the New Age subculture and realized that there was a large Christian witnessing vacuum. In all my years as a New Ager, keeping in touch with the pulse of the movement, I never came across any Christian evangelical programs reaching out into the New Age subculture.

Reports of conversions to the Christian faith are extremely rare in New Age circles. When a New Ager, I personally had not talked with, nor heard about a single one. And when I gave my life to Jesus, the New Age circles I had frequented on a national scale thought that I had *totally* gone round the bend.

Even the possibility of converting to Biblical Christianity is considered preposterous. That subtle but deep-lying New Age superiority complex is pervasive. Satan's voice of lies rules in the New Age, and he is having his way there almost completely.

My heart *breaks* when I think of all the decent people I knew in the New Age. Though there certainly are a plenitude of "rotten apples" in the ranks, there also are many well-meaning people trying to live their "truth" in a positive, constructive way. A heavy burden comes upon me in the Spirit when I think about such souls hanging in the balance.

There are a few Christian evangelical programs for New Agers today. But, so many more are desperately needed to reach out to them, so that some might come to repentance and be raised into life eternal.

There are many souls, thirsting after truth and feeling the pain of inner emptiness that New Age "truth" cannot fill. They thirst and know not the right way. Misdirected, they search in false directions. Some, so parched with the ultimate dust of New Age "truth," will joyously accept the Messiah when they hear of Him—He who said: "whoever drinks of the water that I shall give him shall never thirst; but the water that I shall give him shall become in him a well of water springing up to eternal life"[2]

Part of my testimony is that there is a desperate need for more Christian outreach programs taken to the New Agers themselves.

I earnestly pray that the Lord will call out and raise up a veritable army of Christian evangelists to go forth into New Age "wilderness areas" to shine the Light of Jesus Christ's atoning sacrifice and gift of salvation to the spiritually hungry, thirsty, and deluded New Age masses.

Notes

1. Matthew 7:13.
2. John 4:14.

TWELVE

JESUS CHRIST RETURNS. WELCOME

A portion of the testimony that the Lord has laid upon my heart is to add my small voice to that of so many Christians who have felt the quickening of the Holy Spirit in knowing for a certainty that the personal and visible return of Jesus draws near. Our blessed hope is close at hand as the Lord of lords and King of kings comes on the clouds of the sky with power and great glory to cast down the abominable Antichrist, gather the faithful and to institute the long-awaited millennium that He has promised.

In His own words, Jesus proclaims:

"Behold, I am coming soon! My reward is with me, and I will give everyone according to what he has done. I am the Alpha and the Omega, the First and the Last, the Beginning and the End.

"Blessed are those who wash their robes, that they may have the right to the tree of life and may go through the gates into the city" (Revelation 22:12-14) (NIV).

John's vision of the great multitude from the tribulation who are clothed in white robes is a continual reminder and inspiration for the persevering Christian saints who keep the commandments of the Lord and their faith in Jesus.

"These are the ones who come out of the great tribulation, and they have washed their robes and made them white in the blood of the Lamb.

"For this reason, they are before the throne of God; and they serve Him day and night in His temple; and He who sits on the throne shall spread His tabernacle over them.

"*They shall hunger no more, neither thirst anymore; neither shall the sun beat down on them, nor any heat;*

"*for the Lamb in the center of the throne shall be their shepherd, and shall guide them to springs of the water of life; and God shall wipe every tear from their eyes*" (Revelation 7:14-17).

AN OPEN LETTER
TO NEW AGERS

I f you are a seeker of truth, you must be open-minded. To sincerely seek after truth—ultimate and eternal truth—is to consider *all* possibilities, and to be willing to admit error if it is there to be found. Are you willing to examine the wisdom of your New Age beliefs and practices in view of Jesus Christ's teachings?

Will you *open-mindedly* consider an alternative to New Age philosophy? Will you at least consider what Jesus states about eternal truth?

If you reject this invitation, then you are not as open-minded as you might think.

I would invite and challenge you to read what Jesus did and taught, as it is recorded in the New Testament books of Matthew, Mark, Luke, and John. Please try to leave aside any preconceptions or resistances that you may have, and see for yourself what these books reveal on their own terms. Try to allow the spiritual power contained in these books to speak to your heart, mind and spirit.

This act of reading the Gospels—Matthew, Mark, Luke, and John—in an open-minded way was one of the most important breakthroughs for myself—Randall Baer, a former New Age leader—in seeing how completely different New Age philosophy is from what Jesus taught. On such crucial matters as the nature of man, salvation, the nature of Deity, moral principles, the role of Jesus, and many others, there are deep differences between New Age philosophy and Jesus' teachings.

So many of those in the New Age pick and choose from what Jesus teaches in the Bible, and leave aside the totality of what He says. Try to see clearly, instead, the *whole* of Jesus' teachings, and compare them with New Age philosophy. If you read carefully, you will see that there are profound and irreconcilable differences between Christianity and New Age philosophy.

The issues involved are serious issues indeed. Your soul may very well hang in the balance.

The Lord proclaims: "I AM THE WAY, AND THE TRUTH, AND THE LIFE; NO ONE COMES TO THE FATHER, BUT THROUGH ME (John 14:6). Here, the Biblical person of Jesus states clearly that it is He, and He alone, who is the Savior of all mankind. There are no others.

One of the most commonly held views in the New Age is that Jesus was just one of many "enlightened masters." Jesus, though, in many ways and in many different Bible passages, states clearly that this is definitely *not* the case. This is the most crucial issue that separates Bible-based Christianity from New Age philosophy.

The Bible states that Jesus is the Lord of Lords, King of Kings, and the sole personal Savior. Now, there is not space in this open letter to cover all the complex issues that are raised with this topic.

However, what I have found personally is that, essentially, this issue boils down to a very simple question: Will you or will you not accept Jesus Christ into your life as your Lord and Savior, above all others, and to the exclusion of all others? Please consider this critical question carefully. In Jesus' own words to His disciples: "Go into all the world and preach the gospel to all creation. Whoever believes and is baptized will be saved, but whoever does not believe will be condemned" (Mark 16:15, 16). Also, "And he who does not take his cross and follow after Me is not worthy of Me. He who has found his life shall lose it, and he who has lost his life for my sake shall find it" (Matthew 10:38, 39).

There is a clear and indivisible line drawn here: Choose Jesus and Him alone, and receive salvation unto eternal life through His grace by your faith in Him, or you can choose among the multitudes of New Age paths that may seem right and true but are not, because they do not rest on the Cornerstone of Jesus Christ.

I testify to you in the Spirit of truth that Jesus is exactly who He says He is. And that the fate of your soul hangs in the balance, directly contingent on whether you accept Him fully into your life.

I realize that this message to you may well sound strange, dogmatic, or even totally unenlightened. However, please keep in mind that I am no stranger to the New Age Movement. I was a naturopathic doctor and a leading international expert in the fields of "crystal power" and "sacred science," having authored the books, *Windows of Light: Quartz Crystals and Self-Transformation* (Harper & Row) and *The Crystal Connection: A Guidebook for Personal and Planetary Ascension* (Harper & Row). I spent 15 years of my life in the New Age, and achieved quite a bit of national and international success in it, even as I partook of many and diverse aspects of its teachings and experiences.

What I tell you may sound odd, but it is quite true. There are critical flaws in New Age philosophy and practices that are extremely difficult to see and understand until one turns away from them and embraces the Christian faith. When involved in the New Age, one becomes blinded to these flaws that are sophisticatedly disguised as "light," "love," and "truth." It is as though there are "blind spots" that keep one from seeing the very thing one most needs to see—that Jesus is the only path to eternal life, inner peace, and ultimate fulfillment; and that the New Age is a many-faceted, many-pathed counterfeit designed to keep one sincerely thinking that the truth has been found when, in reality, it has not.

If you scoff at this, I ask you: Would you at least open-mindedly consider the possibility that what I testify to you just might be factual? Giving this thought serious consideration will not do you any harm. So, if you sincerely seek after truth, and are willing to consider all possibilities, why not invest your time in reading Matthew, Mark, Luke, and John?

Believe me, I *know* the thoughts that are probably going through your mind. At one point, they were my thoughts as well. So many doubts and criticisms arise that may try to persuade you not to take up my invitation and challenge. I beseech you though, please don't let these thoughts keep you from following through on reading the Gospel books at the earliest possible opportunity. How about right now? Before something else comes up.

I testify to you, in love and compassion, that what I found when I accepted Jesus as my Lord and personal Savior opened my eyes to seeing truth in a totally different way, a much grander way than anything I ever knew in the New Age. What I have experienced as a Christian *far* surpasses even the most incredible, mind-blowing mystical experiences I had as a New Ager.

This can happen with you, too, and you absolutely will be startled and amazed at how your life is profoundly changed when you accept the gift of salvation by grace through faith that Jesus offers to everyone, if you would only accept His gift. Ask, seek, knock! For Jesus states:

"Behold, I stand at the door and knock; if anyone hears My voice and opens the door, I will come into him, and will dine with him, and he with Me.

"He who overcomes, I will grant to him to sit down with Me on My throne, as I also overcame and sat down with My Father on His throne" (Rev. 3:20, 21).

If and when you decide to accept Jesus into your life, if you do not feel comfortable seeking out Christian counsel quite yet (though this is best), simply follow this basic guideline:

Pray on bended knee in repentance for all your sins, for all persons are sinners in need of redemption. We all must confess our sins to Jesus, and ask for His forgiveness as you renounce all involvements and ties with the New Age Movement as well as all your other sins.

Testify to your belief that Jesus died on the cross of Calvary for your sins, paying the ransom in your place, so that you can escape condemnation through the shedding of His blood.

Tell Him that you are willing to take up the cross, denying yourself, and following His Way, Truth, and Life as His obedient disciple.

Ask Him now to come into your life as your sole Lord and personal Savior, forevermore.

Finding Christian leadership and counsel immediately is your highest priority. They will know how to lead you further. This is imperative. Also, I invite you to read the latter part of Chapter 10 for further insights in fully extricating yourself from all New Age ties. Your path as a newborn Christian will bring you joys untold and also many challenges and opportunities for growth-in-Christ. It will be a new beginning, a new life. Follow the leadership of the Holy Spirit in your life, and He will lead you in all the ways of righteousness and give you the peace that passeth all understanding.

One last thought: the following Bible passage has been of great value to me in my walk with the Lord. Perhaps it may be for you as well:

"Have this attitude in yourselves which was also in Christ Jesus,

"Who, although He existed in the form of God, did not regard equality with God a thing to be grasped,

"But emptied Himself, taking the form of a bond-servant, and being made in the likeness of men.

"And being found in appearance as a man, He humbled Himself by becoming obedient to the point of death, even death on a cross.

"Therefore also God highly exalted Him, and bestowed on Him the name which is above every name,

"That at the name of Jesus every knee should bow, of those who are in heaven, and on earth, and under the earth,

"And that every tongue should confess that Jesus Christ is Lord, to the glory of God the Father" (Phil. 2:5-11).

APPENDICES

Appendix A: Practices and Techniques Advertised or Listed in New Age-Based Magazines, Books, and Newsletters

3HO Superhealth; Acu-massage; Acupressure; Africa Training; Alexander Technique; Alexander Training; Aroma Therapy; Aura Readings; *Ayurveda* Kinesiology; *Ayurveda*: The *Yoga* of Medicine; *Beijing T'ai Chi Gong* Breathing Exercises; Bioenergetics; Body Electronics Acupressure; Bodymind Acupressure; Bodynamic Psychotherapy; Brain Gym Edu-Kinesthetics; Breath Therapy; Breathwork; *Chakra* Harmonization; *Chakra Balancing*; Color Healing; Crystal Healing; Depth Psychology; Dianetics; Domain Shift; Dream Therapy; Electro-Therapy & the Evolving Soul; Emotional Clearing; Ericksonian Hypnosis; Feldenkrais Method; Flower Essences; Food Additives to Enhance Psychic Abilities; Gem Tinctures; Gestalt; Harner Method Shamanic Counseling; Healing Stones; Healing at a Distance; Hellerwork; Hemispheric Synchronization; Herbal Essences; Hoffman Quadrinity Process; Holonomic Touchwork; Holonomic Movement Awareness; Homeopathy; Intuitive Massage; *Jin Shin Do* Acupressure; *Johrei*; Laying on of Stones; Lomi Bodywork; *Looyen* Work; Macrobiotics; Mentastics; Mind-Body Medicine; Movement Psychotherapy; Naturo-Vet Services; Neo-Rechian Massage; NLP—Neuro-Linguistic Programming; *O Sensei* Training; Open Heart Therapy; Ortho-Bionomy; Past Life Regression; Past Life Therapy; Polarity Therapy; Primal Therapy; Psychic Surgery; Psycho-Psi Dynamics; Psycho-Synthesis; Psychospiritual Integration; *Quan Yin* Acupuncture; Radiance Technique; *Rajneesh* Rebalancing; *Rayid Iris* Interpretation; Rebirth Yourself; Rebirthing; Rechian Therapy; Reflexology; *Reiki*; Relaxation Therapy; Rolfing; Rosen Method Bodywork & Psychotherapy; Self-Imagery; Self-Improvement Counseling Classes; Sending Energy at a

Distance; Senoi Dream Education; *Shen*: Physio-emotional Release Therapy; *Shiatsu*; *Soma* Neuro-muscular Integration; Spinning: Energetic Repatterning; Strategic Hypnotherapy; Subliminal Programming; Swedish-*Esalen* Massage; Symmetrical Movement Technique; *T'ai Chi*; Therapeutic Touch; Touch for Health; Traditional Acupuncture; Trager; Trance-Action; Transformational Counseling; Transpersonal Psychology; Transpersonal Hypnotherapy; Vibrational Healing Massage; Whole Brain Learning; *Yoga* for Health; *Zen Shiatsu*.

Appendix B: New Age Buzzwords, Groups, and Potpourri

Academies of Universal Science; Affirmations; Age of Aquarius; *Agni Yoga*; *Aikido*; Akashic Records; Alchemy; Alpha Awareness Techniques; Alpha Pacer II Brain Machine; American Indian Rituals; Amulets; Ancient Crystal Technology; Angelic Music; Anthroposophy; Ascended Masters; Astral Projection; Astrocartography; Astrology; Atlantean Healing Paddles; Atlantis; Attraction Modules; Automatic Writing; Awakening the Master Healer Within; Balancing the Male and Female Within; *Bhakti Yoga*; Bi-Location; Blending *Yoga* and Mysticism; *Bodhisatva*; Brain Machines; Buddhism; Celestial-Seed; Ceremonial Scepters; Channelled Music; Charms; *Chi Kung*: The Act of Mastering the Unseen Life Force; Clairsentience; Clairvoyance; Comics & Cartoons as Transformative Tools; Conscious Conception; Continuum Meditation; Cosmic Consciousness; Council of Twelve; *Course in Miracles*; Create Your Own Reality; Creative Visualization for Achieving Goals; Creative Visualization; Creative Listening; Crystal Skulls; Crystal Visioning; Crystal Dreaming; Crystal Pet Halters; Crystal Gridworks; Crystal Light-Tools; Crystal Flute; Crystal Jewelry; Da Free John—Dawn House Teachings; The Daemon Deck-meditation/therapy cards; Dance the Dance of Your Power Animal; Dances of Universal Peace; *Devas*; *Dharma* Voodoo; Divination; Divine Science; Dolphin Dream-Time Workshop; Dowsing; Dream Crystals; Dream Therapy; Dream Discovery: Diving into the Deep; Dreams and Your Personal Mythology; Druids; Dungeons and Dragons; Dzogchen Contemplation; Earth *Chakra* Activation Pilgrimages; Earth Initiations; Eckankar: The New Age Religion; Egyptian Sand Reading; Egyptology; Equinox Celebrations; *Esalen*; Esoteric Science; ESP; est; Fairies; Feminist Wicca; Finally ... A bridge between ancient and modern technology, The Findhorn; Finding Your Soul-Mate; Firewalking; Form Energy; Forum; Full Moon Rites; Gemstone Elixirs; Genesis II; Geomancy; The Gnostic View of Life; The Great Invocation;

Great White Brotherhood; Handwriting Analysis; Harmonic Convergence; *Hatha Yoga*; Healing Wands; Healing Wands; High Tech Meditation; Higher-Self; Hinduism; How to Become an Angel; Human Potential Movement; Hypnosis; *I Ching*; Imaging; Incan Religion; Inner Peace Movement; Innerquest; Insight Training; Integral *Yoga*; Interdimensional Communication; Invocations; *Iyengar Yoga*; Jewelled Wand Pendants; *Jonathan Livingston Seagull*; *Kabbalah*; *Kahuna*; *Karma* of Vocation; *Karma* Cards; *Ki*; Kirlian Photography; Klark Kent Super Science; *Kripalu Yoga*; *Kriya Yoga*; *Kundalini Yoga*; *Kundalini*; Learn How to Build a Psychic Shield; *Lemuria*; Levitation; Life After Life; Life Purpose; Lifespring; Light Body Activation; Light Ceremonies for World Peace; Light-based Technologies; The Lion's Path; Lost Emerald Tablets; Lucid Dreaming; Magic *Mandalas* from the Right Side of the Brain; Magnetic Alignment of the *Chakras*; *Mandelas*; *Mantras*; Mayan Religion; Medicine Wheels; Mediumship; Megalearning; The Michael Group; Middle Earth; Mind Expansion Without Drugs; Money *Mantras*; Moon Signs; The Motherpeace Tarot Playbook; *Mu*; *Mudras*; Mystery Schools; Necromancy; Neo-Reichian Education; The New Sacred Psychology; New World Ascension Process; New Age Music; New Age Expos; New Age ESP Expo; *Nirvana*; Occult Numerology; *Ooahpse* Bible; Open Relationships; Oracles; Orgone Energy Accumulator Blanket; Ouija Boards; Palmistry; Pendulums; Personal and Planetary Ascension; Personal Transformation through Sound; Physics and Mysticism; Plant Spirits; The Power of the Sacred Pipe; Power Animals; Power Objects; Power Spots; *Prana*; Precognition; Programming Crystals; Prosperity Affirmations; Prosperity Imaging; Psychic Spoon-Bending Parties; Psychokinesis; Psychometry; Psychotronics; Pyramid Power; Radionics; Radix; Rainbow Warriors; *Raja Yoga*; Right Brain, Left Brain Balancing; Runes; Sacred *Scarabs*; Sacred Geometry; Sacred Science; SAGE Seminars; *Samadhi*; *Satori*; Scientology; Scrying; Seances; Secret Spiritual Names; *Sedona*: The Psychic Vortex Experience; Self-Development Using Gemstones, Color, Sound, and Herbs; Sensory Imagery and Meditations to Heal the Mind and Body; The Seven Rays; Sexual Astrology; Shamanic Movement Exploration; Shamanism; *Shamballah*; Silva Mind Control; Solstice Celebrations; Sorcery; Soul-Mates; Spirit Guides; Spiritism; Spiritual Hierarchy of Light; Spontaneous Drawing; Star-Gate; Star-Seed; *Sufi* Dancing; *Sufi*; Summon Wine; Sun Signs; SuperLearning; Supersensonics; Sweat Lodge; Sweat Lodge Ceremonies; Synchronicity; Talisman; *Tantric Yoga*; The *Tao* Way to Total Sexual Fitness for Men; Tarot; Telekinesis; Temples of Light; Third Eye; Tibetan Book of the Dead; TM; Trager Mentastics; Transformational Workshops; UFO Advanced Psychic and Mental

Abilities; UFO Super-Advanced Technologies; UFO "Universal Religion"; UFO "Universal Brotherhood"; UFO Crystal Technologies; UFO Intergalactic Brotherhood of Peace and Love; Ultra Meditation; Unified Energy Fields; Universal Mind; Universal Intelligence; Universarius; *Upanishads*; *Vedas*; *Vipassana* Meditation; Vision Quest; Visionary Art Pictures; Vortexes; Walk-ins; The Way of Cartouche; White Crystal Medicine; White Shamanism; White *Tantric Yoga*; Whole Life Expos; Whole-Light Beings; *Wicca*; Witchcraft; World Hunger Project; World Peace Movement; *Yantras*; *Yin-Yang*; *Zen*.

Appendix C: Some Organizations Advertised or Listed in New Age-Oriented Magazines and Books

Acupressure Institute; Acupressure-Acupuncture Institute; Alchemical Hypnotherapy Institute; Alive and Well!: Institute of Conscious Bodywork; American Society for Psychical Research; American Association of Meta-Science; American Institute of Hypnotherapy; The American Center for the Alexander Technique, Inc.; Ananda Marga; Antioch University San Francisco; Association for Humanistic Psychology; Association for Humanistic Psychology; Association for Holistic Health; Association for Research and Enlightenment; *Astara*; The Aston Training Center; The Body of Knowledge; The Boeing Employees Parapsychology Club; Boulder College; Cadake Industries; California Institute of Integral Studies; California School of Herbal Studies; California Institute of Integral Studies; Camp Lenox; The Center of Light; Center for Transpersonal and Expressive Arts; Center for Shamanic Studies; Center for Applied Institution; *Chinook* Learning Community; Chinook Learning Center; Choices; Dialogue House; Doctor Jay Scherer's Academy of Natural Healing; Dr. Edward Bach Healing Society; *Esalen* Institute; The Esoteric Philosophy Center; Feathered Pipe Foundation; The Female Principle; Flower Essence Society; The Focusing Institute; Foundation for Life Action; Foundation; *Hakomi* Therapy; Harbin Hot Springs; Heart Center; Heartsong Center for Expanded Perception; Heartwood Healing Arts Institute; The Himalayan International Institute of *Yoga*; Holistic Dental Association; Hollyhock Farm; Infinity International School of Hypnotherapy; Institute for Biogenetics and Gestalt; Institute for Evolutionary Research; Institute for Transpersonal Psychology; Institute of Noetic Sciences; Integral *Yoga* Institute; Interdimensional Sciences; Interface; International Rolf Institute; International Foundation for Homeopathy; International Association of Holistic-Health Practitioners; International Association for Psychotronic Research; International Kirlian Research Association; International Medical and Dental Hypnotherapy Association; John Bastyr

College; John F. Kennedy University; John-David Learning Institute; Joy Lake Mountain Seminar Center; Ken Keyes Center; *Kushi* Institute; The *Kushi* Foundation; Lesley College Graduate School; Life Integration Trainings; Life Sciences Counseling Services; The Light Ages Foundation; The Lomi School, Macrobiotic Learning Center; Lorian Association; The Lucis Trust; *Maharishi Ayurveda* Association of America; Melia Foundation; Monroe Institute of Applied Sciences; Mount Madonna Center; The Naropa Institute; National Center for Homeopathy; The New Mexico Academy of Massage and Advanced Healing Arts; New York School of Astrology; New England Sound Healers; New York Open Center; New Life Health Center; New Mexico School of Natural Therapeutics; *Nyingma* Institute; Oasis Center; Oasis Center for Human Potential; Omega Institute for Holistic Studies; Omega Institute for Holistic Studies; The Option Institute; Parapsychological Services Institute; Piedmont *Yoga* Center; Polarity Therapy Center of San Francisco; Potomac MyoTherapy Institute; PSI Research; The Radionic Association; Rocky Mountain *Dharma* Center; Rocky Mountain Peace Center; Rosicrucian Order, AMORC; Rowe Conference Center; The Rudolf Steiner Institute; Rudolf Steiner College; The Sedona Institute; The Self Center; Self Realization Fellowship; *Shakti* Center; Sirius Community; *Sivananda Ashram Yoga* Farm; *Sivanda Yoga Vendanta* Center; The Society of Metaphysicians; Southwestern College of Life Sciences; Spiritual Emergence Network; Spiritual Emergence Network; *Sri Chinmoy* Center; Strong, Stretched, and Centered, Taoist Esoteric *Yoga* Center and Sufi Order; Theosophical Society in America; Three Mountain Foundation; Touch for Health Foundation; Traditional Acupuncture Foundation; The Trager Institute; Transcendental Meditation; Transformation Arts Institute; Vega Study Center; *Vipassana* Meditation Center; Wainwright House; White Lotus Foundation; Windstar Foundation; Wise Woman Center; World College West; World Peace University.

Appendix D: Some New Age-Oriented Journals, Magazines, Resources and Newsletters

Balance Magazine; Beyond Avalon; Body, Mind and Spirit Magazine; Brain/Mind Bulletin Newsletter; Common Ground; Common Boundary Between Spirituality & Psychotherapy; Earth Star/New England; East West Journal; The Essential Whole Earth Catalog; Fate Magazine; Free Spirit; Harmonist Magazine; Holistic Health;

Life Times; The Light Connection; The Loving Brotherhood Newsletter; Magical Blend; Meditation Magazine; The Monk; National New Age Yellow Pages; The New Times; New Age Exchange; New Dimensions Radio Network; New Frontier Magazine; New Frontiers Newsletter; New Age Journal; New Realities; Orange County Resources; Reflections; Whole Again Resource Guide; Whole Life Magazine; Whole Life Monthly; Yoga Journal.

Appendix E: Names of Some of the More Popular Spirits Being Channeled

Adept; Alexander; Alien Soul; Ascended Masters; Ashtar Command; Basher; Celestial Seed; Crystal Woman; Divine Flame Holder; Divine Counterpart; Djwhal Khul; Dr. Peebles; El Morya; Eleutheria; Emmanuel; Enchantment; Enlightened Master; Etherion; Fortuneteller; Global Dreamer; Goddess; *Guru*; Healer; High Priest; Hilarion; Holy One; Initiate; Jaguar Woman; Jason; "Jesus"; John; Jonah; Konar; Kristos; Kuthumi; Lanto; Lazaris; Light Worker; Lilly; Maat; Mafu; Magician; Maitreya; Master R; Master; Medicine Woman; Medicine Man; Medicine Man Sorcerer; Mentor; Mystic; Mystical Traveler; Old Chinese; Oracle; Orion; Power Woman; Prophet; *Quan Yin*; Ra; Ramtha; Saint; Sananda; Savant; Seer; Seth; Shaman; Shepherd; Soli; Soothsayer; Soul Projection; St. Germain; Star Seed Rainbow Warrior; Sunat Kumara; The Michael Entity; Visionary; Warlock; White Eagle; Witch Doctor; Witch; Wizard; Xax; Zosh.

Appendix F: Examples of Some Titles of New Age Workshops

33 Steps Beyond the Earth Plane; A Transpersonal Dream Healing Ceremony; Activating Your Place in God's Plan for Earth; Acupressure for Pregnancy; *Akashic* Records and Reincarnation; Alchemy of Success; and Science; "Angels and Archetypes"; Astral Projection to the Moon, the Other Planets, and Beyond; Awakening the Heart: Relationship as a Transformative Journey; Balancing the Global Energy Network; Change Your Life with Science of Mind; Conscious Evolution and Transforming Personal Rules; Creative Imagination with Colors; Death, Dying, and Transcendence; Developing a Prosperity Consciousness and Learning to Receive; Dialogue with Infinity; Earth Ascending: Preparation for Planetary Empowerment; The Egyptian Mysteries; Emotions and Money; ESP: Extended Sensory Perception is a Natural Function for Everyone; Finding an Authentic Feminine Spirituality; Getting Used to the Idea of Being God; Goddesses is Every Woman; The Harmonics of Health and

Wholeness; Healing Our Relationships Through a "Course in Miracles": Crystal Healing with Breath Using Ancient Egyptian Techniques; Herbs: Sacraments for Spiritual Growth and Healing; Hermetic Wisdom: Qabalistic Path to Wholeness; Holistic Dentistry; Hot Tub Workshop; How to Become an Angel; How to Attract Money; Intuitive Development ... Keys to Inner Self; The Inward Arc: Developing Intuition for Healing and Wholeness; The Joy is in the Journey Through *Hatha Yoga* ... Body, Mind, and Spirit; Learn How to Slow the Aging Process and be Forever Young with Magician, Shaman, Priest, and Priestess: A Look at Esoteric Art Making Love Work: A Personal Growth Seminar; Medicine; Multi-dimensional Energy Transference; Multidimensional Art; Opening the Creative Flow; Overcoming Situations of Love, Sex, Rejection, and Jealousy via Precision Psychodrama; The Path to Mastership; The Path of Power; Peruvian Whistling Vessels; Planetary Herbology: A Training in Clinical Chinese-Western Power Primal Fusion Music; Psychic Aura-Clearing; Relationship Discoveries; Rod Workshop; Sacred Healing Temples of the Past, Present, and Future; The Sacred Science of *Chakra* Balancing and Activation; Secrets of Esoteric Sexuality; Self-hypnosis; Shamanic Healing: Journeying and the Dreamtime Experience; Taoist Internal Alchemical *Yoga*; Theosophical Attitude to Non-violence; Thought-form Technology; Touch for Health Therapy; Tree of Life Study and Meditation; The Unfolding Female Master; Using Crystals as Holographic Computers; The Vision Maker's Workshop; Visualizations: A Powerful Aid to Cancer Rehabilitation; The Way of the Warrior Priest; White *Tantric Yoga*; Women's Mysteries: Discovering the Goddess Within; You are the Light; Your Lover is Your Healer: *Tantra Yoga*.

Appendix G: Power Trips: Ideals and Self-Images of New Agers

Adept; Alien Soul; Causal-Plane Overseer; Celestial Seed; Clairvoyant Channel; Crystal Woman; Divine Counterpart; Divine Flame Holder; Enlightened Master; Fortuneteller; Geomancer; Global Dreamer; Goddess; *Guru*; Healer; High Priest; Holder of the Universal Keys; Initiate; Jaguar Woman; *Kahuna*; Keeper of the Flame; Light Worker; Magician; Master; Medicine Woman; Medicine Man Sorcerer; Medicine Man; Mentalist; Mind-Master; Necromancer; Oracle; Power Woman; Power-Masters; Prince; Princess; Prophet; Psychic Consultant; Saint, Mystic, Holy One; Savant; Seer; Shaman; Shepherd; Soothsayer; Soul Projection; Spiritual Counselor; Star Seed Rainbow Warrior; Trance Channel; Transformational Channel; Upholders of the Light; Visionary; Warlock; Warriors; Witch; Witch Doctor; Wizard.

FOR THE RECORD

Before my conversion to the Christian faith, I was involved in the making of numerous New Age cassette tapes and books. Unfortunately, several of them are still commercially available. In all such cases I do not have the legal right to demand their removal from the market. In these cases, I have: 1) written a formal letter asking the other party to stop making and selling the product, 2) stopped receiving any royalty payments from cassette tapes, 3) donate all royalties from books to charitable Christian causes. Hopefully, in the near future, all these products will stop being offered on the commercial market.

BIBLIOGRAPHY

Ankerburg, John and John Weldon. *The Facts on the New Age Movement*. Eugene, Oregon: Harvest House Publishers. 1988.

Bowen, William. *Globalism: American's Demise*. Lafayette, LA: Huntington House, Inc. 1984.

Carr, Joseph. *The Lucifer Connection*. Lafayette, LA: Huntington House, Inc. 1987.

Chandler, Russell. *Understanding the New Age*. Dallas, TX: Word Publishing. 1988.

Cumbey, Constance. *The Hidden Dangers of the Rainbow*. Lafayette, LA: Huntington House, Inc. 1983.

deParrie, Paul and Mary Pride. *Unholy Sacrifices of the New Age*. Westchester, IL: Crossway Books. 1988.

Groothuis, Douglas. *Unmasking the New Age*. Downers Grove, IL: InterVarsity Press. 1986.

Groothuis, Douglas. *Confronting the New Age*. Downers Grove, IL: InterVarsity Press. 1988.

Hoyt, Karen. *The New Age Rage*. Old Tappan, NJ: Fleming H. Revell Company. 1987.

Hunt, Dave. *Peace, Prosperity, and the Coming Holocaust*. Eugene, OR: Harvest House Publishers. 1983.

Hunt, Dave and T. A. McMahon. *The Seduction of Christianity*. Eugene, OR: Harvest House Publishers, 1985.

Hunt, Dave and T. A. McMahon. *America: The Sorcerer's New Apprentice*. Eugene, OR: Harvest House Publishers. 1988.

Marrs, Texe. *Dark Secrets of the New Age*. Westchester, IL: Crossway Books. 1987.

Marrs, Texe. *Mega Forces: Signs and Wonders of the Coming Chaos*. Austin, TX: Living Truth Publishers. 1988.

McGuire, Paul. *Supernatural Faith in the New Age*. Springdale, PA: Whitaker House. 1987.

Michaelsen, Johanna. *The Beautiful Side of Evil*. Eugene, OR: Harvest House Publishers. 1982.

Larson, Bob. *Larson's Book of Cults*. Wheaton, IL: Tyndale House Publishers, Inc. 1982.

Peretti, Frank. *This Present Darkness*. Westchester, IL: Crossway Books. 1986.

Phillips, Phil. *Turmoil in the Toy Box*. Lancaster, PA: Starburst Publishers. 1986.

Reisser, Paul, M. D., Teri Reisser, and John Weldon. *New Age Medicine: A Christian Perspective in Holistic Health*. Chattanooga, TN: Global Publishers, Inc. 1988.

Smith, F. LaGard. *Out on a Broken Limb*. Eugene, OR: Harvest House Publishers. 1986.

MORE GOOD BOOKS FROM HUNTINGTON HOUSE

Personalities in Power: The Making of Great Leaders
by Florence Littauer

You'll laugh and cry as Florence Littauer shares with you heart warming accounts of the personal lives of some of our greatest leaders. Learn of their triumphs and tragedies, and become aware of the different personality patterns that exist and how our leaders have been influenced by them.

Discover your own strengths and weaknesses by completing the Personality Chart included in this book. "Personalities in Power" lets you understand yourself and others and helps you live up to your full potential.

ISBN 0-910311-56-0 $8.95

The Deadly Deception: Freemasonry Exposed by One of Its Top Leaders *by Jim Shaw and Tom McKenney*

Presents a frank look at Freemasonry and its origin. Learn of the "secrets" and "deceptions" that are practiced daily around the world. Find out why masonry teaches that it is the true religion, that all other religions are but corrupted and perverted forms of masonry. For the first time the 33rd degree ritual is made public!

ISBN 0-910311-54-4 $6.95

Hidden Dangers of the Rainbow *by Constance Cumbey*

This national #1 bestseller paved the way for all other books on the subject, as it was the first to uncover and expose the New Age Movement. It has become the literary giant in its category. This book provides a vivid exposé of the New Age Movement which the author reveals is dedicated to wiping out Christianity and establishing a one world order. This movement, a vast network of occult and pagan organizations meets the test of prophecy concerning the Antichrist.

ISBN 0-910311-03-X $6.95

Exposing the Aids Scandal: What You Don't Know Can Kill You
by Dr. Paul Cameron

Where do you turn when those who control the flow of information in this country withhold the truth? Why is the national media hiding facts from the public? Can Aids be spread in ways we're not being told? Finally . . . a book that gives you a total account of the Aids epidemic, and what steps can be taken to protect yourself. What you don't know can kill you!

ISBN 0-910311-52-8 $6.95

The Delicate Balance *by John Zajac*

Did you know that the Apostle John, George Washington and Nostradamus had revealed to them many of the same end-time events. It's true!

Accomplished scientist, inventor, and speaker John Zajac asserts that science and religion are not opposed. He uses science to demonstrate the newly understood relevance of the book of Revelations. Read about the catastrophic forces at work today that the ancient prophets and others foretold. You'll wonder at George Washington's description of an angelic being which appeared to him and showed him end-time events that were to come—the accuracy of Nostradamus (who converted to Christianity) and the warnings of St. John that are revealed in the Book of Revelations—earthquakes, floods, terrorism—what does it all mean??? No other author has examined these topics from Zajac's unique perspective and presented such a reasonable and concise picture of the whole.

ISBN 0-910311-57-9 $7.95

Plague In Our Midst: Sexuality, Aids and the Christian Family
by Dr. Gregg Albers

The sexual revolution is taking its toll on the American family—where do concerned parents turn? Written by a medical authority, this book is oriented toward the family, their need to know the issues, with information concerning promiscuity, sexuality and AIDS. Included, a biblically based guide to help parents teach sex education to their teens.

ISBN 0-910311-51-X $7.95

The Responsible Parent's Guide to TV: A Noted Expert Looks at Television's Role in Changing Our Children's Values *by Colonel Doner*

Exposes the methods that the TV networks are employing on our youth and suggests guidelines for your children's viewing habits. Learn how Hollywood producers are intentionally using "entertainment" programming to "sell" homosexuality, abortion, promiscuity and humanism. Find out about the media elite's secret agenda for your family and nation—and what you can do about it!

ISBN 0-910311-50-1 $6.95

Devil Take the Youngest *by Winkie Pratney*

A history of Satan's hatred of innocence and his historical treachery against the young. Pratney begins his journey in ancient Babylon and carries through to modern-day America where infants are murdered daily and children are increasingly victimized through pornography, prostitution and humanism.

ISBN 0-910311-29-3 $7.95

Backward Masking Unmasked *by Jacob Aranza*

Rock music affects millions of young people and adults—with lyrics exalting drugs, Satan, violence and immorality. But there is even a more sinister threat: hidden messages that exalt the Prince of Darkness!

ISBN 0-910311-04-8 $6.95

On cassette tape! Hear authentic demonic backward masking from rock music.

ISBN 0-910311-23-4 $6.95

The Lucifer Connection *by Joseph Carr*

Shirley MacLaine and other celebrities are persuading millions that the New Age Movement can fill the spiritual emptiness in their lonely lives. Joseph Carr explains why the New Age Movement is the most significant and potentially destructive challenge to the church today. But is it new? How should Christians protect themselves and their children from this insidious threat? This book is a prophetic, information-packed examination by one of the most informed authors in America.

ISBN 0-910311-42-0 $6.95

The Last Days Collection *by Last Days Ministries*
Heartstirring, faith-challenging messages from Keith Green, David Wilkerson, Melody Green, Leonard Ravenhill, Winkie Pratney, Charles Finney and William Booth are designed to awaken complacent Christians to action.
ISBN 0-961-30020-5 $8.95

Jubilee on Wall Street *by David Knox Barker*
On October 19, 1987, the New York Stock Exchange suffered its greatest loss in history—twice that of the 1929 crash. Will this precipitate a new Great Depression? This riveting book is a look at what the author believes is the inevitable collapse of the world's economy. Using the biblical principle of the Year of Jubilee, a refreshing dose of optimism and an easy-to-read style, the author shows readers how to avoid economic devastation.
ISBN 0-933-451-03-2 $6.95

Where Were You When I Was Hurting? *by Nicky Cruz*
An exciting series of adventures as delinquent-turned-evangelist Nicky Cruz takes the reader on a trek through the Third World, behind the Iron Curtain and into the streets of America's cities.
ISBN 0-910311-41-2 $6.95

A Reasonable Reason to Wait *by Jacob Aranza*
God speaks specifically about premarital sex. Aranza provides a definite, frank discussion on premarital sex. He also provides a Biblical healing message for those who have already been sexually involved before marriage. This book delivers an important message for young people, as well as their parents.
ISBN 0-910311-21-8 $5.95

Pat Robertson: A Biography *by Neil Eskelin*
Behind-the-scenes accounts of the man, the author, the attorney and political scion viewed by millions daily on *The 700 Club*. An unblinking, dramatic look at the Yale law graduate who took up a ministry in the New York slums, the penniless visionary who launched the Christian Broadcasting Network.
ISBN 0-910311-47-1 $6.95

The Great Falling Away Today *by Milton Green*
One of today's most talked-about teachers probes the spiritual condition of God's people. Thought-provoking reading for those concerned about sin and its effect on our fulfilling the Great Commission.
ISBN 0-910311-40-4 $6.95

ORDER THESE BOOKS FROM HUNTINGTON HOUSE!

_____ America Betrayed — *Marlin Maddoux* .... $6.95 _____

_____ Backward Masking Unmasked — *Jacob Aranza* .... 6.95 _____

_____ Backward Masking Unmasked Audiotapes
       — *Jacob Aranza* .... 6.95 _____

_____ Computers and the Beast of Revelation
       — *Webber & Hutchings* .... 6.95 _____

_____ *Deadly Deception: Freemasonry — *Tom McKenney* .... 6.95 _____

_____ *Delicate Balance — *John Zajac* .... 7.95 _____

_____ Devil Take the Youngest — *Winkie Pratney* .... 7.95 _____

_____ *Exposing the Aids Scandal — *Dr. Paul Cameron* .... 6.95 _____

_____ Great Falling Away Today — *Milton Green* .... 6.95 _____

_____ Hand of Death-On Cults & Satanism — *Max Call* ...... 12.95 _____

_____ Hidden Dangers of the Rainbow
       — *Constance Cumbey* .... 6.95 _____

_____ *Inside the New Age Nightmare
       — *Randall Baer* .... 7.95 _____

_____ Jubilee on Wall Street — *David Knox Barker* .... 6.95 _____

_____ Last Days Collection — *Last Days Ministries* .... 8.95 _____

_____ Lucifer Connection — *Joseph Carr* .... 6.95 _____

_____ *Plague in Our Midst — *Dr. Gregg Albers* .... 7.95 _____

_____ A Reasonable Reason to Wait — *Jacob Aranza* .... 5.95 _____

_____ *Responsible Parent's Guide to T.V.
       — *Colonel V. Doner* .... 6.95 _____

_____ *Personalities in Power — *Florence Littauer* .... 8.95 _____

_____ Twisted Cross — *Joseph Carr* .... 7.95 _____

_____ Where Were You When I Was Hurting?
       — *Nicky Cruz* .... 6.95 _____

Shipping and Handling _____

*New titles   TOTAL _____

AVAILABLE AT BOOKSTORES EVERYWHERE or order direct from:
Huntington House, Inc., P.O. Box 53788, Lafayette, LA 70505.

Send check/money order. **For faster service use
VISA/Mastercard, call toll-free 1-800-572-8213.**

Add: Freight and handling, $2.00 for the first book
ordered, and $.50 for each additional book.

Enclosed is $_____ including postage.
Card type:
VISA/Mastercard #_____ Expiration date_____

NAME _____

ADDRESS_____

CITY, STATE, ZIP _____